INDIA BOOKVARSITY

LOTUS CHOICES

Editor: Mahendra Kulasrestha

THE LOTUS SUTRA

English translation of

SADDHARMA PUNDARIKA

Other Works
in the Buddha Pitaka Series
by the same publisher

— • —

The Golden Book of Buddhism

The Life of Lord Buddha: Asvaghosa's
Buddha Charita

The Discourses of Lord Buddha
Sutta Nipata

TThe Last Days of Lord Buddha
Mahaparinibbana Sutta

The Dhammapada

India in China: The Gift of Buddha

Lotus PRESS

4735/22, Prakash Deep Building
Ansari Road, Darya Ganj,
New Delhi-110002

THE LOTUS SUTRA

The BIBLE of MAHAYANA BUDDHISM

The Sixth Book of the Nine Dharmas
SADDHARMA PUNDARIKA

Translated by
H.KERN

Source: Saddharma Pundarika
or The Lotus of the True Law,
Translated by H. Kern,
Sacred Books of the East, Vol. 21,
U.S.A., 1884.

THE LOTUS SUTRA

New First Edition, 2012

ISBN: 978-81-8382-283-1 (H/B)

Published by:
Lotus Press Publishers & Distributors
Unit No. 220, Second Floor, 4735/22, Prakash Deep Building,
Ansari Road, Darya Ganj, New Delhi-10002
Ph.: 011-23280047, 32903912 • Mob.: 098118-38000
E-mail: lotus_press@sify.com

Printed at: **Concept Imprint**, Delhi

Editorspeak

NAM MYOHO RENGE KYO

The title given above is the regular chant of the Japanese Buddhist sect started in the 13th century by a fisherman named Nichiren, made popular under his own name, an essentially nationalist and relatively militant group of Mahayana Buddhism, which in its modern avatar of Soka Gakkai, led by the formidable Daisaku Ikeda, has during the past few decades, made its mark in many countries of the West—well, the chant means 'Homage to the Lotus Sutra', our present work, and its followers believe that salvation could be attained by just reciting the holy name of this Sutra. The present writer has known a Japanese nun belonging to this sect and active in Delhi, who while tapping over her flat round drum, kept reciting the holy chant. It is mentionable that her guru, the famous Fuji Guruji, chanted with no less a person than Mahatma Gandhi in earlier times, and presented to him the well known three monkeys with closed eyes and ears. Gandhiji, in return, made this Odaimoku mantra a part of his ashram prayers and it was he who gave him the honorofic 'Guruji.' We may therefore say that the Lotus Sutra is a significant part of current Indian history.

Originally known as Saddharma Pundarika, it holds a most significant position in Mahayana Buddhism, and is greatly valued in China, Japan and Korea, forming the basis of their many important schools such as Tien-tai and Tendai, in addition to the Nichiren-shu. It is a discourse in over 25 chapters said to have been delivered by Lord Buddha himself—called Sakya muni in these countries—on the famous Gridhrakuta, or Vulture Peak, where the Lord usually took his seat and addressed his followers.

The central message of the Lotus Sutra is that though there are several paths that lead to enlightenment and Salvation—three in particular, one that of the Sravaka, the second that of Pratyeka Buddha or individual Buddha, and the third that of Bodhisattva—there is in fact only one real path, or one vehicle, or Ekyana. This vehicle includes both the other vehicles known as Hinayana and Mahayana. It is well known that Mahayana or the large vehicle was a later development of Buddhism, which took a distinct ideological turn to include every human being in its hold, whose salvation became the duty of Bodhisattvas who will forego their personal salvation in order to push every other being into it. It was a great ideal indeed and did help bring humanity together in a big way. No wonder, Buddhism became the first great religion of the world to spread all over the then known countries. China took the lead in this process, sending teachers in neighbouring countries, and seekers like Fa Hian, Sun Yung, It-sing, Huen Tsang, etc., to India one after the other in search of the original books of laws and philosophy at the very great cost of physical and other suffering. It may be mentioned that Fa Hian did not agree to write a book on his experiences because it would encourage others to take up the hard journey; and Huen Tsang was attacked by robbers many a time, and was caught to be sacrified at the altar of Durga somewhere in India.

This idea is illustrated with a number of parables, such as that of a burning house, a blind man and a prodigal son.

The nature of the Tathagata has been exemplified by means of developing skillfulness in how to utilise wisdom and growing the qualities of Bodhisattva. The Japanese monk Nichiren in particular emphasised the importance of the Lotus Sutra and promoting the recitation of the chant noted in the beginning, which simply means 'Homage to the Scripture of the Lotus of the Good Teaching' which is all the more effective if done with looking at the Gohouzon, a mandala-like diagram with the words written over it. Amen!

Translatorspeak

THE CROWN JEWEL OF THE SUTRAS

The Saddharma Pundarika is one of the nine Dharmas known by the titles of—1. Ashtasahasrika Prajnaparamita; 2. Gandavyuha; 3. Dasabhumisvara; 4. Samadhiraja; 5. Lankavatara 6. Saddharma Pundarika; 7. Tathgata-guhyaka; 8. Lalitavistara; and 9. Suvarna-prabhasa.

These nine works embrace, in the first an abstract of the philosophy of Buddhism; in the seventh, a treatise on the esoteric doctrines; and in the seven remaining ones, a full illustration of every point of the ordinary doctrine and discipline, taught in the easy and effective way of example and anecdote, interspersed with occasional instances of instruction. With the exception of the first, these works are therefore of a narrative kind, but interwoven with much occasional speculative matter.

The Saddharma Pundarika bears the character of a dramatic performance, in which the chief interlocutor, not the only one, is Sakyamuni, the Lord. It consists of a series of dialogues, brightened by the magic effects of a would-be supernatural scenery. The phantasmagorical parts of the whole are as clearly intended to impress us with the idea of the might and glory of the Buddha, as his speeches are to set forth his all-surpassing wisdom.

There exist various Chinese translations of the Saddharma Pundarika, or parts of it, the dates of which are well ascertained. The oldest Chinese translation, known by

the title of Kan-fa-hwa-kin, is from Ku Fa-hu (Dharmaraksha), of the Western Tsin dynasty, A.D. 265-316, in 28 chapters. Equally old is an incomplete translation entitled Sa-than- fan-tho-li-kin, of an unknown author. Next in time comes the Miao-fa-lien-hwa-kiti, by Kumarajiva, of the latter Tshin dynasty, A. D. 384-417. It agrees with the Tibetan version, and contains 28 chapters. The last translation in order of time, entitled Thien-phin-miao-fa-lien-hwa-kin, is from Jnanagupta and Dharmagupta, A.D. 601, of the Sui dynasty, in 27 chapters.

It is perfectly true that **Sakya does not receive the simple title of Deva, because that title is far too poor for so exalted a personage who is the Devatideva, the paramount god of gods. So he is called in the Lotus, and innumerable times in the whole range of Buddhist literature.** The title of Adibuddha does not occur in the Lotus, but it is intimated that Sakya is identical with Adibuddha in these words:' 'From the very beginning have I roused, brought to maturity, fully developed the innumerable Bodhisattvas to be fit for their Bodhisattva position.' The Buddha most solemnly declares that he reached Bodhi an immense time ago, not as people fancy, first at Gaya. From the whole manner in which Sakya speaks of his existence in former times, it is perfectly clear that the author wished to convey the meaning that the Lord had existed from eternity or, what comes to the same, from the very beginning, from time immemorial.

Sakya has not only lived an infinite number of Aeons in the past, he is to live for ever. Common people fancy that he enters Nirvana, but in reality he only makes a show of Nirvana out of regard for the weakness of men. He, the Father of the world, the self-born One, the Chief and Saviour of creatures, produces a semblance of Nirvana, whenever he sees them given to error and folly. In reality his being is not subject to complete Nirvana; it is only by a skilful devise that he makes a show of it; and repeatedly he appears in the world of the living, though his real abode is on the summit of the Gridhrakuta.

The Buddha is anthropomorphic, of course; what god is not? **The Lotus, far from giving prominence to the unavoidable human traits, endeavours as superhuman beings.** In Chap. XIV there is a great pause, as in a drama, of no less than fifty intermediate kalpas, during which Sakyamuni and all his hearers, keep silence. A second pause of 1000, or according to a various reading, 100,000 years, is held in Chap. XX. Now it is difficult to conceive that any author, wilfully and ostentatiously, would mention such traits if he wished to impress the reader with the notion that the narrative refers to human beings.

It will not be necessary to multiply examples. There is, to my comprehension, not the slightest doubt that the Saddharma Pundarika intends to represent Sakya as the supreme being as the god of gods, almighty and all-wise.

The Sakyamuni of the Lotus is an ideal, a personification, and not a person. Traits borrowed, or rather surviving, from an older cosmological mythology, abound in the Lotus. It is possible that the ancient doctors of the Mahayana have believed that such an ideal one walked in the flesh here on earth, but the impression left by the spirit and the letter of the whole work does not favour that supposition. In later times fervent adherents of the Mahayana really held that belief, as we know from the example of the pious Huen Tsang, who was evidently as earnest in his belief that the Lord once trod the soil of India as he was convinced of Manjusri, Maitreya, and Avalokitesvara existing as animated beings. The book must be acknowledged as the very cream of orthodoxy; **it is the last, the supreme, the most sublime of the Sutras exposed by the Lord; it is, so to say, the Siromani, the crown jewel, of all Sutras.**

The compilers of the Sutra intended giving as exposition of the principal truths of their religion in general, and of the peculiar tenets of their system in particular, the whole with anxious care arranged in such a form that the Sutra admitted of an exoterical and esoterical interpretation. It contains a revelation of the state of things in the present, as well as in the past and the future, a revelation derived from a virtually eternal source, so that the doctrine taught in it must be deemed valid not only for a certain spiritual brotherhood or church, but for the human race at large.

The Lotus being one of the standard works of the Mahayana, the study of it cannot but be useful for the right appreciation of that remarkable system. In general it may be said that the spirit of Mahayana is more universal, its ideal less monastical than the Hinayana's. According to Professor Rhys Davids, we must not seek the superior vital power which enabled the Great Vehicle to outlive the earlier teaching in certain metaphysical subtleties, but in the idea of a desire to save all living creatures; 'the idea,' to quote his own words, 'as summarised in the theory of Bodisatship, is the keynote of the later school, just as Arahatship is the keynote of early Buddhism.' The Mahayana doctors said in effect: 'We grant you all you say about the bliss of attaining Nirvana in this life. But it produces advantage only to yourselves; and according to your own theory, there will be a necessity for Buddhas in the future as much as there has been for Buddhas in the past. Greater, better, nobler then, than the attainment of Arahatship must be the attainment of Bodisatship from a desire to save all living creatures in the ages that will come.'

The teaching of the Lotus, however, is different, and comes to this, that everyone should try to become a Buddha. These means are, in plain language, piety, philosophy or rather Yogism, and striving for the enlightenment and weal of our fellow creatures; these means are designated by the terms of Vehicle of obedient hearers or disciples, of Pratyeka Buddhas, and of Bodhisattvas. Higher than piety is true and self-acquired knowledge of the eternal laws; higher than knowledge is devoting oneself to the spiritual weal of others. The higher unity embracing the three separate Vehicles is the Buddha-vehicle.

The title of Bodhisattva is not always used in the same acceptation. Apart from a broad distinction we can draw between human and superhuman Bodhisattvas—we find sometimes the word applied to as styled Sravakas, hearers, learners. This appears to be the case at least in Nepal. 'The Buddha is the adept in the wisdom of Buddhism (Bodhisasana), whose first duty, so long as he remains on earth, is to communicate his wisdom to those who are willing to receive it. These willing learners are the "Bodhisattvas," so called from their hearts being inclined to the wisdom of Buddhism, and "Sanghas," from their companionship with one another, and with their Buddha or teacher, in the viharas or cohabitical establishments. The Bodhisattva or Sangha continues to be such until he has surmounted the very last grade of that vast and laborious ascent by which he is instructed that he can "scale the heavens," and pluck immortal wisdom from its resplendent source: which achievement performed, he becomes a Buddha, that is, an Omniscient Being.

The Bodhisattvas were charged with the office of preaching. They are persons who deserve to be honoured both by mendicant monks and lay devotees, and formed, it would seem, a kind of learned clergy. Taranatha considers it to be the equivalent of the older Mahabhadanta; he distinguishes 'Bodhisattvas' from 'common Panditas' and 'Arhats'. The Vehicle of the Bodisattvas is the loftiest; they must be considered as occupying the highest rank. Arhats are sages of the past, canonized saints; human Bodhisattvas are sages, wise men of the present, most reverend worthies who should live a saintly life and generally do so, but who, however sanctimonious, are not acknowledged saints. The Arhats being dead, they cannot be active; the Bodhisattvas as living persons, can. The remark of Professor Rhys Davids holds good:

the Bodhisattvas represent the ideal of spiritual activity, the Arhats of inactivity. The Lotus breathes a less monastic and ascetic spirit; it does not go the length to speak of ascetism and mortification in scornful terms but at the same time, it never extols it. There are in the book many indications that the art of preaching was made much of and highly developed, and it may be supposed that a greater proficiency in hermeneutics combined with superior mental activity has enabled the Mahayana to supplant its rival, the Hinayana, and to extend its spiritual conquests from the snows of Siberia to the luxuriant islands of the Indian Archipelago.

The base of my translation has been an old manuscript on palm leaves, belonging to Dr. D. Wright's collection, in the University Library of Cambridge. It is one of the most ancient Sanskrit MSS existing in Europe, and therefore I thought that if was advisable to follow its readings as much as possible, except in such passages as were evidently corrupt. A second MS, unfortunately incomplete, from the same collection, is of unknown date since the latter part of the codex is lost.

I beg to offer my sincere thanks of Professors William Wright and E.B. Cowell, at Cambridge, for the generous way in which they have enabled me to use the MSS.

—Leiden

CONTENTS

Lord Buddha, Thailand

—Nam Myoho Renge Kyo—
Homage to the Scripture of the Lotus
of the Good Teaching

1

THE GREAT ASSEMBLY

At Rajagriha, on Gridhrakuta, gather a large number of men, monks and kings, to hear the venerable Buddha deliver his Great Exposition.

Thus have I heard. Once upon a time the Lord was staying at Rajagriha, on the Gridhrakuta mountain with a numerous assemblage of monks, twelve hundred monks, all of them Arhats, stainless, free from depravity, self-controlled, thoroughly emancipated in thought and knowledge, of noble breed, like unto great elephants, having done their task, done their duty, acquitted their charge, reached the goal; in whom the ties which bound them to existence were wholly destroyed, whose minds were thoroughly emancipated by perfect knowledge, who had reached the utmost perfection in subduing all their thoughts; who were possessed of the transcendent faculties; eminent disciples, such as the venerable Ajnata-Kaundinya, the venerable Asvajit, the venerable Vashpa, the venerable Mahanaman, the venerable Bhadrika, the venerable Maha-Kasyapa, the venerable Kasyapa of Uruvilva, the venerable Kasyapa of Nadi, the venerable Kasyapa of Gaya, the venerable Sariputra, the venerable Maha-Maudgalyayana, the venerable Maha-Katayana, the venerable Aniruddha, the venerable Revata, the venerable Kapphina, the venerable Gavampati, the venerable Pulindavatsa, the venerable Vakula, the venerable Bharadvaja, the venerable Maha-Kaushthila, the venerable Nanda, the venerable Upananda, the venerable Sundara-Nanda, the venerable Purna Maitrayaniputra, the venerable Subhuti, the venerable Rahula; with them yet other great disciples, as the venerable Ananda, still under training, and two thousand other monks, some of whom still under training, the others masters; with six thousand nuns having at their head Mahaprjapati, and the nun Yasodhara, the mother of Rahula along with her train; further with eighty thousand Bodhisattvas, all unable to slide back, endowed with the spells of supreme, perfect enlightenment, firmly standing in wisdom; who moved onward the never deviating wheel of the law; who had propitiated many hundred thousands of Buddhas; who under many hundred thousands of Buddhas had planted the roots of goodness, had been intimate with many hundred thousands of Buddhas, were in body and mind fully penetrated with the feeling of charity; able in communicating the wisdom of the Tathagatas; very wise, having reached the perfection of wisdom; renowned in many hundred thousands of worlds; having saved many hundred thousand myriads of kotis of beings; such as the Bodhisattva Mahasattva Manjusri, as prince royal; the Bodhisattvas Mahasattvas Avalokitesvara, Mahasthamaprapta, Sarvarthanaman, Nityodyukta, Anikshiptadhura, Ratnapani, Bhaishajyaraja, Pradanasura, Ratnachandra, Ratnaprabha, Purnachandra, Mahavikramin, Trailokavikramin, Anantavikramin, Mahapratibhana, Satatasamitabhiyukta, Dharanidhara, Akshayamati, Padmasri, Nakshatraraja, the Bodhisattva Mahasattva Maitreya, the Bodhisattva Mahasattva Simha.

With them were also the sixteen virtuous men to begin with Bhadrapala, to wit, Bhadrapala, Ratnakara, Susarthavaha, Naradatta, Guhagupta, Varunadatta, Indradatta, Uttaramati, Viseshamati, Vardhamanamati, Amoghadarsin, Susamsthita, Suvikranta-vikramin, Anupamamati, Suryagarbha, and Dharanidhara; besides eighty thousand Bodhisattvas, among whom the forementioned were the chiefs; further Sakra, the ruler of the celestials, with twenty thousand gods, his followers, such as the god Chandra (the Moon), the god Surya (the Sun), the god Samantagandha (the Wind), the god Ratnaprabha, the god Avabhasaprabha, and others; further, the four great rulers of the cardinal points with thirty thousand gods in their train, viz., the great ruler Virudhaka, the great ruler Virupaksha, the great ruler Dhritarashtra, and the great ruler Vaisravana; the god Isvara and the god Mahesvara, each followed by thirty thousand gods; further, Brahma Sahampati and his twelve thousand followers, the Brahmakayika gods, amongst whom Brahma Sikhin and Brahma Jyotishprabha, with the other twelve thousand Brahmakayika gods; together with the eight Naga kings and many hundred thousand myriads of kotis of Nagas in their train, viz., the Naga king Nanda, the Naga king Upananda, Sagara, Vasuki, Takshaka, Manasvin, Anavatapta, and Utpalaka; further, the four Kinnara kings with many hundred thousand myriads of kotis of followers, viz., the Kinnara king Druma, the Kinnara king Mahadharma, the Kinnara king Sudharma, and the Kinnara king Dharmadhara; besides, the four divine beings called Gandharvakayikas with many hundred thousand Gandharvas in their suite, viz., the Gandharva Manojna, the Gandharva Manojnasvara, the Gandharva Madhura, and the Gandharva Madhurasvara; further, the four chiefs of the demons followed by many hundred thousand myriads of kotis of demons, viz., the chief of the demons Bali, Kharaskandha, Vemachitri, and Rahu; along with the four Garuda chiefs followed by many hundred thousand myriads of kotis of Garudas, viz., the Garuda chiefs Mahatejas, Mahakaya, Mahapurna, and Mahariddhiprapta, and with Ajatasatru, king of Magadha, the son of Vaidehi.

Now at that time it was that the Lord surrounded, attended, honoured, revered, venerated, worshipped by the four classes of hearers, after expounding the Dharmaparyaya called 'the Great Exposition,' a text of great development, serving to instruct Bodhisattvas and proper to all Buddhas, sat cross-legged on the seat of the law and entered upon the meditation termed 'the station of the exposition of Infinity;' his body was motionless and his mind had reached perfect tranquillity. And as soon as the Lord had entered upon his meditation, there fell a great rain of divine flowers, Mandaravas and great Mandaravas, Manjushakas and great Manjushakas, covering the Lord and the four classes of hearers, while the whole Buddha-field shook in six ways: it moved, removed, trembled, trembled from one end to the other, tossed, tossed along.

Then did those who were assembled and sitting together in that congregation, monks, nuns, male and female lay devotees, gods, Nagas, goblins, Gandharvas, demons, Garudas, Kinnaras, great serpents, men, and beings not human, as well as governors of a region, rulers of armies and rulers of four continents, all of them with their followers, gaze on the Lord in astonishment, in amazement, in ecstasy.

And at that moment there issued a ray from within the circle of hair between the eyebrows of the Lord. It extended over eighteen hundred thousand Buddha-fields in the eastern quarter, so that all those Buddha-fields appeared wholly illuminated by its radiance, down to the great hell Avichi and up to the limit of existence. And the beings in any of the six states of existence became visible, all without exception. Likewise the Lords Buddhas staying, living, and existing in those Buddha-fields became all visible, and the law preached by them could be entirely heard by all beings. And the monks, nuns, lay devotees male and female, Yogins and students of Yoga, those who had obtained the fruition of the Paths of sanctification and those who had not, they, too, became visible. And the Bodhisattvas Mahasattvas in those Buddha-fields who plied the Bodhisattva-course with ability, due to their earnest belief in numerous and various lessons and the fundamental ideas, they, too, became all visible. Likewise the Lords Buddhas in those Buddha-fields who had reached final Nirvana became visible, all of them. And the Stupas made of jewels and containing the relics of the extinct Buddhas became all visible in those Buddha-fields.

Then rose in the mind of the Bodhisattva Mahasattva Maitreya this thought: O how great a wonder does the Tathagata display! What may be the cause, what the reason of the Lord producing so great a wonder as this? And such astonishing, prodigious, inconceivable, powerful miracles now appear, although the Lord is absorbed in meditation! Why, let me inquire about this matter; who would be able here to explain it to me? He then thought: Here is Manjusri, the prince royal, who has plied his office under forme Jinas and planted the roots of goodness, while worshipping many Buddhas. This Manjusri, the prince royal, must have witnessed before such signs of the former Tathagatas, those Arhats, those perfectly enlightened Buddhas; of yore he must have enjoyed the grand conversations on the law. Therefore will I inquire about this matter with Manjusri, the prince royal.

And the four classes of the audience, monks, nuns, male and female lay devotees, numerous gods, Nagas, goblins, Gandharvas, demons, Garudas, Kinnaras, great serpents, men, and beings not human, on seeing the magnificence of this great miracle of the Lord, were struck with astonishment, amazement and curiosity, and thought: Let us inquire why this magnificent miracle has been produced by the great power of the Lord.

At the same moment, at that very instant, the Bodhisattva Mahasattva Maitreya knew in his mind the thoughts arising in the minds of the four classes of hearers and he spoke to Manjusri, the prince royal: What, O Manjusri, is the cause, what is the reason of this wonderful, prodigious, miraculous shine having been produced by the Lord? Look, how these eighteen thousand Buddha-fields appear variegated, extremely beautiful, directed by Tathagatas and superintended by Tathagatas.

Then it was that Maitreya, the Bodhisattva Mahasattva, addressed Manjusri, the prince royal, in the following stanzas:

1. Why, Manjusri, does this ray darted by the guide of men shine forth from between his brows? This single ray issuing from the circle of hair? and why this abundant rain of Mandaravas?
2. The gods, overjoyed, let drop Manjushakas and sandal powder, divine, fragrant, and delicious.
3. This earth is, on every side, replete with splendour, and all the four classes of the assembly are filled with delight, while the whole field shakes in six different ways, frightfully.
4. And that ray in the eastern quarter illuminates the whole of eighteen thousand Buddha-fields, simultaneously, so that those fields appear as gold-coloured.
5. The universe as far as the hell Avichi and the extreme limit of existence, with all beings of those fields living in any of the six states of existence, those who are leaving one state to be born in another;

6. Their various and different actions in those states have become visible; whether they are in a happy, unhappy, low, eminent, or intermediate position, all that I see from this place.
7. I see also the Buddhas, those lions of kings, revealing and showing the essence of the law, comforting many kotis of creatures and emitting sweet-sounding voices.
8. They let go forth, each in his own field, a deep, sublime, wonderful voice, while proclaiming the Buddha-laws by means of myriads of kotis of illustrations and proofs.
9. And to the ignorant creatures who are oppressed with toils and distressed in mind by birth and old age, they announce the bliss of Rest, saying: This is the end of trouble, O monks.
10. And to those who are possessed of strength and vigour and who have acquired merit by virtue or earnest belief in the Buddhas, they show the vehicle of the Pratyeka Buddhas, by observing this rule of the law.
11. And the other sons of the Sugata who, striving after superior knowledge, have constantly accomplished their various tasks, them also they admonish to enlightenment.
12. From this place, O Manjughosha, I see and hear such things and thousands of kotis of other particulars besides; I will only describe some of them.
13. I see in many fields Bodhisattvas by many thousands of kotis, like sands of the Ganges, who are producing enlightenment according to the different degree of their power.
14. There are some who charitably bestow wealth, gold, silver, gold money, pearls, jewels, conch shells, stones, coral, male and female slaves, horses, and sheep;
15. As well as litters adorned with jewels. They are spending gifts with glad hearts, developing themselves for superior enlightenment, in the hope of gaining the vehicle.
16. Thus they think: 'The best and most excellent vehicle in the whole of the threefold world is the Buddha-vehicle magnified by the Sugatas. May I, forsooth, soon gain it after my spending such gifts.'

17. Some give carriages yoked with four horses and furnished with benches, flowers, banners, and flags; others give objects made of precious substances.
18. Some, again, give their children and wives; others their own flesh; offer, when bidden, their hands and feet, striving to gain supreme enlightenment.
19. Some give their heads, others their eyes, others theif dear own body, and after cheerfully bestowing their gifts they aspire to the knowledge of the Tathagatas.
20. Here and there, O Manjusri, I behold beings who have abandoned their flourishing kingdoms, harems, and continents, left all their counsellors and kinsmen,
21. And betaken themselves to the guides of the world to ask for the most excellent law, for the sake of bliss; they put on reddish-yellow robes, and shave hair and beard.
22. I see also many Bodhisattvas like monks, living in the forest, and others inhabiting the empty wilderness, engaged in reciting and reading.
23. And some Bodhisattvas I see, who, full of wisdom or constancy, betake themselves to mountain caves, where by cultivating and meditating the Buddha-knowledge they arrive at its perception.
24. Others who have renounced all sensual desires, by purifying their own self, have cleared their sphere and obtained the five transcendent faculties, live in the wilderness, as true sons of the Sugata.
25. Some are standing firm, the feet put together and the hands joined in token of respect towards the leaders, and are praising joyfully the king of the leading Jinas in thousands of stanzas.
26. Some thoughtful, meek, and tranquil, who have mastered the niceties of the course of duty, question the highest of men about the law, and retain in their memory what they have learnt.
27. And I see here and there some sons of the principal Jina who, after completely developing their own self, are preaching the law to many kotis of living beings with many myriads of illustrations and reasons.

28. Joyfully they proclaim the law, rousing many Bodhisattvas; after conquering the Evil One with his hosts and vehicles, they strike the drum of the law.
29. I see some sons of the Sugata, humble, calm, and quiet in conduct, living under the command of the Sugatas, and honoured by men, gods, goblins, and Titans.
30. Others, again, who have retired to woody thickets, are saving the creatures in the hells by emitting radiance from their body, and rouse them to enlightenment.
31. There are some sons of the Jina who dwell in the forest, abiding in vigour, completely renouncing sloth, and actively engaged in walking; it is by energy that they are striving for supreme enlightenment.
32. Others complete their course by keeping a constant purity and an unbroken morality like precious stones and jewels; by morality do these strive for supreme enlightenment
33. Some sons of the Jina, whose strength consists in forbearance, patiently endure abuse, censure, and threats from proud monks. They try to attain enlightenment by dint of forbearance.
34. Further, I see Bodhisattvas, who have forsaken all wanton pleasures, shun unwise companions and delight in having intercourse with genteel men (aryas);
35. Who, with avoidance of any distraction of thoughts and with attentive mind, during thousands of kotis of years have meditated in the caves of the wilderness; these strive for enlightenment by dint of meditation.
36. Some, again, offer in presence of the Jinas and the assemblage of disciples gifts consisting in food hard and soft, meat and drink, medicaments for the sick, in plenty and abundance.
37. Others offer in presence of the Jinas and the assemblage of disciples hundreds of kotis of clothes, worth thousands of kotis, and garments of priceless value.
38. They bestow in presence of the Sugatas hundreds of kotis of monasteries which they have caused to be built of precious substances and sandalwood, and which are furnished with numerous lodgings or couches.

39. Some present the leaders of men and their disciples with neat and lovely gardens abounding with fruits and beautiful flowers, to serve as places of daily recreation.
40. When they have, with joyful feelings, made such various and splendid donations, they rouse their energy in order to obtain enlightenment; these are those who try to reach supreme enlightenment by means of charitableness.
41. Others set forth the law of quietness, by many myriads of illustrations and proofs; they preach it to thousands of kotis of living beings; these are tending to supreme enlightenment by science.
42. There are sons of the Sugata who try to reach enlightenment by wisdom; they understand the law of indifference and avoid acting at the antinomy of things, unattached like birds in the sky.
43. Further, I see, O Manjughosha, many Bodhisattvas who have displayed steadiness under the rule of the departed Sugatas, and now are worshipping the relics of the Jinas.
44. I see thousands of kotis of Stupas, numerous as the sand of the Ganges, which have been raised by these sons of the Jina and now adorn kotis of grounds.
45. Those magnificent Stupas, made of seven precious substances, with their thousands of kotis of umbrellas and banners, measure in height no less than 5000 yojanas and 2000 in circumference.
46. They are always decorated with flags; a multitude of bells is constantly heard sounding; men, gods, goblins, and Titans pay their worship with flowers, perfumes, and music.
47. Such honour do the sons of the Sugata render to the relics of the Jinas, so that all directions of space are brightened as by the celestial coral trees in full blossom.
48. From this spot I behold all this; those numerous kotis of creatures; both this world and heaven covered with flowers, owing to the single ray shot forth by the Jina.
49. O how powerful is the Leader of men! how extensive and bright is his knowledge! that a single beam darted by him over the world renders visible so many thousands of fields!

50. We are astonished at seeing this sign and this wonder, so great, so incomprehensible. Explain to me the matter, O Manjusvara! the sons of Buddha are anxious to know it.
51. The four classes of the congregation in joyful expectation gaze on thee, O hero, and on me; gladden their hearts; remove their doubts; grant a revelation, O son of Sugata!
52. Why is it that the Sugata has now emitted such a light? O how great is the power of the Leader of men! O how extensive and holy is his knowledge!
53. That one ray extending from him all over the world makes visible many thousands of fields. It must be for some purpose that this great ray has been emitted.
54. Is the Lord of men to show the primordial laws which he, the Highest of men, discovered on the terrace of enlightenment? Or is he to prophesy the Bodhisattvas their future destiny?
55. There must be a weighty reason why so many thousands of fields have been rendered visible, variegated, splendid, and shining with gems, while Buddhas of infinite sight are appearing.
56. Maitreya asks the son of Jina; men, gods, goblins, and Titans, the four classes of the congregation, are eagerly awaiting what answer Maujusvara shall give in explanation.

Whereupon Manjusrt, the prince royal, addressed Maitreya, the Bodhisattva Mahasattva, and the whole assembly of Bodhisattvas in these words: It is the intention of the Tathagata, young men of good family, to begin a grand discourse for the teaching of the law, to pour the great rain of the law, to make resound the great drum of the law, to raise the great banner of the law, to kindle the great torch of the law, to blow the great conch trumpet of the law, and to strike the great tymbal of the law. Again, it is the intention of the Tathagata, young men of good family, to make a grand exposition of the law this very day. Thus it appears to me, young men of good family, as I have witnessed a similar sign of the former Tathagatas, the Arhats, the perfectly enlightened. Those former Tathagatas, etc., they, too, emitted a lustrous ray, and I am convinced that the

Tathagata is about to deliver a grand discourse for the teaching of the law and make his grand speech on the law everywhere heard, he having shown such a foretoken. And because the Tathagata, etc., wishes that this Dharmaparyaya meeting opposition in all the world be heard everywhere, therefore does he display so great a miracle and this foretoken consisting in the lustre occasioned by the emission of a ray.

I remember, young men of good family, that in the days of yore, many immeasurable, inconceivable, immense, infinite, countless Aeons, more than countless Aeons ago, nay, long and very long before, there was born a Tathagata called Chandrasuryapradipa, an Arhat, etc., endowed with science and conduct, a Sugata, knower of the world, an incomparable tamer of men, a teacher and ruler of gods and men, a Buddha and Lord. He showed the law; he revealed the duteous course which is holy at its commencement, holy in its middle, holy at the end, good in substance and form, complete and perfect, correct and pure. That is to say, to the disciples he preached the law containing the four Noble Truths, and starting from the chain of causes and effects, tending to overcome birth, decrepitude, sickness, death, sorrow, lamentation, woe, grief, despondency, and finally leading to Nirvana; and to the Bodhisattvas he preached the law connected with the six Perfections, and terminating in the knowledge of the Omniscient, after the attainment of supreme, perfect enlightenment.

Now, young men of good family, long before the time of that Tathagata Kandrasuryapradipa, the Arhat, etc., there had appeared a Tathagata, etc., likewise called Kandrasurya-pradipa, after whom, O Ajita, there were twenty thousand Tathagatas, etc., all of them bearing the name of Kandrasurya-pradipa, of the same lineage and family name, of Bharadvaja. All those twenty thousand Tathagatas, O Ajita, from the first to the last, showed the law, revealed the course which is holy at its commencement, holy in its middle, holy at the end, etc.

The aforesaid Lord Kandrasuryapradipa, the Tathagata, etc., when a young prince and not yet having left home to embrace the ascetic life, had eight sons, viz., the young princes Sumati,

Anantamati, Ratnamati, Viseshamati, Vimatisamudghatin, Ghoshamati, and Dharmamati. These eight young princes, Ajita, sons to the Lord Kandrasuryapradipa, the Tathagata, had an immense fortune. Each of them was in possession of four great continents, where they exercised the kingly sway. When they saw that the Lord had left his home to become an ascetic, and heard that he had attained supreme, perfect enlightenment, they forsook all of them the pleasures of royalty and followed the example of the Lord by resigning the world; all of them strove to reach superior enlightenment and became preachers of the law. While constantly leading a holy life, those young princes planted roots of goodness under many thousands of Buddhas.

It was at that time, Ajita, that the Lord Kandrasuryapradipa, the Tathagata, etc., after expounding the Dharmaparyaya called 'the Great Exposition,' a text of great extension, serving to instruct Bodhisattvas and proper to all Buddhas, at the same moment and instant, at the same gathering of the classes of hearers, sat cross-legged on the same seat of the law, and entered upon the meditation termed 'the Station of the Exposition of Infinity;' his body was motionless, and his mind had reached perfect tranquillity. And as soon as the Lord had entered upon meditation, there fell a great rain of divine flowers, Mandaravas and great Mandaravas, Manjushakas and great Manjshakas, covering the Lord and the four classes of hearers, while the whole Buddha-field shook in six ways; it moved, removed, trembled, trembled from one end to the other, tossed, tossed along.

Then did those who were assembled and sitting together at that congregation, monks, nuns, male and female lay devotees, gods, Nagas, goblins, Gandharvas, demons, Garudas, Kinnaras, great serpents, men and beings not human, as well as governors of a region, rulers of armies and rulers of four continents, all of them with their followers gaze on the Lord in astonishment, in amazement, in ecstasy.

And at that moment there issued a ray from within the circle of hair between the eyebrows of the Lord. It extended over eighteen hundred thousand Buddha-fields in the eastern quarter, so that all those Buddha-fields appeared wholly illuminated by its radiance, just like the Buddha-fields do now, O Ajita.

At that juncture, Ajita, there were twenty kotis of Bodhisattvas following the Lord. All hearers of the law in that assembly, on seeing how the world was illuminated by the lustre of that ray, felt astonishment, amazement, ecstasy, and curiosity.

Now it happened, Ajita, that under the rule of the aforesaid Lord there was a Bodhisattva called Varaprabha, who had eight hundred pupils. It was to this Bodhisattva Varaprabha that the Lord, on rising from his meditation, revealed the Dharmaparyaya called 'the Lotus of the True Law.' He spoke during fully sixty intermediate kalpas, always sitting on the same seat, with immovable body and tranquil mind. And the whole assembly continued sitting on the same seats, listening to the preaching of the Lord for sixty intermediate kalpas, there being not a single creature in that assembly who felt fatigue of body or mind.

As the Lord Kandrasuryapradipa, the Tathagata, etc., during sixty intermediate kalpas had been expounding the Dharmaparyaya called 'the Lotus of the True Law,' a text of great development, serving to instruct Bodhisattvas and proper to all Buddhas, he instantly announced his complete Nirvana to the world, including the gods, Maras and Brahmas, to all creatures, including ascetics, Brahmins, gods, men and demons, saying: To-day, O monks, this very night, in the middle watch, will the Tathagata, by entering the element of absolute Nirvana, become wholly extinct.

Thereupon, Ajita, the Lord Kandrasuryapradipa, the Tathagata, etc., predestinated the Bodhisattva called Srigarbha to supreme, perfect enlightenment, and then spoke thus to the whole assembly: O monks, this Bodhisattva Srigarbha here shall immediately after me attain supreme, perfect enlightenment, and become Vimalanetra, the Tathagata, etc.

Thereafter, Ajita, that very night, at that very watch, the Lord Kandrasuryapradipa, the Tathagata, etc., became extinct by entering the element of absolute Nirvana. And the aforementioned Dharmaparyaya, termed 'the Lotus of the True Law,' was kept in memory by the Bodhisattva Mahasattva Varaprabha; during eighty intermediate kalpas did the Bodhisattva Varaprabha keep and reveal the commandment of the Lord who had entered Nirvana. Now it so happened, Ajita, that the eight sons of the Lord Kandrasuryapradipa, Mati and the rest, were pupils to that very Bodhisattva Varaprabha. They were by him made ripe for supreme, perfect enlightenment, and in after times they saw and worshipped many hundred thousand myriads of kotis of Buddhas, all of whom had attained supreme, perfect enlightenment, the last of them being Dipankara, the Tathagata, etc.

Amongst those eight pupils there was one Bodhisattva who attached an extreme value to gain, honour and praise, and was fond of glory, but all the words and letters one taught him faded from his memory, did not stick. So he got the appellation of Yasaskama. He had propitiated many hundred thousand myriads of kotis of Buddhas by that root of goodness, and afterwards esteemed, honoured., respected, revered, venerated, worshipped them. Perhaps, Ajita, thou feelest some doubt, perplexity or misgiving that in those days, at that time, there was another Bodhisvattva Mahasattva Varaprabha, preacher of the law. But do not think so. Why? because it is myself who in those days, at that time, was the Bodhisattva Mahasattva Varaprabha, preacher of the law; and that Bodhisattva named Yasaskama, the lazy one, it is thyself, Ajita, who in those days, at that time, were the Bodhisattva named Yasaskama, the lazy one.

And so, Ajita, having once seen a similar foretoken of the Lord, I infer from a similar ray being emitted just now, that the Lord is about to expound the Dharmaparyaya called 'the Lotus of the True Law.'

And on that occasion, in order to treat the subject more copiously, Manjusri, the prince royal, uttered the following stanzas:

57. I remember a past period, inconceivable, illimited kalpas ago, when the highest of beings, the Jina of the name of Kandrasuryapradipa, was in existence.
58. He preached the true law, he, the leader of creatures; he educated an infinite number of kotis of beings, and roused inconceivably many Bodhisattvas to acquiring supreme Buddha-knowledge.

59. And the eight sons born to him, the leader, when he was prince royal, no sooner saw that the great sage had embraced ascetic life, than they resigned worldly pleasures and became monks.

60. And the Lord of the world proclaimed the law, and revealed to thousands of kotis of living beings the Sutra, the development, which by name is called 'the excellent Exposition of Infinity.'

61. Immediately after delivering his speech, the leader crossed his legs and entered upon the meditation of 'the excellent Exposition of the Infinite.' There on his seat of the law the eminent seer continued absorbed in meditation.

62. And there fell a celestial rain of Mandaravas, while the drums of heaven resounded without being struck; the gods and elves in the sky paid honour to the highest of men.

63. And simultaneously all the fields of Buddha began trembling. A wonder it was, a great prodigy. Then the chief emitted from between his brows one extremely beautiful ray,

64. Which moving to the eastern quarter glittered, illuminating the world all over the extent of eighteen thousand fields. It manifested the vanishing and appearing of beings.

65. Some of the fields then seemed jewelled, others showed the hue of lapis lazuli, all splendid, extremely beautiful, owing to the radiance of the ray from the leader.

66. Gods and men, as well as Nagas, goblins, Gandharvas, nymphs, Kinnaras, and those occupied with serving the Sugata became visible in the spheres and paid their devotion.

67. The Buddhas also, those self-born beings, appeared of their own accord, resembling golden columns; like unto a golden disk (within lapis lazuli), they revealed the law in the midst of the assembly.

68. The disciples, indeed, are not to be counted: the disciples of Sugata are numberless. Yet the lustre of the ray renders them all visible in every field.

69. Energetic, without breach or flaw in their course, similar to gems and jewels, the sons of the leaders of men are visible in the mountain caves where they are dwelling.
70. Numerous Bodhisattvas, like the sand of the Ganges, who are spending all their wealth in giving alms, who have the strength of patience, are devoted to contemplation and wise, become all of them visible by that ray.
71. Immovable, unshaken, firm in patience, devoted to contemplation, and absorbed in meditation are seen the true sons of the Sugatas while they are striving for supreme enlightenment by dint of meditation.
72. They preach the law in many spheres, and point to the true, quiet, spotless state they know. Such is the effect produced by the power of the Sugata.
73. And all the four classes of hearers on seeing the power of the mighty Kandrarkadipa were filled with joy and asked one another: How is this?
74. And soon afterwards, as the Leader of the world, worshipped by men, gods, and goblins, rose from his meditation, he addressed his son Varaprabha, the wise Bodhisattva and preacher of the law:
75. 'Thou art wise, the eye and refuge of the world; thou art the trustworthy keeper of my law, and canst bear witness as to the treasure of laws which I am to lay bare to the weal of living beings.'
76. Then, after rousing and stimulating, praising and lauding many Bodhisattvas, did the Jina proclaim the supreme laws during fully sixty intermediate kalpas.
77. And whatever excellent supreme law was proclaimed by the Lord of the world while continuing sitting on the very same seat, was kept in memory by Varaprabha, the son of Jina, the preacher of the law.
78. And after the Jina and Leader had manifested the supreme law and stimulated the numerous crowd, he spoke, that day, towards the world including the gods as follows:
79. 'I have manifested the rule of the law; I have shown the nature of the law; now, O monks, it is the time of my Nirvana; this very night, in the middle watch.

80. 'Be zealous and strong in persuasion; apply yourselves to my lessons; for the Jinas, the great seers, are but rarely met with in the lapse of myriads of kotis of Aeons.'
81. The many sons of Buddha were struck with grief and filled with extreme sorrow when they heard the voice of the highest of men announcing that his Nirvana was near at hand.
82. To comfort so inconceivably many kotis of living beings the king of kings said: 'Be not afraid, O monks; after my Nirvana there shall be another Buddha.
83. 'The wise Bodhisattva Srigarbha, after finishing his course in faultless knowledge, shall reach highest, supreme enlightenment, and become a Jina under the name of Vimalagranetra.'
84. That very night, in the middle watch, he met complete extinction, like a lamp when the cause of its burning is exhausted. His relics were distributed, and of his Stupas there was an infinite number of myriads of kotis.
85. The monks and nuns at the time being, who strove after supreme, highest enlightenment, numerous as sand of the Ganges, applied themselves to the commandment of the Sugata.
86. And the monk who then was the preacher of the law and the keeper of the law, Varaprabha, expounded for fully eighty intermediate kalpas the highest laws according to the commandment of the Sugata.
87. He had eight hundred pupils, who all of them were by him brought to full development. They saw many kotis of Buddhas, great sages, whom they worshipped.
88. By following the regular course they became Buddhas in several spheres, and as they followed one another in immediate succession they successively foretold each other's future destiny to Buddhaship.
89. The last of these Buddhas following one another was Dipankara. He, the supreme god of gods, honoured by crowds of sages, educated thousands of kotis of living beings.

90. Among the pupils of Varaprabha, the son of Jina, at the time of his teaching the law, was one slothful, covetous, greedy of gain and cleverness.
91. He was also excessively desirous of glory, but very fickle, so that the lessons dictated to him and his own reading faded from his memory as soon as learnt.
92. His name was Yasaskama, by which he was known everywhere. By the accumulated merit of that good action, spotted as it was,
93. He propitiated thousands of kotis of Buddhas, whom he rendered ample honour. He went through the regular course of duties and saw the present Buddha Sakyasimha.
94. He shall be the last to reach superior enlightenment and become a Lord known by the family name of Maitreya, who shall educate thousands of kotis of creatures.
95. He who then, under the rule of the extinct Sugata, was so slothful, was thyself, and it was I who then was the preacher of the law.
96. As on seeing a foretoken of this kind I recognise a sign such as I have seen manifested of yore, therefore and on that account I know,
97. That decidedly the chief of Jinas, the supreme king of the Sakyas, the All-seeing, who knows the highest truth, is about to pronounce the excellent Sutra which I have heard before.
98. That very sign displayed at present is a proof of the skilfulness of the leaders; the Lion of the Sakyas is to make an exhortation, to declare the fixed nature of the law.
99. Be well prepared and well minded; Join your hands: he who is affectionate and merciful to the world is going to speak, is going to pour the endless rain of the law and refresh those that are waiting for enlightenment.
100. And if some should feel doubt, uncertainty, or misgiving in any respect, then the Wise One shall remove it for his children, the Bodhisattvas here striving after enlightenment.

◆ ◆ ◆ ◆ ◆

2

THE LORD SPEAKS OF SKILFULNESS

Awakening of the Lord from his mystic trance, display of his transcendent skilfulness, proved by the apparent trinity of vehicles, whereas in reatity there is but one vehicle.

The Lord then rose with recollection and consciousness from his meditation, and forthwith addressed the venerable Sariputra: The Buddha-knowledge, Sariputra, is profound, difficult to understand, difficult to comprehend. It is difficult for all disciples and Pratyeka Buddhas to fathom the knowledge arrived at by the Tathagatas, etc., and that, Sariputra, because the Tathagatas have worshipped many hundred thousand myriads of kotis of Buddhas; because they have fulfilled their course for supreme, complete enlightenment, during many hundred thousand myriads of kotis of Aeons; because they have wandered far, displaying energy and possessed of wonderful and marvellous properties; possessed of properties difficult to understand; because they have found out things difficult to understand.

The mystery of the Tathagatas, etc., is difficult to understand, Sariputra, because when they explain the, laws or phenomena, things, that have their causes in themselves they do so by means of skilfulness, by the display of knowledge, by arguments, reasons, fundamental ideas, interpretations, and suggestions. By a variety of skilfulness they are able to release creatures that are attached to one point or another. The Tathagatas, etc., Sariputra, have acquired the highest perfection in skilfulness and the display of knowledge; they are endowed with wonderful properties, such as the display of free and unchecked knowledge; the powers; the absence of hesitation;

the independent conditions; the strength of the organs; the constituents of Bodhi; the contemplations; emancipations; meditations; the degrees of concentration of mind. The Tathigatas, etc., Sariputra, are able to expound various things and have something wonderful and marvellous. Enough, Sariputra, let it suffice to say, that the Tathagatas, etc., have something extremely wonderful, Sariputra. None but a Tathagata, Sariputra, can impart to a Tathagata those laws which the Tathagata knows. And all laws, Sariputra, are taught by the Tathagata, and by him alone; no one but he knows all laws, what they are, how they are, like what they are, of what characteristics and of what nature they are.

And on that occasion, to set forth the same subject more copiously, the Lord uttered the following stanzas:

1. Innumerable are the great heroes in the world that embraces gods and men; the totality of creatures is unable to completely know the leaders.
2. None can know their powers and states of emancipation, their absence of hesitation and Buddha-properties, such as they are.
3. Of yore have I followed in the presence of kotis of Buddhas the good course which is profound, subtle, difficult to understand, and most difficult to find.
4. After pursuing that career during an inconceivable number of kotis of Aeons, I have on the terrace of enlightenment discovered the fruit thereof.
5. And therefore I recognise, like the other chiefs of the world, how it is, like what it is, and what are its characteristics.
6. It is impossible to explain it; it is unutterable; nor is there such a being in the world.
7. To whom this law could be explained or who would be able to understand it when explained, with exception of the Bodhisattvas, those who are firm in resolve.

5. As to the disciples of the Knower of the world, those who have done their duty and received praise from the Sugatas, who are freed from faults and have arrived at the last stage of bodily existence, the Jina-knowledge lies beyond their sphere.

9. If this whole sphere were full of beings like Sariputra, and if they were to investigate with combined efforts, they would be unable to comprehend the knowledge of the Sugata.
10. Even if the ten points of space were full of sages like thee, ay, if they were full of such as the rest of my disciples,
11. And if those beings combined were to investigate the knowledge of the Sugata, they would, all together, not be able to comprehend the Buddha-knowledge in its whole immensity.
12. If the ten points of space were filled with Pratyeka Buddhas, free from faults, gifted with acute faculties, and standing in the last stage of their existence, as numerous as reeds and bamboos in the woods;
13. And if combined for an endless number of myriads of kotis of Aeons, they were to investigate a part only of my superior laws, they would never find out its real meaning.
14. If the ten points of space were full of Bodhisattvas who, after having done their duty under many kotis of Buddhas, investigated all things and preached many sermons, after entering a new vehicle;
15. If the whole world were full of them, as of dense reeds and bamboos, without any interstices, and if all combined were to investigate the law which the Sugata has realised;
16. If they were going on investigating for many kotis of Aeons, as incalculable as the sand of the Ganges, with undivided attention and subtle wit, even then that knowledge would be beyond their ken.
17. If such Bodhisattvas as are unable to fall back, numerous as the sand of the Ganges, were to investigate it with undivided attention, it would prove to lie beyond their ken.
18. Profound are the laws of the Buddhas, and subtle; all inscrutable and faultless. I myself know them as well as the Jinas do in the ten directions of the world.
19. Thou, Sariputra, be full of trust in what the Sugata declares. The Jina speaks no falsehood, the great Seer who has so long preached the highest truth.

20. I address all disciples here, those who have set out to reach the enlightenment of Pratyeka Buddhas, those who are roused to activity at my Nirvana, and those who have been released from the series of evils.
21. It is by my superior skilfulness that I explain the law at great length to the world at large. I deliver whosoever are attached to one point or another, and show the three vehicles.

The eminent disciples in the assembly headed by Ajnata Kaundinya, the twelve hundred Arhats faultless and self-controlled, the other monks, nuns, male and female lay devotees using the vehicle of disciples, and those who had entered the vehicle of Pratyeka Buddhas, all of them made this reflection: What may be the cause, what the reason of the Lord so extremely extolling the skilfulness of the Tathagatas of his extolling it by saying, 'Profound is the law by me discovered;' of his extolling it by saying, 'It is difficult for all disciples and Pratyeka Buddhas to understand it.' But as yet the Lord has declared no more than one kind of emancipation, and therefore we also should acquire the Buddha laws on reaching Nirvana. We do not catch the meaning of this utterance of the Lord.

And the venerable Sariputra, who apprehended the doubt and uncertainty of the four classes of the audience and guessed their thoughts from what was passing in his own mind, himself being in doubt about the law, then said to the Lord: What, O Lord, is the cause, what the reason of the Lord so repeatedly and extremely extolling the skilfulness, knowledge, and preaching of the Tathagata? Why does he repeatedly extol it by saying, ' Profound is the law by me discovered; it is difficult to understand the mystery of the Tathagatas.' Never before have I heard from the Lord such a discourse on the law. These four classes of the audience, O Lord, are overcome with doubt and perplexity. Therefore may the Lord be pleased to explain what the Tatha-gata is alluding to, when repeatedly extolling the profound law of the Tathagatas.

On that occasion the venerable Sariputra uttered the following stanzas:

22. Now first does the Sun of men utter such a speech: 'I have acquired the powers, emancipations, and numberless meditations.'
23. And thou mention est the terrace of enlightenment without anyone asking thee; thou mention est the mystery, although no one asks thee.
24. Thcu speakest unasked and laudest thine own course; thou mentionest thy having obtained knowledge and pronounces profound words.
25. Today a question rises in my mind and of these self-controlled, faultless beings striving after Nirvana: Why does the Jina speak in this manner?
26. Those who aspire to the enlightenment of Pratyeka Buddhas, the nuns and monks, gods, Nagas, goblins, Gandharvas, and great serpents, are talking together, while looking up to the highest of men,
27. And ponder in perplexity. Give an elucidation, great Sage, to all the disciples of Sugata here assembled.
28. Myself have reached the perfection of virtue, have been taught by the supreme Sage; still, O highest of men! even in my position I feel some doubt whether the course of duty shown to me shall receive its final sanction by Nirvana.
29. Let thy voice be heard, O thou whose voice resounds like an egregious kettle-drum! proclaim thy law such as it is. The legitimate sons of Jina here standing and gazing at the Jina, with joined hands;
30. As well as the gods, Nagas, goblins, Titans, numbering thousands of kotis, like sand of the Ganges; and those that aspire to superior enlightenment, here standing, fully eighty thousand in number;
31. Further, the kings, rulers of provinces and paramount monarchs, who have flocked hither from thousands of kotis of countries, are now standing with joined hands, and respectful, thinking: How are we to fulfil the course of duty?

The venerable Sariputra having spoken, the Lord said to him: Enough, Sariputra; it is of no use explaining this matter. Why? Because, Sariputra, the world, including the gods, would be frightened if this matter were expounded.

But the venerable Sariputra entreated the Lord a second time, saying: Let the Lord expound, let the Sugata expound this matter, for in this assembly, O Lord, there are many hundreds, many thousands, many hundred thousands, many hundred thousand myriads of kotis of living beings who have seen former Buddhas, who are intelligent, and will believe, value, and accept the words of the Lord.

The venerable Sariputra addressed the Lord with this stanza:

32. Speak clearly, O most eminent of Jinas! in this assembly there are thousands of living beings trustful, affectionate, and respectful towards the Sugata; they will understand the law by thee expounded.

And the Lord said a second time to the venerable Sariputra: Enough, Sariputra; it is of no use explaining this matter, for the world, including the gods, would be frightened, Sariputra, if this matter were expounded, and some monks might be proud and come to a heavy fall.

And on that occasion uttered the Lord the following stanza:

33. Speak no more of it that I should declare this law! This knowledge is too subtle, inscrutable, and there are so many unwise men who in their conceit and foolishness would scoff at the law revealed.

A third time the venerable Sariputra entreated the Lord, saying: Let the Lord expound, let the Sugata expound this matter. In this assembly, O Lord, there are many hundreds of living beings my equals, and many hundreds, many thousands, many hundred thousands, many hundred thousand myriads of kotis of other living beings more, who in former births have been brought by the Lord to full ripeness. They will believe, value, and accept what the Lord declares, which shall tend to their advantage, weal, and happiness in length of time.

On that occasion the venerable Sariputra uttered the following stanzas:

34. Explain the law, O thou most high of men! I, thine eldest son, beseech thee. Here are thousands of kotis of beings who are to believe in the law by thee revealed.

35. And those beings that in former births so long and constantly have by thee been brought to full maturity and now are all standing here with joined hands, they, too, are to believe in this law.
36. Let the Sugata, seeing the twelve hundred, my equals, and those who are striving after superior enlightenment, speak to them and produce in them an extreme joy.

When the Lord for the third time heard the entreaty of the venerable Sariputra, he spoke to him as follows: Now that thou entreatest the Tathagata a third time, Sariputra, I will answer thee. Listen then, Sariputra, take well and duly to heart what I am saying; I am going to speak.

Now it happened that five thousand proud monks, nuns, and lay devotees of both sexes in the congregation rose from their seats and, after saluting with their heads the Lord's feet, went to leave the assembly. Owing to the principle of good which there is in pride they imagined having attained what they had not, and having understood what they had not. Therefore, thinking themselves aggrieved, they went to leave the assembly, to which the Lord by his silence showed assent.

Thereupon the Lord addressed the venerable Sariputra: My congregation, Sariputra, has been cleared from the chaff, freed from the trash; it is firmly established in the strength of faith. It is good, Sariputra, that those proud ones are gone away. Now I am going to expound the matter, Sariputra. 'Very well, Lord,' replied the venerable Sariputra. The Lord then began and said:

It is but now and then, Sariputra, that the Tathagata preaches such a discourse on the law as this. Just as but now and then is seen the blossom of the glamorous fig-tree, Sariputra, so does the Tathagata but now and then preach such a discourse on the law. Believe me, Sariputra; I speak what is real, I speak what is truthful, I speak what is right. It is difficult to understand the exposition of the mystery of the Tathagata, Sariputra; for in elucidating the law, Sariputra, I use hundred thousands of various skilful means, such as different interpretations, indications, explanations, illustrations. It is not by reasoning, Sariputra, that the law is to be found: it is beyond the pale of reasoning, and must be learnt from the Tathagata. For,

Sariputra, it is for a sole object, a sole aim, verily a lofty object, a lofty aim that the Buddha, the Tathagata, etc., appears in the world. **And what is that sole object, that sole aim; that lofty object, that lofty aim of the Buddha, the Tathagata, etc. appearing in the world? To show all creatures the sight of Tathagata-knowledge does the Buddha, the Tathagata, etc., appear in the world; to open the eyes of creatures for the sight of Tathagata-knowledge does the Buddha, the Tathagata, etc., appear in the world.** This, O Sariputra, is the sole object, the sole aim, the sole purpose of his appearance in the world. Such then, Sariputra, is the sole object, the sole aim, the lofty object, the lofty aim of the Tathagata. And it is achieved by the Tathagata. Fot, Sariputra, I do show all creatures the sight of Tathagata-knowledge; I do open the eyes of creatures for the sight of Tathagata-knowledge, Sariputra; I do firmly establish the teaching of Tathagata-knowledge, Sariputra; I do lead the teaching of Tathagata-knowledge on the right path, Sariputra.

By means of one sole vehicle, to wit, the Buddha-vehicle, Sariputra, do I teach creatures the law; there is no second vehicle, nor a third. This is the nature of the law, Sariputra, universally in the world, in all directions. For, Sariputra, all the Tathagatas, etc., who in times past existed in countless, innumerable spheres in all directions for the weal of many, the happiness of many, out of pity to the world, for the benefit, weal, and happiness of the great body of creatures, and who preached the law to gods and men with able means, such as several directions and indications, various arguments, reasons, illustrations, fundamental ideas, interpretations, paying regard to the dispositions of creatures whose inclinations and temperaments are so manifold, all those Buddhas and Lords, Sariputra, have preached the law to creatures by means of only one vehicle, the Buddha-vehicle, which finally leads to omniscience; it is identical with showing all creatures the sight of Tathagata-knowledge; with opening the eyes of creatures for the sight of Tathagata-knowledge; with the awakening or admonishing by the display or sight of Tathagata-knowledge; with leading the teaching of Tathagata-knowledge on the right path. Such is the law they have preached to creatures. And those creatures, Sariputra, who have heard the law from the past Tathagatas, etc., have all of them reached supreme, perfect enlightenment.

And the Tathagatas, etc., who shall exist in future, Sariputra, in countless, innumerable spheres in all directions for the weal of many, the happiness of many, out of pity to the world, for the benefit, weal, and happiness of the great body of creatures, and who shall preach the law to gods and men, etc., as above till the right path. Such is the law they shall preach to creatures. And those creatures, Sariputra, who shall hear the law from the future Tathagatas, etc., shall all of them reach supreme, perfect enlightenment.

And the Tathagatas, etc., who now at present are staying, living, existing, Sariputra, in countless, innumerable spheres in all directions, etc., and who are preaching the law to gods and men etc., as above till the right path. Such is the law they are preaching to creatures. And those creatures, Sariputra, who are hearing the law from the present Tathagatas, etc., shall all of them reach supreme, perfect enlightenment.

I myself also, Sariputra, am at the present period a Tathagata, etc., for the weal of many etc., till manifold; I myself also, Sariputra, am preaching the law to creatures, etc., till the right path. Such is the law I preach to creatures. And those creatures, Sariputra, who now are hearing the law from me, shall all of them reach supreme, perfect enlightenment. In this sense, Sariputra, **it must be understood that nowhere in the world a second vehicle is taught, far less a third.**

Yet, Sariputra, when the Tathagatas, etc., happen to appear at the decay of the epoch, the decay of creatures, the decay of besetting sins, the decay of views, or the decay of lifetime; when they appear amid such signs of decay at the disturbance of the epoch; when creatures are much tainted, full of greed and poor in roots of goodness; then, Sariputra, the Tathagatas, etc., use, skilfully, to designate that one and sole Buddha-vehicle by the appellation of the threefold vehicle. Now, Sariputra, such disciples, Arhats, or Pratyeka Buddhas who do not hear their actually being called to the Buddha-vehicle by the Tathagata, who do not perceive, nor heed it, those, Sariputra, should not be acknowledged as disciples of the Tathagata, nor as Arhats, nor as Pratyeka Buddhas.

Again, Sariputra, if there be some monk or nun pretending to Arhatship without an earnest vow to reach supreme, perfect enlightenment and saying, 'I am standing too high for the Buddha-vehicle, I am in my last appearance in the body before complete Nirvana,' then, Sariputra, consider such a one to be, conceited. For, Sariputra, it is unfit, it is improper that a monk, a faultless Arhat, should not believe in the law which he hears from the Tathagata in his presence. I leave out of question when the Tathagata shall have reached complete Nirvana; for at that period, that time, Sariputra, when the Tathagata shall be wholly extinct, there shall be none who either knows by heart or preaches such Sutras as this. It will be under other Tathagatas, etc., that they are to be freed from doubts. In respect to these things believe my words, Sariputra, value them, take them to heart; for there is no falsehood in the Tathagatas, Sariputra. **There is but one vehicle, Sariputra, and that is the Buddha-vehicle.**

And on that occasion to set forth this matter more copiously the Lord uttered the following stanzas:

37. No less than five thousand monks, nuns, and lay devotees of both sexes, full of unbelief and conceit,
38. Remarking this slight, went, defective in training and foolish as they were, away in order to beware of damage.
39. The Lord, who knew them to be the dregs of the congregation, exclaimed: They have no sufficient merit to hear this law.
40. My congregation is now pure, freed from chaff; the trash is removed and the pith only remains.
41. Hear from me, Sariputra, how this law has been discovered by the highest man, and how the mighty Buddhas are preaching it with many hundred proofs of skilfulness.
42. I know the disposition and conduct, the various inclinations of kotis of living beings in this world; I know their various actions and the good they have done before.
43. Those living beings I initiate in this law by the aid of manifold interpretations and reasons; and by hundreds of

arguments and illustrations have I, in one way or another, gladdened all creatures.

44. I utter both Sutras and stanzas; legends, Jatakas, and prodigies, besides hundreds of introductions and curious parables.
45. I show Nirvana to the ignorant with low dispositions, who have followed no course of duty under many kotis of Buddhas, are bound to continued existence and wretched.
46. The self-born one uses such means to manifest Buddha-knowledge, but he shall never say to them, Ye also are to become Buddhas.
47. Why should not the mighty one, after having waited for the right time, speak, now that he perceives the right moment is come? This is the fit opportunity, met somehow, of commencing the exposition of what really is.
48. Now the word of my commandment, as contained in nine divisions, has been published according to the varying degrees of strength of creatures: Such is the device I have shown in order to introduce creatures to the knowledge of the giver of boons.
49. And to those in the world who have always been pure, wise, good-minded, compassionate sons of Buddha and done their duty under many kotis of Buddhas will I make known amplified Sutras.
50. For they are endowed with such gifts of mental disposition and such advantages of a blameless outward form that I can announce to them: in future ye shall become Buddhas benevolent and compassionate.
51. Hearing which, all of them will be pervaded with delight at the thought: We shall become Buddhas pre-eminent in the world. And I, perceiving their conduct, will again reveal amplified Sutras.
52. And those are the disciples of the Leader, who have listened to my word of command. One single stanza learnt or kept in memory suffices, no doubt of it, to lead all of them to enlightenment.

53. There is, indeed, but one vehicle; there is no second, nor a third anywhere in the world, apart from the case of the Purushottamas using an expedient to show that there is a diversity of vehicles.

54. The Chief of the world appears in the world to reveal the Buddha-knowledge. He has but one aim, indeed, no second; the Buddhas do not bring over creatures by an inferior vehicle.

55. There where the self-born one has established himself, and where the object of knowledge is, of whatever form or kind; where the powers, the stages of meditation, the emancipations, the perfected faculties are; there the beings also shall be established.

56. I should be guilty of envy, should I, after reaching the spotless eminent state of enlightenment, establish anyone in the inferior vehicle. That would not beseem me.

57. There is no envy whatever in me; no jealousy, no desire, nor passion. Therefore I am the Buddha, because the world follows my teaching.

58. When, splendidly marked with the thirty-two characteristics, I am illuminating this whole world, and, worshipped by many hundreds of beings, I show the unmistakable stamp of the nature of the law;

59. Then, Sariputra, I think thus: How will all beings by the thirty-two characteristics mark the self-born Seer, who of his own accord sheds his lustre all over the world?

60. And while I am thinking and pondering, when my wish has been fulfilled and my vow accomplished, I no more reveal Buddha-knowledge.

61. If, O son of Sari, I spoke to the creatures, 'Vivify in your minds the wish for enlightenment,' they would in their ignorance all go astray and never catch the meaning of my good words.

62. And considering them to be such, and that they have not accomplished their course of duty in previous existences, I see how they are attached and devoted to sensual pleasures, infatuated by desire and blind with delusion.

63. From lust they run into distress; they are tormented in the six states of existence and people the cemetery again and again; they are overwhelmed with misfortune, as they possess little virtue.
64. They are continually entangled in the thickets of sectarian theories, such as, 'It is and it is not; it is thus and it is not thus.' In trying to get a decided opinion on what is found in the sixty-two heretical theories they come to embrace falsehood and continue in it.
65. They are hard to correct, proud, hypocritical, crooked, malignant, ignorant, dull; hence they do not hear the good Buddha-call, not once in kotis of births.
66. To those, son of Sari, I show a device and say: Put an end to your trouble. When I perceive creatures vexed with mishap I make them see Nirvana.
67. And so do I reveal all those laws that are ever holy and correct from the very first. And the son of Buddha who has completed his course shall once be a Jina.
68. It is but my skilfulness which prompts me to manifest three vehicles; for there is but one vehicle and one track; there is also but one instruction by the leaders.
69. Remove all doubt and uncertainty; and should there be any who feel doubts, let them know that the Lords of the world speak the truth; this is the only vehicle, a second there is not.
70. The former Tathagatas also, living in the past for innumerable Aeons, the many thousands of Buddhas who are gone to final rest, whose number can never be counted,
71. Those highest of men have all of them revealed most holy laws by means of illustrations, reasons, and arguments, with many hundred proofs of skilfulness.
72. And all of them have manifested but one vehicle and introduced but one on earth; by one vehicle have they led to full ripeness inconceivably many thousands of kotis of beings.
73. Yet the Jinas possess various and manifold means through which the Tathagata reveals to the world, including the

gods, superior enlightenment, in consideration of the inclinations and dispositions of the different beings.

74. And all in the world who are hearing or have heard the law from the mouth of the Tathagatas, given alms, followed the moral precepts, and patiently accomplished the whole of their religious duties;
75. Who have acquitted themselves in point of zeal and meditation, with wisdom reflected on those laws, and performed several meritorious actions, have all of them reached enlightenment.
76. And such beings as were living patient, subdued, and disciplined, under the rule of the Jinas of those times, have all of them reached enlightenment.
77. Others also, who paid worship to the relics of the departed Jinas, erected many thousands of Stupas made of gems, gold, silver, or crystal,
78. Or built Stupas of emerald, cat's eye, pearls, egregious lapis lazuli, or sapphire; they have all of them reached enlightenment.
79. And those who erected Stupas from marble, sandalwood, or eaglewood; constructed Stupas from Deodar or a combination of different sorts of timber;
80. And who in gladness of heart built for the Jinas Stupas of bricks or clay; or caused mounds of earth to be raised in forests and wildernesses in dedication to the Jinas;
81. The little boys even, who in playing erected here and there heaps of sand with the intention of dedicating them as Stupas to the Jinas, they have all of them reached enlightenment.
82. Likewise have all who caused jewel images to be made and dedicated, adorned with the thirty-two characteristic signs, reached enlightenment.
83. Others who had images of Sugatas made of the seven precious substances, of copper or brass, have all of them reached enlightenment.
84. Those who ordered beautiful statues of Sugatas to be made of lead, iron, clay, or plaster have... etc.

85. Those who made images of the Sugatas on painted walls, with complete limits and the hundred holy signs, whether they drew them themselves or had them drawn by others, have... etc.

86. Those even, whether men or boys, who during the lesson or in play, by way of amusement, made upon the walls such images with the nail or a piece of wood,

87. Have all of them reached enlightenment; they have become compassionate, and, by rousing many Bodhisattvas, have saved kotis of creatures.

88. Those who offered flowers and perfumes to the relics of the Tathagatas, to Stupas, a mound of earth, images of clay or drawn on a wall;

89. Who caused musical instruments, drums, conch trumpets, and noisy great drums to be played, and raised the rattle of tymbals at such places in order to celebrate the highest enlightenment;

90. Who caused sweet lutes, cymbals, tabors, small drums, reed-pipes, flutes or sugarcane to be made, have all of them reached enlightenment.

91. Those who to celebrate the Sugatas made iron cymbals resound, or small drums; who sang a song sweet and lovely;

92. They have all of them reached enlightenment. By paying various kinds of worship to the relics of the Sugatas, by doing but a little for the relics, by making resound were it but a single musical instrument;

93. Or by worshipping were it but with a single flower, by drawing on a wall the images of the Sugatas, by doing worship were it even with distracted thoughts, one shall in course of time see kotis of Buddhas.

94. Those who, when in presence of a Stupa, have offered their reverential salutation, be it in a complete form or by merely joining the hands; who, were it but for a single moment, bent their head or body;

95. And who at Stupas containing relics have one single time said: Homage be to Buddha! albeit they did it with distracted thoughts, all have attained superior enlightenment.

96. The creatures who in the days of those Sugatas, whether already extinct or still in existence, have heard no more than the name of the law, have all of them reached enlightenment.

97. Many kotis of future Buddhas beyond imagination and measure shall likewise reveal this device as Jinas and supreme Lords.

98. Endless. shall be the skilfulness of these leaders of the world, by which they shall educate kotis of beings to that Buddha-knowledge which is free from imperfection.

99. Never has there been any being who, after hearing the law of those leaders, shall not become Buddha; for this is the fixed vow of the Tathagatas: Let me, by accomplishing my course of duty, lead others to enlightenment.

100. They are to expound in future days many thousand kotis of heads of the law; in their Tathagataship they shall teach the law by showing the sole vehicle before-mentioned.

101. The line of the law forms an unbroken continuity and the nature of its properties is always manifest. Knowing this, the Buddhas, the highest of men, shall reveal this single vehicle.

102. They shall reveal the stability of the law, its being subjected to fixed rules, its unshakeable perpetuity in the world, the awaking of the Buddhas on the elevated terrace of the earth, their skilfulness.

103. In all directions of space are standing Buddhas, like sand of the Ganges, honoured by gods and men; these also do, for the weal of all beings in the world, expound superior enlightenment.

104. Those Buddhas while manifesting skilfulness display various vehicles though, at the same time, indicating the one single vehicle: the supreme place of blessed rest.

105. Acquainted as they are with the conduct of all mortals, with their peculiar dispositions and previous actions; with due regard to their strenuousness and vigour, as well as their inclination, the Buddhas impart their lights to them.

106. By dint of knowledge the leaders produce many illustrations, arguments, and reasons; and considering how the creatures have various inclinations they impart various directions.
107. And myself also, the leader of the chief Jinas, am now manifesting, for the weal of creatures now living, this Buddha enlightenment by thousands of kotis of various directions.
108. I reveal the law in its multifariousness with regard to the inclinations and dispositions of creatures. I use different means to rouse each according to his own character. Such is the might of my knowledge.
109. I likewise see the poor wretches, deficient in wisdom and conduct, lapsed into the mundane whirl, retained in dismal places, plunged in affliction incessantly renewed.
110. Fettered as they are by desire like the yak by its tail, continually blinded by sensual pleasure, they do not seek the Buddha, the mighty one; they do not seek the law that leads to the end of pain.
111. Staying in the six states of existence, they are benumbed in their senses, stick unmoved to the low views, and suffer pain on pain. For those I feel a great compassion.
112. On the terrace of enlightenment I have remained three weeks in full, searching and pondering on such a matter, steadily looking up to the tree there standing.
113. Keeping in view that king of trees with an unwavering gaze I walked round at its foot thinking: This law is wonderful and lofty, whereas creatures are blind with dullness and ignorance.
114. Then it was that Brahma entreated me, and so did Indra, the four rulers of the cardinal points, Mahesvara, Isvara, and the hosts of Maruts by thousands of kotis.
115. All stood with joined hands and respectful, while myself was revolving the matter in my mind and thought: What shall I do? At the very time that I am uttering syllables, beings are oppressed with evils.
116. In their ignorance they will not heed the law I announce, and in consequence of it they will incur some penalty. It

would be better were I never to speak. May my quiet extinction take place this very day!

117. But on remembering the former Buddhas and their skilfulness, I thought: Nay, I also will manifest this tripartite Buddha-enlightenment.

118. When I was thus meditating on the law, the other Buddhas in all the directions of space appeared to me in their own body and raised their voice, crying 'Amen.

119. 'Amen, Solitary, first Leader of the world! now that thou hast come to unsurpassed knowledge, and art meditating on the skilfulness of the leaders of the world, thou repeatest their teaching.

120. 'We also, being Buddhas, will make clear the highest word, divided into three parts; for men occasionally have low inclinations, and might perchance from ignorance not believe us, when we say, Ye shall become Buddhas.

121. 'Hence we will rouse many Bodhisattvas by the display of skilfulness and the encouraging of the wish of obtaining fruits.'

122. And I was delighted to hear the sweet voice of the leaders of men; in the exultation of my heart I said to the blessed saints, 'The words of the eminent sages are not spoken in vain.

123. 'I, too, will act according to the indications of the wise leaders of the world; having myself been born in the midst of the degradation of creatures, I have known agitation in this dreadful world.

124. When I had come to that conviction, O son of Sari, I instantly went to Benares, where I skilfully preached the law to the five Solitaries, that law which is the base of final beatitude.

125. From that moment the wheel of my law has been moving, and the name of Nirvana made its appearance in the world, as well as the name of Arhat, of Dharma, and Sangha.

126. Many years have I preached and pointed to the stage of Nirvana, the end of wretchedness and mundane existence. Thus I used to speak at all times.

127. And when I saw, Sariputra, the children of the highest of men by many thousands of kotis, numberless, striving after the supreme, the highest enlightenment;
128. And when such as had heard the law of the Jinas, owing to the many-sidedness of their skilfulness, had approached me and stood before my face, all of them with joined hands, and respectful;
129. Then I conceived the idea that the time had come for me to announce the excellent law and to reveal supreme enlightenment, for which task I had been born in the world.
130. This event today will be hard to be understood by the ignorant who imagine they see here a sign, as they are proud and dull. But the Bodhisattvas, they will listen to me.
131. And I felt free from hesitation and highly cheered; putting aside all timidity, I began speaking in the assembly of the sons of Sugata, and roused them to enlightenment.
132. On beholding such worthy sons of Buddha I said: Thy doubts also will be removed, and these twelve hundred disciples of mine, free from imperfections, will all of them become Buddhas.
133. Even as the nature of the law of the former mighty saints and the future Jinas is, so is my law free from any doubtfulness, and it is such as I today preach it to thee.
134. At certain times, at certain places, somehow do the leaders appear in the world, and after their appearance will they, whose view is boundless, at one time or another preach a similar law.
135. It is most difficult to meet with this superior law, even in myriads of kotis of Aeons; very rare are the beings who will adhere to the superior law which they have heard from me.
136. Just as the blossom of the glamerous fig-tree is rare, albeit sometimes, at some places, and somehow it is met with, as something pleasant to see for everybody, as a wonder to the world including the gods;

137. So wonderful and far more wonderful is the law I proclaim. Anyone who, on hearing a good exposition of it, shall cheerfully accept it and recite but one word of it, will have done honour to all the Buddhas.

138. Give up all doubt and uncertainty in this respect; I declare that I am the king of the law, Dharmaraja.; I am urging others to enlightenment, but I am here without disciples.

139. Let this mystery be for thee, Sariputra, for all disciples of mine, and for the eminent Bodhisattvas, who are to keep this mystery.

140. For the creatures, when at the period of the five depravities, are vile and bad; they are blinded by sensual desires, the fools, and never turn their minds to enlightenment.

141. Some beings, having heard this one and sole vehicle manifested by the Jina, will in days to come swerve from it, reject the Sutra, and go down to hell.

142. But those beings who shall be modest and pure, striving after the supreme and the highest enlightenment, to them shall I unhesitatingly set forth the endless forms of this one and sole vehicle.

143. Such is the mastership of the leaders; that is, their skilfulness. They have spoken in many mysteries; hence it is difficult to understand them.

144. Therefore try to understand the mystery of the Buddhas, the holy masters of the world; forsake all doubt and uncertainty: you shall become Buddhas; rejoice!

◆ ◆ ◆ ◆ ◆

3

PARABLE: A BIG HOUSE WITH ONE DOOR ON FIRE

Prophecy of the Lord regarding the future destiny of Sariputra, second turn of the wheel of the Law on that occasion, with incidental commemoration of the first turn in Benares. Parable of a burning house to show from the burning pains of existence.

Then the venerable Sariputra, pleased, glad, charmed, cheerful, thrilling with delight and joy, stretched his joined hands towards the Lord, and, looking up to the Lord with a steady gaze, addressed him in this strain: I am astonished, amazed, O Lord! I am in ecstasy to hear such a call from the Lord. For when, before I had heard of this law from the Lord, I saw other Bodhisattvas, and heard that the Bodhisattvas would in future get the name of Buddhas, I felt extremely sorry, extremely vexed to be deprived from so grand a sight as the Tathagata-knowledge. And whenever, O Lord, for my daily recreation I was visiting the caves of rocks or mountains, wood thickets, lovely gardens, rivers, and roots of trees, I always was occupied with the same and ever-recurring thought: 'Whereas the entrance into the fixed points of the law is nominally equal, we have been dismissed by the Lord with the inferior vehicle.'

Instantly, however, O Lord, I felt that it was our own fault, not the Lord's. For had we regarded the Lord at the time of his giving the all-surpassing demonstration of the law, that is, the exposition of supreme, perfect enlightenment, then, O Lord, we should have become adepts in those laws. But because, without understanding the mystery of the Lord, we, at .the moment of the Bodhisattvas not being assembled, heard only in a hurry, caught, meditated, minded, took to heart the first lessons pronounced on the law, therefore, O Lord, I used to pass day and night in self-reproach. But to-day, O Lord, I have reached complete extinction; to-day, O Lord, I have become calm; to-day, O Lord, I am wholly come to rest; to-day, O Lord, I have reached Arhatship; to-day, O Lord, I am the Lord's eldest son, born from his law, sprung into existence by the law, made by the law, inheriting from the law, accomplished by the law. My burning has left me, O Lord, now that I have heard this wonderful law, which I had not learnt before, announced by the voice from the mouth of the Lord.

And on that occasion the venerable Sariputra addressed the Lord in the following stanzas:

1. I am astonished, great Leader, I am charmed to hear this voice; I feel no doubt any more; now am I fully ripe for the superior vehicle.
2. Wonderful is the voice of the Sugatas; it dispels the doubt and pain of living beings; my pain also is all gone now that I, freed from imperfections, have heard that voice (or, call).
3. When I was taking my daily recreation or was walking in woody thickets, when betaking myself to the roots of trees or to mountain caves, I indulged in no other thought but this:
4. 'O how am I deluded by vain thoughts! whereas the faultless laws are, nominally, equal, shall I in future not preach the superior law in the world?
5. 'The thirty-two characteristic signs have failed me, and the gold colour of the skin has vanished; all the ten powers and emancipations have likewise been lost. O how have I gone astray at the equal laws!
6. 'The secondary signs also of the great Seers, the eighty excellent specific signs, and the eighteen uncommon properties have failed me. O how am I deluded!'
7. And when I had perceived thee, so benign and merciful to the world, and was lonely walking to take my daily recreation, I thought: 'I am excluded from that inconceivable, unbounded knowledge!'
8. Days and nights, O Lord, I passed always thinking of the same subject; I would ask the Lord whether I had lost my rank or not.

9. In such reflections, O Chief of Jinas, I constantly passed my days and nights; and on seeing many other Bodhisattvas praised by the Leader of the world,
10. And on hearing this Buddha-law, I thought: 'To be sure, this is expounded mysteriously; it is an inscrutable, subtle. and faultless science, which is announced by the Jinas on the terrace of enlightenment.'
11. Formerly I was attached to heretical theories, being a wandering monk and in high honour or, of the same opinions with the heretics; afterwards has the Lord, regarding my disposition, taught me Nirvana, to detach me from perverted views.
12. After having completely freed myself from all heretical views and reached the laws of void, I conceive that I have become extinct; yet this is not deemed to be extinction.
13. But when one becomes Buddha, a superior being, honoured by men, gods, goblins, Titans, and adorned with the thirty-two characteristic signs, then one will be completely extinct.
14. All those former cares have now been dispelled, since I have heard the voice. Now am I extinct, as thou announcest my destination to Nirvana before the world including the gods.
15. When I first heard the voice of the Lord, I had a great terror lest it might be Mara, the evil one, who on this occasion had adopted the disguise of Buddha.
16. But when the unsurpassed Buddha-wisdom had been displayed in and established with arguments, reasons, and illustrations, by myriads of kotis, then I lost all doubt about the law I heard.
17. And when thou hadst mentioned to me the thousands of kotis of Buddhas, the past Jinas who have come to final rest, and how they preached this law by firmly establishing it through skilfulness;
18. How the many future Buddhas and those who are now existing, as knowers of the real truth, shall expound or are expounding this law by hundreds of able devices;

19. And when thou were, mentioning thine own course after leaving home, how the idea of the wheel of the law presented itself to thy mind and how thou decidedst upon preaching the law;
20. Then I was convinced: This is not Mara; it is the Lord of the world, who has shown the true course; no Maras can here abide. So then my mind for a moment was overcome with perplexity;
21. But when the sweet, deep, and lovely voice of Buddha gladdened me, all doubts were scattered, my perplexity vanished, and I stood firm in knowledge.
22. I shall become a Tathagata, undoubtedly, worshipped in the world including the gods; I shall manifest Buddha-wisdom, mysteriously rousing many Bodhisattvas.

After this speech of the venerable Sariputra, the Lord said to him: I declare to thee, Sariputra, I announce to thee, in presence of this world including the gods, Maras, and Brahmas, in presence of this people, including ascetics and Brahmins, that thou, Sariputra, hast been by me made ripe for supreme, perfect enlightenment, in presence of twenty hundred thousand myriads of kotis of Buddhas, and that thou, Sariputra, hast for a long time followed my commandments. Thou, Sariputra, art, by the counsel of the Bodhisattva, by the decree of the Bodhisattva, reborn here under my rule. Owing to the mighty will of the Bodhisattva thou, Sariputra, hast no recollection of thy former vow to observe the religious course; of the counsel of the Bodhisattva, the decree of the Bodhisattva. Thou thinkest that thou hast reached final rest. I, wishing to revive and renew in thee the knowledge of thy former vow to observe the religious course, will reveal to the disciples the Dharmaparyaya called 'the Lotus of the True Law,' this Sutranta, etc.

Again, Sariputra, at a future period, after innumerable, inconceivable, immeasurable Aeons, when thou shalt have learnt the true law of hundred thousand myriads of kotis of Tathagatas, showed devotion in various ways, and achieved the present Bodhisattva-course, thou shalt become in the world a Tathagata, etc., named Padmaprabha, endowed with science and conduct, a Sugata, a knower of the world, an unsurpassed tamer of men, a master of gods and men, a Lord Buddha.

At that time then, Sariputra, the Buddha-field of that Lord, the Tathagata Padmaprabha, to be called Viraja, will be level, pleasant, delightful, extremely beautiful to see, pure, prosperous, rich, quiet, abounding with food, replete with many races of men; it will consist of lapis lazuli, and contain a checker-board of eight compartments distinguished by gold threads, each compartment having its jewel tree always and perpetually filled with blossoms and fruits of seven precious substances.

Now that Tathagata Padmaprabha, etc., Sariputra, will preach the law by the instrumentality of three vehicles. Further, Sariputra, that Tathagata will not appear at the decay of the Aeon, but preach the law by virtue of a vow.

That Aeon, Sariputra, will be named Maharatnapratimandita, i.e, ornamented with magnificent jewels. Knowest, thou, Sariputra, why that Aeon is named Maharatnapratimandita? The Bodhisattvas of a Buddha-field, Sariputra, are called ratnas, jewels, and at that time there will be many Bodhisattvas in that sphere called Viraja; innumerable, incalculable, beyond computation, abstraction made from their being computed by the Tathagatas. On that account is that Aeon called Maharatnapratimandita.

Now, to proceed, Sariputra, at that period the Bodhisattvas of that field will in walking step on jewel lotuses. And these Bodhisattvas will not be plying their work for the first time, they having accumulated roots of goodness and observed the course of duty under many hundred thousand Buddhas; they are praised by the Tathagatas for their zealous application to Buddha-knowledge; are perfectioned in the rites preparatory to transcendent knowledge; accomplished in the direction of all true laws; mild, thoughtful. Generally, Sariputra, will that Buddha-region teem with such Bodhisattvas.

As to the lifetime, Sariputra, of that Tathagata Padmaprabha, it will last twelve intermediate kalpas, if we leave out of account the time of his being a young prince. And the lifetime of the creatures then living will measure eight intermediate kalpas. At the expiration of twelve intermediate kalpas, Sariputra, the Tathagata Padmaprabha, after announcing the future destiny of the Bodhisattva called Dhritiparipurna to superior perfect enlightenment, is to enter complete Nirvana. 'This Bodhisattva Mahasattva Dhritiparipurna, O monks, shall immediately after me come to supreme, perfect enlightenment. He shall become in the world a Tathagata named Padmavrishabhavikramin, an Arhat, etc., endowed with science and conduct, etc., etc.

Now the Tathagata Padmavrishabhavikramin, Sariputra, will have a Buddha-field of quite the same description. The true law, Sariputra, of that Tathagata Padmavrishabhavikramin will, after his extinction, last thirty-two intermediate kalpas, and the counterfeit of his true law will last as many intermediate kalpas.

And on that occasion the Lord uttered the following stanzas:

23. Thou also, son of Sari, shalt in future be a Jina, a Tathagata named Padmaprabha, of illimited sight; thou shalt educate thousands of kotis of living beings.

24. After paying honour to many kotis of Buddhas, makings strenuous efforts in the course of duty, and after having produced in thyself the ten powers, thou shalt reach supreme, perfect enlightenment.

25. Within a period inconceivable and immense there shall be an Aeon rich in jewels and a sphere named Viraja, the pure field of the highest of men;

26. And its ground will consist of lapis lazuli, and be set off with gold threads; it will have hundreds of jewel trees, very beautiful, and covered with blossoms and fruits.

27. Bodhisattvas of good memory, able in showing the course of duty which they have been taught under hundreds of Buddhas, will come to be born in that field.

28. And the aforementioned Jina, then in his last bodily existence, shall, after passing the state of prince royal, renounce sensual pleasures, leave home to become a wandering ascetic, and thereafter reach the supreme and the highest enlightenment.

29. The lifetime of that Jina will be precisely twelve intermediate kalpas, and the life of men will then last eight intermediate kalpas.
30. After the extinction of the Tathagata the true law will continue thirty-two Aeons in full, for the benefit of the world, including the gods.
31. When the true law shall have come to an end, its counterfeit will stand for thirty-two intermediate kalpas. The dispersed relics of the holy one will always be honoured by men and gods.
32. Such will be the fate of that Lord. Rejoice, O son of Sari, for it is thou who shalt be that most excellent of men, so unsurpassed.

The four classes of the audience, monks, nuns, lay devotees male and female, gods, Nagas, goblins, Gandharvas, demons, Garudas, Kinnaras, great serpents, men and beings not human, on hearing the announcement of the venerable Sariputra's destiny to supreme, perfect enlightenment, were so pleased, glad, charmed, thrilling with delight and joy, that they covered the Lord severally with their own robes, while Indra, the chief of gods, Brahma Sahampati, besides hundred thousands of kotis of other divine beings, covered him with heavenly garments and bestrewed him with flowers of heaven, Mandaravas and great Mandaravas. High aloft they whirled celestial clothes and struck hundred thousands of celestial musical instruments and cymbals, high in the sky; and after pouring a great rain of flowers they uttered these words: The wheel of the law has been put in motion by the Lord, the first time at Benares at Rishipatana in the Deer-Park; to-day has the Lord again put in motion the supreme wheel of the law.

And on that occasion those divine beings uttered the following stanzas:

33. The wheel of the law was put in motion by thee, O thou that art unrivalled in the world, at Benares, O great hero! that wheel which is the rotation of the rise and decay of all aggregates.

34. There it was put in motion for the first time; now, a second time, is it turned here, O Lord. To-day, O Master, thou hast preached this law, which is hard to be received with faith.
35. Many laws have we heard near the Lord of the world, but never before did we hear a law like this.
36. We receive with gratitude, O great hero, the mysterious speech of the great Sages, such as this prediction regarding the self-possessed Arya Sariputra.
37. May we also become such incomparable Buddhas in the world, who by mysterious speech announce supreme Buddha-enlightenment.
38. May we also, by the good we have done in this world and in the next, and by our having propitiated the Buddha, be allowed to make a vow for Buddhaship.

Thereupon the venerable Sariputra thus spoke to the Lord: My doubt is gone, O Lord, my uncertainty is at an end on hearing from the mouth of the Lord my destiny to supreme enlightenment. But these twelve hundred self-controlled disciples, O Lord, who have been placed by thee on the stage of Saikshas, those under training have been thus admonished and instructed: 'My preaching of the law, O monks, comes to this, that deliverance from birth, decrepitude, disease, and death is inseparably connected with Nirvana;' and these two thousand monks, O Lord, thy disciples, both those who are still under training and adepts, who all of them are free from false views about the soul, false views about existence, false views about cessation of existence, free, in short, from all false views, who are fancying themselves to have reached the stage of Nirvana, these have fallen into uncertainty by hearing from the mouth of the Lord this law which they had not heard before. Therefore, O Lord, please speak to these monks, to dispel their uneasiness, so that the four classes of the audience, O Lord, may be relieved from their doubt and perplexity.

On this speech of the venerable Sariputra the Lord said to him the following: Have I not told thee before, Sariputra, that the Tathagata, etc., preaches the law by able devices, varying directions and indications, fundamental ideas, interpretations, with due regard to the different dispositions and inclinations of creatures whose temperaments are so various? All his preachings of the law have no other end but supreme and perfect enlightenment, for which he is rousing beings to the Bodhisattva-course. But, Sariputra, to elucidate this matter more at large, I will tell thee a parable, for men of good understanding will generally readily enough catch the meaning of what is taught under the shape of a parable.

Let us suppose the following case, Sariputra. In a certain village, town, borough, province, kingdom, or capital, there was a certain housekeeper, old, aged, decrepit, very advanced in years, rich, wealthy, opulent; he had a great house, high, spacious, built a long time ago and old, inhabited by some two, three, four, or five hundred living beings. The house had but one door, and a thatch; its terraces were tottering, the bases of its pillars rotten, the coverings and plaster of the walls loose. On a sudden the whole house was from every side put in conflagration by a mass of fire. Let us suppose that the man had many little boys, say five, or ten, or even twenty, and that he himself had come out of the house.

Now, Sariputra, that man, on seeing the house from every side wrapt in a blaze by a great mass of fire, got afraid, frightened, anxious in his mind, and made the following reflection: I myself am able to come out from the burning house through the door, quickly and safely, without being touched or scorched by that great mass of fire; but my children, those young boys, are staying in the burning house, playing, amusing, and diverting themselves with all sorts of sports. They do not perceive, nor know, nor understand, nor mind that the house is on fire, and do not get afraid. Though scorched by that great mass of fire, and affected with such a mass of pain, they do not mind the pain, nor do they conceive the idea of escaping.

The man, Sariputra, is strong, has powerful arms, and so he makes this reflection: I am strong, and have powerful arms; why, let me gather all my little boys and take them to my breast to effect their escape from the house. A second reflection then presented itself to his mind: This house has but one opening; the door is shut; and those boys, fickle, unsteady, and childlike as they are, will, it is to be feared, run hither and thither, and come to grief and disaster in this mass of fire. Therefore I will warn them. So resolved, he calls to the boys: Come, my children; the house is burning with a mass of fire; come, lest ye be burnt in that mass of fire, and come to grief and disaster. But the ignorant boys do not heed the words of him who is their well-wisher; they are not afraid, not alarmed, and feel no misgiving; they do not care, nor fly, nor even know nor understand the purport of the word 'burning;' on the contrary, they run hither and thither, walk about, and repeatedly look at their father; all, because they are so ignorant.

Then the man is going to reflect thus: The house is burning, is blazing by a mass of fire. It is to be feared that myself as well as my children will come to grief and disaster. Let me therefore by some skilful means get the boys out of the house. The man knows the disposition of the boys, and has a clear perception of their inclinations. Now these boys happen to have many and manifold toys to play with, pretty, nice, pleasant, dear, amusing, and precious. The man, knowing the disposition of the boys, says to them: My children, your toys, which are so pretty, precious, and admirable, which you are so loth to miss, which are so various and multifarious, such as bullock-carts, goat-carts, deer-carts, which are so pretty, nice, dear, and precious to you, have all been put by me outside the house-door for you to play with. Come, run out, leave the house; to each of you I shall give what he wants. Come soon; come out for the sake of these toys. And the boys, on hearing the names mentioned of such playthings as they like and desire, so agreeable to their taste, so pretty, dear, and delightful, quickly rush out from the burning house, with eager effort and great alacrity, one having no time to wait for the other, and pushing each other on with the cry of 'Who shall arrive first, the very first?'

The man, seeing that his children have safely and happily escaped, and knowing that they are free from danger, goes and sits down in the open air on the square of the village, his heart filled with joy and delight, released from trouble and hindrance, quite at ease. The boys go up to the place where their father is sitting, and say: 'Father, give us those toys to play with, those bullock-carts, goat-carts, and deer-carts.' Then, Sariputra, the man gives to his sons, who run swift as the wind, bullock-carts only made of seven precious substances, provided with benches, hung with a multitude of small bells, lofty, adorned with rare and wonderful jewels, embellished with jewel wreaths, decorated with garlands of flowers, carpeted with cotton mattresses and woollen coverlets, covered with white cloth and silk, having on both sides rosy cushions, yoked with white, very fair and fleet bullocks, led by a multitude of men. To each of his children he gives several bullock-carts of one appearance and one kind, provided with flags, and swift as the wind. That man does so, Sariputra, because being rich, wealthy, and in possession of many treasures and granaries, he rightly thinks: Why should I give these boys inferior carts, all these boys being my own children, dear and precious? I have got such great vehicles, and ought to treat all the boys equally and without partiality. As I own many treasures and granaries, I could give such great vehicles to all beings, how much more then to my own children. Meanwhile the boys are mounting the vehicles with feelings of astonishment and wonder. Now, Sariputra, what is thy opinion? Has that man made himself guilty of a falsehood by first holding out to his children the prospect of three vehicles and afterwards giving to each of them the greatest vehicles only, the most magnificent vehicles?

Sariputra answered: By no means, Lord; by no means, Sugata. That is not sufficient, O Lord, to qualify the man as a speaker of falsehood, since it only was a skilful device to persuade his children to go out of the burning house and save their lives. Nay, besides recovering their very body, O Lord, they have received all those toys. If that man, O Lord, had given no single cart, even then he would not have been a speaker of falsehood, for he had previously been meditating on saving the little boys from a great mass of pain by some able device. Even in this case, O Lord, the man would not have been guilty of falsehood, and far less now that he, considering his having plenty of treasures and prompted by no other motive but the love of his children, gives to all, to coax them, vehicles of one kind, and those the greatest vehicles. That man, Lord, is not guilty of falsehood.

The venerable Sariputra having thus spoken, the Lord said to him: Very well, very well, Sariputra, quite so; it is even as thou sayest. So, too, Sariputra, the Tathagata, etc., is free from all dangers, wholly exempt from all misfortune, despondency, calamity, pain, grief, the thick enveloping dark mists of ignorance. He, the Tathagata, endowed with Buddha-knowledge, forces, absence of hesitation, uncommon properties, and mighty by magical power, is the father of the world, who has reached the highest perfection in the knowledge of skilful means, who is most merciful, long-suffering, benevolent, compassionate. He appears in this triple world, which is like a house the roof and shelter whereof are decayed, a house burning by a mass of misery, in order to deliver from affection, hatred, and delusion the beings subject to birth, old age, disease, death, grief, wailing, pain, melancholy, despondency, the dark enveloping mists of ignorance, in order to rouse them to supreme and perfect enlightenment.

Once born, he sees how the creatures are burnt, tormented, vexed, distressed by birth, old age, disease, death, grief, wailing, pain, melancholy, despondency; how for the sake of enjoyments, and prompted by sensual desires, they severally suffer various pains. In consequence both of what in this world they are seeking and what they have acquired, they will in a future state suffer various pains, in hell, in the brute creation, in the realm of Yama; suffer such pains as poverty in the world of gods or men, union with hateful persons or things, and separation from the beloved ones. And whilst incessantly whirling in that mass of evils they are sporting, playing, diverting themselves; they do not fear, nor dread, nor are they seized with terror; they do not know, nor mind; they are not startled, do not try to escape, but are enjoying themselves in that triple world which is like unto a burning house, and run hither and thither. Though overwhelmed by that mass of evil, they do not conceive the idea that they must beware of it.

Under such circumstances, Sariputra, the Tathagata reflects thus: Verily, I am the father of these beings; I must save them from this mass of evil, and bestow on them the immense, inconceivable bliss of Buddha-knowledge, wherewith they shall sport, play, and divert themselves, wherein they shall find their rest.

Then, Sariputra, the Tathagata reflects thus: If, in the conviction of my possessing the power of knowledge and magical faculties, I manifest to these beings the knowledge, forces, and absence of hesitation of the Tathagata, without availing myself of I some device, these beings will not escape. For they are attached to the pleasures of the five senses, to worldly pleasures; they will not be freed from birth, old age, disease, death, grief, wailing, pain, melancholy, despondency, by which they are burnt, tormented, vexed, distressed. Unless they are forced to leave the triple world which is like a house of shelter and roof whereof is in a blaze, how are they to get acquainted with Buddha-knowledge?

Now, Sariputra, even as that man with powerful arms, without using the strength of his arms, attracts his children out of the burning house by an able device, and afterwards gives them magnificent, great carts, so, Sariputra, the Tathagata, the Arhat, etc., possessed of knowledge and freedom from all hesitation, without using them, in order to attract the creatures out of the triple world which is like a burning house with decayed roof and shelter, shows, by his knowledge of able devices, three vehicles, viz., the vehicle of the disciples, the vehicle of the Pratyeka Buddhas, and the vehicle of the, Bodhisattvas. By means of these three vehicles he attracts the creatures and speaks to them thus:

Do not delight in this triple world, which is like a burning house, in these miserable forms, sounds, odours, flavours, and contacts. For in delighting in this triple world ye are burnt, heated, inflamed with the thirst inseparable from the pleasures of the five senses. Fly from this triple world; betake yourselves to the three vehicles: the vehicle of the disciples, the vehicle of the Pratyeka Buddhas, the vehicle of the Bodhisattvas. I give you my pledge for it, that I shall give you these three vehicles; make an effort to run out of this triple world. And to attract them I say: These vehicles are grand, praised by the Aryas, and provided with most pleasant things; with such you are to sport, play, and divert yourselves in a noble manner. Ye will feel the great delight of the families, powers, constituents of Bodhi, meditations, the eight degrees of emancipation, self-concentration, and the results of self-concentration, and ye will become greatly happy and cheerful.

Now, Sariputra, the beings who have become wise have faith in the Tathagata, the father of the world, and consequently apply themselves to his commandments. Amongst them there are some who, wishing to follow the dictate of an authoritative voice, apply themselves to the commandment of the Tathagata to acquire the knowledge of the four great truths, for the sake of their own complete Nirvana. These one may say to be those who, coveting the vehicle of the disciples, fly from the triple world, just as some of the boys will fly from that burning house, prompted by a desire of getting a cart yoked with deer. Other beings desirous of the science without a master, of self-restraint and tranquillity, apply themselves to the commandment of the Tathagata to learn to understand causes and effects, for the sake of their own complete Nirvana. These one may say to be those who, coveing the vehicle of the Pratyeka Buddhas, fly from the triple world, just as some of the boys fly from the burning house, prompted by the desire of getting a cart yoked with goats. Others again desirous of the knowledge of the all-knowing, the knowledge of Buddha, the knowledge of the self-born one, the science without a master, apply themselves to the commandment of the Tathagata to learn to understand the knowledge, powers, and freedom from hesitation of the Tathagata, for the sake of the common weal and happiness, out of compassion to the world, for the benefit, weal, and happiness of the world at large, both gods and men, for the sake of the complete Nirvana of all beings. These one may say to be those who, coveting the great vehicle, fly from the triple world. Therefore they are called Bodhisattvas Mahasattvas. They may be likened to those among the boys who have fled from the burning house prompted by the desire of getting a cart yoked with bullocks.

In the same manner, Sariputra, as that man, on seeing his children escaped from the burning house and knowing them safely and happily rescued and out of danger, in the consciousness of his great wealth, gives the boys one single grand cart; so, too, Sariputra, the Tathagata, the Arhat, etc., on seeing many kotis of beings recovered from the triple world, released from sorrow, fear, terror, and calamity, having escaped owing to the command of the Tathagata, delivered from all fears, calamities, and difficulties, and having reached the bliss of Nirvana, so, too, Sariputra, the Tathagata, the Arhat, etc., considering that he possesses great wealth of knowledge, power, and absence of hesitation, and that all beings are his children, leads them by no other vehicle but the Buddha-vehicle to full development. But he does not teach a particular Nirvana for each being; he causes all beings to reach complete Nirvana by means of the complete Nirvana of the Tathagata. And those beings, Sariputra, who are delivered from the triple world, to them the Tathagata gives as toys to amuse themselves with the lofty pleasures of the Aryas, the pleasures of meditation, emancipation, self-concentration, and its results; toys all of the same kind.

Even as that man, Sariputra, cannot be said to have told a falsehood for having held out to those boys the prospect of three vehicles and given to all of them but one great vehicle, a magnificent vehicle made of seven precious substances, decorated with all sorts of ornaments, a vehicle of one kind, the most egregious of all, so, too, Sariputra, the Tathagata, the Arhat, etc., tells no falsehood when by an able device he first holds forth three vehicles and afterwards leads all to complete Nirvana by the one great vehicle. For the Tathagata, Sariputra, who is rich in treasures and storehouses of abundant knowledge, powers, and absence of hesitation, is able to teach all beings the law which is connected with the knowledge of the all-knowing. In this way, Sariputra, one has to understand how the Tathagata by an able device and direction shows but one vehicle, the great vehicle.

And on that occasion the Lord uttered the following stanzas:

39. A man has an old house, large, but very infirm; its terraces are decaying and the columns rotten at their bases.
40. The windows and balconies are partly ruined, the wall as well as its coverings and plaster decaying; the coping shows rents from age; the thatch is everywhere pierced with holes.

41. It is inhabited by no less than five hundred beings; containing many cells and closets filled with excrements and disgusting.
42. Its roof-rafters are wholly ruined; the walls and partitions crumbling away; kotis of vultures nestle in it, as well as doves, owls, and other birds.
43. There are in every corner dreadful snakes, most venomous and horrible; scorpions and mice of all sorts; it is the abode of very wicked creatures of every description.
44. Further, one may meet in it here and there beings not belonging to the human race. It is defiled with excrement and urine, and teeming with worms, insects, and fireflies; it resounds from the howling of dogs and jackals.
45. In it are horrible hyenas that are wont to devour human carcasses; many dogs and jackals greedily seeking the matter of corpses.
46. Those animals weak from perpetual hunger go about in several places to feed upon their prey, and quarrelling fill the spot with their cries. Such is that most horrible house.
47. There are also very malign goblins, who violate human corpses in several spots there are centipedes, huge snakes, and vipers.
48. Those animals creep into all corners, where they make nests to deposit their brood, which is often devoured by the goblins.
49. And when those cruel-minded goblins are satiated with feeding upon the flesh of other creatures, so that their bodies are big, then they commence sharply fighting on the spot.
50. In the wasted retreats are dreadful, malign urchins, some of them measuring one span, others one cubit or two cubits, all nimble in their movements.
51. They are in the habit of seizing dogs by the feet, throwing them upside down upon the floor, pinching their necks and using them ill.

52. There also live yelling ghosts naked, black, wan, tall, and high, who, hungry and in quest of food, are here and there emitting cries of distress.
53. Some have a mouth like a needle, others have a face like a cow's; they are of the size of men or dogs, go with entangled hair, and utter plaintive cries from want of food.
54. Those goblins, ghosts, imps, like vultures, are always looking out through the windows and loopholes, in all directions in search of food.
55. Such is that dreadful house, spacious and high, but very infirm, full of holes, frail and dreary. Let us suppose that it is the property of a certain man,
56. And that while he is out of doors the house is reached by a conflagration, so that on a sudden it is wrapt in a blazing mass of fire on every side.
57. The beams and rafters consumed by the fire, the columns and partitions in flame are crackling most dreadfully, whilst goblins and ghosts are yelling.
58. Vultures are driven out by hundreds; urchins withdraw with parched faces; hundreds of mischievous beasts of prey run, scorched, on every side, crying and shouting.
59. Many poor devils move about, burnt by the fire; while burning they tear one another with the teeth, and bespatter each other with their blood.
60. Hyenas also perish there, in the act of eating one another. The excrements burn, and a loathsome stench spreads in all directions.
61. The centipedes, trying to fly, are devoured by the urchins. The ghosts, with burning hair, hover about, equally vexed with hunger and heat.
62. In such a state is that awful house, where thousands of flames are breaking out on every side. But the man who is the master of the house looks on from without.
63. And he hears his own children, whose minds are engaged in playing with their toys, in their fondness of which they amuse themselves, as fools do in their ignorance.

64. And as he hears them he quickly steps in to save his children, lest his ignorant children might perish in the flames.
65. He tells them the defect of the house, and says: This, young man of good family, is a miserable house, a dreadful one; the various creatures in it, and this fire to boot, form a series of evils.
66. In it are snakes, mischievous goblins, urchins, and ghosts in great number; hyenas, troops of dogs and jackals, as well as vultures, seeking their prey.
67. Such beings live in this house, which, apart from the fire, is extremely dreadful, and miserable enough; and now comes to it this fire blazing on all sides.
68. The foolish boys, however, though admonished, do not mind their father's words, deluded as they are by their toys; they do not even understand him.
69. Then the man thinks: I am now in anxiety on account of my children. What is the use of my having sons if I lose them? No, they shall not perish by this fire.
70. Instantly a device occurred to his mind: These young and ignorant children are fond of toys, and have none just now to play with. Oh, they are so foolish!
71. He then says to them: Listen, my sons, I have carts of different sorts, yoked with deer, goats, and excellent bullocks, lofty, great, and completely furnished.
72. They are outside the house; run out, do with them what you like; for your sake have I caused them to be made. Run out all together, and rejoice to have them.
73. All the boys, on hearing of such carts, exert themselves, immediately rush out hastily, and reach, free from harm, the open air.
74. On seeing that the children have come out, the man betakes himself to the square in the centre of the village and there from the throne he is sitting on he says: Good people, now I feel at ease.
75. These poor sons of mine, whom I have recovered with difficulty, my own dear twenty young children, were

in a dreadful, wretched, horrible house. full of many animals.

76. As it was burning and wrapt in thousands of flames, they were amusing themselves in it with playing, but now I have rescued them all. Therefore I now feel most happy.
77. The children, seeing their father happy, approached him, and said: Dear father, give us, as you have promised, those nice vehicles of three kinds;
78. And make true all that you promised us in the house when saying, 'I will give you three sorts of vehicles.' Do give them; it is now the right time.
79. Now the man, as we have supposed, had a mighty treasure of gold, silver, precious stones, and pearls; he possessed bullion, numerous slaves, domestics, and vehicles of various kinds;
80. Carts made of precious substances, yoked with bullocks, most excellent, with benches and a row of tinkling bells, decorated with umbrellas and flags, and adorned with a network of gems and pearls.
81. They are embellished with gold, and artificial wreaths hanging down here and there; covered all around with excellent cloth and fine white muslin.
82. Those carts are moreover furnished with choice mattresses of fine silk, serving for cushions, and covered with choice carpets showing the images of cranes and swans, and worth thousands of kotis.
83. The carts are yoked with white bullocks, well fed, strong, of great size, very fine, who are tended by numerous persons.
84. Such excellent carts that man gives to all his sons, who, overjoyed and charmed, go and play with them in all directions.
85. In the same manner, Sariputra, I, the great Seer, am the protector and father of all beings, and all creatures who, childlike, are captivated by the pleasures of the triple world, are my sons.
86. This triple world is as dreadful as that house, overwhelmed with a number of evils, entirely inflamed on every side by a hundred different sorts of birth, old age, and disease.

87. But I, who am detached from the triple world and serene, am living in absolute retirement in a wood. This triple world is my domain, and those who in it are suffering from burning heat are my sons.
88. And I told its evils because I had resolved upon saving them, but they would not listen to me, because all of them were ignorant and their hearts attached to the pleasures of sense.
89. Then I employ an able device, and tell them of the three vehicles, so showing them the means of evading the numerous evils of the triple world which are known to me.
90. And those of my sons who adhere to me, who are mighty in the six transcendent faculties (Abhijnas) and the triple science, the Pratyeka Buddhas, as well as the Bodhisattvas unable to slide back;
91. And those others who equally are my sons, to them I just now am showing, by means of this excellent allegory, the single Buddha-vehicle. Receive it; ye shall all become Jinas.
92. It is most excellent and sweet, the most exalted in the world, that knowledge of the Buddhas, the most high among men; it is something sublime and adorable.
93. The powers, meditations, degrees of emancipation and self-concentration by many hundreds of kotis, that is the exalted vehicle in which the sons of Buddha take a never-ending delight.
94. In playing with it they pass days and nights, fortnights, months, seasons, years, intermediate kalpas, nay, thousands of kotis of kalpas.
95. This is the lofty vehicle of jewels which sundry Bodhisattvas and the disciples listening to the Sugata employ to go and sport on the terrace of enlightenment.
96. Know then, Tishya, that there is no second vehicle in this world anywhere to be found, in whatever direction thou shalt search, apart from the device shown by the most high among men.
97. Ye are my children, I am your father, who has removed you from pain, from the triple world, from fear and danger, when you had been burning for many kotis of Aeons.

98. And I am teaching blessed rest Nirvana, in so far as, though you have not yet reached final rest, you are delivered from the trouble of the mundane whirl, provided you seek the vehicle of the Buddhas.
99. Any Bodhisattvas here present obey my Buddha-rules. Such is the skilfulness of the Jina that he disciplines many Bodhisattvas.
100. When the creatures in this world delight in low and contemptible pleasures, then the Chief of the world, who always speaks the truth, indicates **pain as the first great truth.**
101. And to those who are ignorant and too simple-minded to discover the root of that pain I lay open the way: **'Awaking of full consciousness, strong desire is the origin of pain.'**
102. **Always try, unattached, to suppress desire. This is my third truth, that of suppression. It is an infallible means of deliverance; for by practising this method one shall become emancipated.**
103. And from what are they emancipated, Sariputra? They are emancipated from chimeras. Yet they are not wholly freed; the Chief declares that they have not yet reached final and complete rest in this world.
104. Why is it that I do not pronounce one to be delivered before one's having reached the highest, supreme enlightenment? Because such is my will; I am the ruler of the law, who is born in this world to lead to beatitude.
105. This, Sariputra, is the closing word of my law which now at the last time I pronouncest for the weal of the world including the gods. Preach it in all quarters.
106. And if someone speaks to you these words, 'I joyfully accept,' and with signs of utmost reverence receives this Sutra, thou mayst consider that man to be unable to slide back.
107. To believe in this Sutra one must have seen former Tathagatas, paid honour to them, and heard a law similar to this.
108. To believe in my supreme word one must have seen me; thou and the assembly of monks have seen all these Bodhisattvas.

109. This Sutra is apt to puzzle the ignorant, and I do not pronounce it before having penetrated to superior knowledge. Indeed, it is not within the range of the disciples, nor do the Pratyeka Buddhas come to it.
100. But thou, Sariputra, hast good will, not to speak of my other disciples here. They will walk in my faith, though each cannot have his individual knowledge.
111. But do not speak of this matter to haughty persons, nor to conceited ones, nor to Yogins who are not self-restrained; for the fools, always revelling in sensual pleasures, might in their blindness scorn the law manifested.
112. Now hear the dire results when one scorns my skilfulness and the Buddha-rules for ever fixed in the world; when one, with sullen brow, scorns the vehicle.
113. Hear the destiny of those who have scorned such a Sutra like this, whether during my lifetime or after my Nirvana, or who have wronged the monks.
114. After having disappeared from amongst men, they shall dwell in the lowest hell (Avichi) during a whole kalpa, and thereafter they shall fall lower and lower, the fools, passing through repeated births for many intermediate kalpas.
115. And when they have vanished from amongst the inhabitants of hell, they shall further descend to the condition of brutes, be even as dogs and jackals, and become a sport to others.
116. Under such circumstances they shall grow blackish of colour, spotted, covered with sores, itchy; moreover, they shall be hairless and feeble, all those who have an aversion to my supreme enlightenment.
117. They are ever despised amongst animals; hit by clods or weapons they yell; everywhere they are threatened with sticks, and their bodies are emaciated from hunger and thirst.
118. Sometimes they become camels or asses, carrying loads, and are beaten with whips and sticks; they are constantly occupied with thoughts of eating, the fools who have scorned the Buddha-rule.

119. At other times they become ugly jackals, half blind and crippled; the helpless creatures are vexed by the village boys, who throw clods and weapons at them.
120. Again shooting off from that place, those fools become animals with bodies of five hundred yojanas, whirling round, dull and lazy.
121. They have no feet, and creep on the belly; to be devoured by many kotis of animals is the dreadful punishment they have to suffer for having scorned a Sutra like this.
122. And whenever they assume a human shape, they are born crippled, maimed, crooked, one-eyed, blind, dull, and low, they having no faith in my Sutra.
123. Nobody keeps their side; a putrid smell is continually issuing from their mouths; an evil spirit has entered the body of those who do not believe in this supreme enlightenment.
124. Needy, obliged to do menial labour, always in another's service, feeble, and subject to many diseases they go about in the world, unprotected.
125. The man whom they happen to serve is unwilling to give them much, and what he gives is soon lost. Such is the fruit of sinfulness.
126. Even the best-prepared medicaments, administered to them by able men, do, under those circumstances, but increase their illness, and the disease has no end.
127. Some commit thefts, affrays, assaults, or acts of hostility, whereas others commit robberies of goods; all this befalls the sinner.
128. Never does he behold the Lord of the world, the King of kings ruling the earth, for he is doomed to live at a wrong times, he who scorns my Buddha-rule.
129. Nor does that foolish person listen to the law; he is deaf and senseless; he never finds rest, because he has scorned this enlightenment.
130. During many hundred thousand myriads of kotis of Aeons equal to the sand of the Ganges he shall be dull and defective; that is the evil result from scorning this Sutra.

131. Hell is his garden, or monastery, a place of misfortune his abode; he is continually living amongst asses, hogs, jackals, and dogs.

132. And when he has assumed a human shape he is to be blind, deaf, and stupid, the servant of another, and always poor.

133. Diseases, myriads of kotis of wounds on the body, scab itch, scurvy, leprosy, blotch, a foul smell are, in that condition, his covering and apparel.

134. His sight is dim to distinguish the real. His anger appears mighty in him, and his passion is most violent; he always delights in animal wombs.

135. Were I to go on, Sariputra, for a whole Aeon, enumerating the evils of him who shall scorn my Sutra, I should not come to an end.

136. And since I am fully aware of it, I command thee, Sariputra, that thou shalt not expound a Sutra like this before foolish people.

137. But those who are sensible, instructed, thoughtful, clever, and learned, who strive after the highest supreme enlightenment, to them expound its real meaning.

138. Those who have seen many kotis of Buddhas, planted immeasurably many roots of goodness, and undertaken a strong vow, to them expound its real meaning.

139. Those who, full of energy and ever kindhearted, have a long time been developing the feeling of kindness, have given up body and life, in their presence thou mayst preach this Sutra.

140. Those who show mutual love and respect, keep no intercourse with ignorant people, and are content to live in mountain caverns, to them expound this hallowed Sutra.

141. If thou see sons of Buddha who attach themselves to virtuous friends and avoid bad friends, then reveal to them this Sutra.

142. Those sons of Buddha who have not broken the moral vows, are pure like gems and jewels, and devoted to the study of the great Sutras, before those thou mayst propound this Sutra.

143. Those who are not irascible, ever sincere, full of compassion for all living beings, and respectful towards the Sugata, before those thou mayst propound this Sutra.
144. To one who in the congregation, without any hesitation and distraction of mind, speaks to expound the law, with many myriads of kotis of illustrations, thou mayst manifest this Sutra.
145. And he who, desirous of acquiring all-knowingness, respectfully lifts his joined hands to his head, or who seeks in all directions to find some monk of sacred eloquence;
146. And he who keeps in memory the great Sutras, while he never shows any liking for other books, nor even knows a single stanza from another work; to all of them thou mayst expound this sublime Sutra.
147. He who seeks such an excellent Sutra as this, and after obtaining it devoutly worships it, is like the man who wears a relic of the Tathagata he has eagerly sought for.
148. Never mind other Sutras nor other books in which a profane philosophy is taught; such books are fit for the foolish; avoid them and preach this Sutra.
149. During a full Aeon, Sariputra, I could speak of thousands of kotis of connected points, but this suffices; thou mayst reveal this Sutra to all who are striving after the highest supreme enlightenment.

◆ ◆ ◆ ◆ ◆

4

ON A PERSON'S DISPOSITION

Another parable showing the skill of the wise father in leading a child that has gone astray and lost all self-respect to a feeling of his innate nobility and to happiness.

As the venerable Subhuti, the venerable Maha-Katyayana, the venerable Maha-Kasyapa, and the venerable Maha-Maudgalyayana heard this law unheard of before, and as from the mouth of the Lord they heard the future destiny of Sariputra to superior perfect enlightenment, they were struck with wonder, amazement, and rapture. They instantly rose from their seats and went up to the place where the Lord was sitting; after throwing their cloak over one shoulder, fixing the right knee on the ground and lifting up their joined hands before the Lord, looking up to him, their bodies bent, bent down and inclined, they addressed the Lord in this strain:

Lord, we are old, aged, advanced in years; honoured as seniors in this assemblage of monks. Worn out by old age we fancy that we have attained Nirvana; we make no efforts, O Lord, for supreme perfect enlightenment; our force and exertion are inadequate to it. Though the Lord preaches the law and has long continued sitting, and though we have attended to that preaching of the law, yet, O Lord, as we have so long been sitting and so long attended the Lord's service, our greater and minor members, as well as the joints and articulations, begin to ache. Hence, O Lord, we are unable, in spite of the Lord's preaching, to realise the fact that all is vanity or void, purposeless, or causeless, or unconditioned, and unfixed; we have conceived no longing after the Buddha-laws, the divisions of the Buddha-fields, the sports of the Bodhisattvas or Tathagatas. For by having fled out of the triple world, O Lord, we imagined having attained Nirvana, and we are decrepit from old age. Hence, O Lord, though we have exhorted other Bodhisattvas and instructed them in supreme perfect enlightenment, we have in doing so never conceived a single thought of longing. And just now, O Lord, we are hearing from the Lord that disciples also may be predestined to supreme perfect enlightenment. We are astonished and amazed, and deem it a great gain, O Lord, that today, on a sudden, we have heard from the Lord a voice such as we never heard before. We have acquired a magnificent jewel, O Lord, an incomparable jewel. We had not sought, nor searched, nor expected, nor required so magnificent a jewel. It has become clear to us, O Lord; it has become clear to us, O Sugata.

It is a case, O Lord, as if a certain man went away from his father and betook himself to some other place. He lives there in foreign parts for many years, twenty or thirty or forty or fifty. In course of time the father becomes a great man; the son is poor; in seeking a livelihood for the sake of food and clothing he roams in all directions and goes to some place, whereas his father removes to another country. The latter has much wealth, gold, corn, treasures, and granaries; possesses much wrought gold and silver, many gems, pearls, lapis lazuli, conch shells, and, corals, gold and silver; many slaves male and female, servants for menial work and journeymen; is rich in elephants, horses, carriages, cows, and sheep. He keeps a large retinue; has his money invested in great territories, and does great things in business, moneylending, agriculture, and commerce.

In course of time, Lord, that poor man, in quest of food and clothing, roaming through villages, towns, boroughs, provinces, kingdoms, and royal capitals, reaches the place where his father, the owner of much wealth and gold, treasures and granaries, is residing. Now the poor man's father, Lord, the owner of much wealth and gold, treasures and granaries, who was residing in that town, had always and ever been thinking of the son he had lost fifty years ago, but he gave no utterance to his thoughts before others, and was only pining in himself and thinking: I am old, aged, advanced in years, and possess abundance of bullion, gold, money and corn, treasures and granaries, but have no son. It is to be feared lest death shall overtake me and an this perish unused. Repeatedly he was thinking of that son: O how happy should I be, were my son to enjoy this mass of wealth!

Meanwhile, Lord, the poor man in search of food and clothing was gradually approaching the house of the rich man, the owner of abundant bullion, gold, money and corn, treasures and granaries. And the father of the poor man happened to sit at the door of his house, surrounded and waited upon by a great crowd of Brahmins, Kshatriyas, Vaisyas, and Sudras; he was sitting on a magnificent throne with a footstool decorated with gold and silver, while dealing with hundred thousands of kotis of gold-pieces, and fanned with a chowrie, on a spot under an extended awning inlaid with pearls and flowers and adorned with hanging garlands of jewels; sitting in great pomp. The poor man, Lord, saw his own father in such pomp sitting at the door of the house, surrounded with a great crowd of people and doing a householder's business. The poor man frightened, terrified, alarmed, seized with a feeling of horripilation all over the body, and agitated in mind, reflects thus: Unexpectedly have I here fallen in with a king or grandee. People like me have nothing to do here; let me go; in the street of the poor I am likely to find food and clothing without much difficulty. Let me no longer tarry at this place, lest I be taken to do forced labour or incur some other injury.

Thereupon, Lord, the poor man quickly departs, runs off, does not tarry from fear of a series of supposed dangers. But the rich man, sitting on the throne at the door of his mansion, has recognised his son at first sight, in consequence whereof he is content, in high spirits, charmed, delighted, filled with joy and cheerfulness. He thinks: Wonderful! he who is to enjoy this plenty of bullion, gold, money and corn, treasures and granaries, has been found! He of whom I have been thinking again and again, is here now that I am old, aged, advanced in years.

At the same time, moment, and instant, Lord, he despatches couriers, to whom he says: Go, sirs, and quickly fetch me that man. The fellows thereon all run forth in full speed and overtake the poor man, who, frightened, terrified, alarmed, seized with a feeling of horripilation all over his body, agitated in mind, utters a lamentable cry of distress, screams, and exclaims: I have given you no offence. But the fellows drag the poor man, however lamenting, violently with them. He, frightened, terrified, alarmed, seized with a feeling of horripilation all over his body, and agitated in mind, thinks by himself: I fear lest I shall be punished with capital punishment; I am lost. He faints away, and falls on the earth. His father dismayed and near despondency says to those fellows: Do not carry the man in that manner. With these words he sprinkles him with cold water without addressing him any further. For that householder knows the poor man's humble disposition and his own elevated position; yet he feels that the man is his son.

The householder, Lord, skilfully conceals from everyone that it is his son. He calls one of his servants and says to him: Go, sirrah, and tell that poor man: Go, sirrah, whether thou likest; thou art free. The servant obeys, approaches the poor man and tells him: Go, sirrah, whether thou likest; thou art free. The poor man is astonished and amazed at hearing these words; he leaves that spot and wanders to the street of the poor in search of food and clothing. In order to attract him the householder practises an able device. He employs for it two men ill-favoured and of little splendour. Go, says he, go to the man you saw in this place; hire him in your own name for a double daily fee, and order him to do work here in my house. And if he asks: What work shall I have to do? tell him: Help us in clearing the heap of dirt. The two fellows go and seek the poor man and engage him for such work as mentioned. Thereupon the two fellows conjointly with the poor man clear the heap of dirt in the house for the daily pay they receive from the rich man, while they take up their abode in a hovel of straw in the neighbourhood of the rich man's dwelling. And that rich man beholds through a window his own son clearing the heap of dirt, at which sight he is anew struck with wonder and astonishment.

Then the householder descends from his mansion, lays off his wreath and ornaments, parts with his soft, clean, and gorgeous attire, puts on dirty raiment, takes a basket in his right hand, smears his body with dust, and goes to his son, whom he greets from afar, and thus addresses: Please, take the baskets and without delay remove the dust. By this device he manages to speak to his son, to have a talk with him and say: Do, sirrah, remain here in my service; do not go again to another place; I will give thee extra pay, and whatever thou wantest thou mayst confidently ask me, be it the price of a pot, a smaller pot, a boiler or wood, or be it the price of salt, food, or clothing. I have got an old cloak, man; if thou shouldst want it, ask me for it, I will give it. Any utensil of such sort, when thou wantest to have it, I will give thee. Be at ease, fellow; look upon me as if I were thy father, for I am older and thou art younger, and thou hast rendered me much service by clearing this heap of dirt, and as long as thou hast been in my service thou hast never shown nor art showing wickedness, crookedness, arrogance, or hypocrisy; I have discovered in thee no vice at all of such as are commonly seen in other man-servants. From henceforward thou art to me like my own son.

From that time, Lord, the householder addresses the poor man by the name of son, and the latter feels in presence of the householder as a son to his father. In this manner, Lord, the householder affected with longing for his son employs him for the clearing of the heap of dirt during twenty years, at the end of which the poor man feels quite at ease in the mansion to go in and out, though he continues taking his abode in the hovel of straw.

After a while, Lord, the householder falls sick, and feels that the time of his death is near at hand. He says to the poor man: Come hither, man, I possess abundant bullion, gold, money and corn, treasures and granaries. I am very sick, and wish to have one upon whom to bestow my wealth; by whom it is to be received, and with whom it is to be deposited. Accept it. For in the same manner as I am the owner of it, so art thou, but thou shalt not suffer anything of it to be wasted.

And so, Lord, the poor man accepts the abundant bullion, gold, money and corn, treasures and granaries of the. rich man, but for himself he is quite indifferent to it, and requires nothing from it, not even so much as the price of a prastha of flour; he continues living in the same hovel of straw and considers himself as poor as before.

After a while, Lord, the householder perceives that his son is able to save, mature and mentally developed; that in the consciousness of his nobility he feels abashed, ashamed, disgusted, when thinking of his former poverty. The time of his death approaching, he sends for the poor man, presents him to a gathering of his relations, and before the king or king's peer and in the presence of citizens and country-people makes the following speech: Hear, gentlemen! this is my own son, by me begotten. It is now fifty years that he disappeared from such and such a town. He is called so and so, and myself am called so and so. In searching after him I have from that town come hither. He is my son, I am his father. To him I leave all my revenues, and all my personal or private wealth shall he acknowledge his own.

The poor man, Lord, hearing this speech was astonished and amazed; he thought by himself: Unexpectedly have I obtained this bullion, gold, money and corn, treasures and granaries.

Even so, O Lord, do we represent the sons of the Tathagata, and the Tathagata says to us: Ye are my sons, as the householder did. We were oppressed, O Lord, with three difficulties, the difficulty of pain, the difficulty of conceptions, the difficulty of transition and in the worldly whirl we were disposed to what is low. Then have we been prompted by the Lord to ponder on the numerous inferior laws, or conditions, things, that are similar to a heap of dirt. Once directed to them we have been practising, making efforts, and seeking for nothing but Nirvana as our fee. We were content, O Lord, with the Nirvana obtained, and thought to have gained much at the hands of the Tathagata because of our having applied ourselves to these laws, practised, and made efforts. But the Lord takes no notice of us, does not mix with us, nor tell us that this treasure of the Tathagata's knowledge shall belong to us, though the Lord skilfully appoints us as heirs to this treasure of the knowledge of the Tathagata. And we, O Lord, are not impatiently longing to enjoy it, because we deem it a great gain already to receive from the Lord Nirvana as our fee. We preach to the Bodhisattvas Mahasattvas a sublime sermon about the knowledge of the Tathagata; we explain, show, demonstrate the knowledge of the Tathagata, O Lord, without longing. For the Tathagata by his skilfulness knows our disposition, whereas we ourselves do not know, nor apprehend. It is for this very reason that the Lord just now tells us that we are to him as sons, and that he reminds us of being heirs to the Tathagata. For the case stands thus: we are as sons to the Tathagata, but low, or humble, of disposition; the Lord perceives the strength of our disposition and applies to us the denomination of Bodhisattvas; we are, however, charged with a double office in so far as in presence of Bodhisattvas we are called persons of low disposition and at the same time have to rouse them to Buddha-enlightenment. Knowing the strength of our disposition the Lord has thus spoken, and in this way, O Lord, do we say that we have obtained unexpectedly and without longing the jewel of omniscience, which we did not desire, nor seek, nor search after, nor expect, nor require; and that inasmuch as we are the sons of the Tathagata.

On that occasion the venerable Maha-Kasyapa uttered the following stanzas:

1. We are stricken with wonder, amazement, and rapture at hearing a voice; it is the lovely voice, the leader's voice, that so unexpectedly we hear to-day.

2. In a short moment we have acquired a great heap of precious jewels such as we were not thinking of, nor requiring. All of us are astonished to hear it.

3. It is like the history of a young person who, seduced by foolish people, went away from his father and wandered to another country far distant.

4. The father was sorry to perceive that his son had run away and in his sorrow roamed the country in all directions during no less than fifty years.

5. In search of his son he came to some great city, where he built a house and dwelt, blessed with all that can gratify the five senses.

6. He had plenty of bullion and gold, money and corn, conch shells, stones, and coral; elephants, horses, and footboys; cows, cattle, and sheep;

7. Interests, revenues, landed properties; male and female slaves and a great number of servants; was highly honoured by thousands of kotis and a constant favourite of the king's.
8. The citizens bow to him with joined hands, as well as the villagers in the rural districts; many merchants come to him, and persons charged with numerous affairs.
9. In such a way the man becomes wealthy, but he gets old, aged, advanced in years, and he passes days and nights always sorrowful in mind on account of his son.
10. It is fifty years since that foolish son has run away. I have got plenty of wealth and the hour of my death draws near:
11. Meanwhiie that foolish son is wandering from village to village, poor and miserable, seeking food and clothing.
12. When begging, he at one time gets something, another time he does not. He grows lean in his travels, the unwise boy, while his body is vitiated with scabs and itch.
13. In course of time he in his rovings reaches the town where his father is living, and comes to his father's mansion to beg for food and raiment.
14. And the wealthy, rich man happens to sit at the door on a throne under a canopy expanded in the sky and surrounded with many hundreds of living beings.
15. His trustees stand round him, some of them counting money and bullion, Some writing bills, some lending money on interest.
16. The poor man, seeing the splendid mansion of the householder, thinks within himself: Where am I here? This man must, be a king or a grandee.
17. Let me not incur some injury and be caught to do forced labour. With these reflections he hurried away inquiring after the road to the street of the poor.
18. The rich man on the throne is glad to see his own son, and despatches messengers, with the order to fetch that poor man.
19. The messengers immediately seize the man, but he is no sooner caught than he faints away (as he thinks): These

are certainly executioners who have approached me; what do I want, clothing or food?

20. On seeing it, the rich, sagacious man thinks: This ignorant and stupid person is of low disposition and will have no faith in my magnificence, nor believe that I am his father.
21. Under those circumstances he orders persons of low character, crooked, one-eyed, maimed, ill-clad, and blackish, to go and search that man who shall do menial work.
22. 'Enter my service and cleanse the putrid heap of dirt, replete with faeces and urine; I will give thee a double salary', are the words of the message.
23. On hearing this call the poor man comes and cleanses the said spot; he takes up his abode there in a hovel near the mansion.
24. The rich man continually observes him through the windows and thinks: There is my son engaged in a low occupation, cleansing the heap of dirt.
25. Then he descends, takes a basket, puts on dirty garments, and goes near the man. He chides him, saying: Thou dost not perform thy work.
26. I will ,give thee double salary and twice more ointment for the feet; I will give thee food with salt, potherbs, and, besides, a cloak.
27. So he chides him at the time, but afterwards he wisely conciliates him by saying: Thou dost thy work very well, indeed; thou art thy son, surely; there is no doubt of it.
28. Little by little he makes the man enter the house, and employs him in his service for fully twenty years, in the course of which time he succeeds in inspiring him with confidence.
29. At the same time he lays up in the house gold, pearls, and crystal, draws up the sum total, and is always occupied in his mind with all that property.
30. The ignorant man, who is living outside the mansion, alone in a hovel, cherishes no other ideas but of poverty, and thinks to himself: Mine are no such possessions!

31. The rich man perceiving this of him thinks: My son has arrived at the consciousness of being noble. He calls together a gathering of his friends and relatives and says: I will give all my property to this man.
32. In the midst of the assembly where the king, burghers, citizens, and many merchantmen were present, he speaks thus: This is my son whom I lost a long time ago.
33. It is now fully fifty years—and twenty years more during which I have seen him—that he disappeared from such and such a place and that in his search I came to this place.
34. He is owner of all my property; to him I leave it all and entirely; let him do with it what he wants; I give him my whole family property.
35. And the poor man is struck with surprise; remembering his former poverty, his low disposition and as he receives those good things of his father's and the family property, he thinks: Now am I a happy man.
36. In like manner has the leader, who knows our low disposition or position, declared to us: Ye shall become Buddhas,' but, 'Ye are, certainly, my disciples and sons.
37. And the Lord of the world enjoins us: Teach, Kasyapa, the superior path to those that strive to attain the highest summit of enlightenment, the path by following which they are to become Buddhas.
38. Being thus ordered by the Sugata, we show the path to many Bodhisattvas of great might by means of myriads of kotis of illustrations and proofs.
39. And by hearing us the sons of Jina realise that eminent path to attain enlightenment, and in that case receive the prediction that they are to become Buddhas in this world.
40. Such is the work we are doing strenuously, preserving this law-treasure and revealing it to the sons of Jina, in the manner of that man who had deserved the confidence of that other man.
41. Yet, though we diffuse the Buddha-treasure we feel ourselves to be poor; we do not require the knowledge of the Jina, and yet, at the same time, we reveal it.

42. We fancy an individual Nirvana; so far, no further does our knowledge reach; nor do we ever rejoice at hearing of the divisions of Buddha-fields.
43. All these laws are faultless, unshaken, exempt from destruction and commencement; but there is no law in them. When we hear this, however, we cannot believe.
44. We have put aside all aspiration to superior Buddha-knowledge a long time ago; never have we devoted ourselves to it. This is the last and decisive word spoken by the Jina.
45. In this bodily existence, closing with Nirvana, we have continually accustomed our thoughts to the void; we have been released from the evils of the triple world we were suffering from, and have accomplished the command of the Jina.
46. To whomsoever among the sons of Jina who in this world are on the road to superior enlightenment we revealed the law and whatever law we taught, we never had any predilection for it.
47. And the Master of the world, the Self-born one, takes no notice of us; waiting his time; he does not explain the real connection of the things; as he is testing our disposition.
48. Able in applying devices at the right time, like that rich man he says: Be constant in subduing your low disposition and to those who are subdued he gives his wealth.
49. It is a very difficult task which the Lord of the world is performing, a task in which he displays his skilfulness, when he tames his sons of low disposition and thereupon imparts to them his knowledge.
50. On a sudden have we to-day been seized with surprise. just as the poor man who acquired riches; now for the first time have we obtained the fruit under the rule of Buddha, a fruit as excellent as faultless.
51. As we have always observed the moral precepts under the rule of the Knower of the world, we now receive the fruit of that morality which we have formerly practised.
52. Now have we obtained the egregious, hallowed, exalted, and perfect fruit of our having observed an excellent and pure spiritual life under the rule of the Leader.

53. Now, O Lord, are we disciples, and we shall proclaim supreme enlightenment everywhere, reveal the word of enlightenment, by which we are formidable disciples.
54. Now have we become Arhats, O Lord; and deserving of the worship of the world, including the gods, Maras and Brahmas, in short, of all beings.
55. Who is there, even were he to exert himself during kotis of Aeons, able to thwart thee, who accomplishes in this world of mortals such difficult things as those, and others even more difficult?
56. It would be difficult to offer resistance with hands, feet, head, shoulder, or breast, even were one to try during as many complete Aeons as there are grains of sand in the Ganges.
57. One may charitably give food, soft and solid, clothing, drink, a place for sleeping and sitting, with clean coverlets; one may build monasteries of sandalwood, and after furnishing them with double pieces of fine white muslin present them;
58. One may be assiduous in giving medicines of various kinds to the sick, in honour of the Sugata; one may spend alms during as many Aeons as there are grains of sand in the Ganges, even then one will not be able to offer resistance.
59. Of sublime nature, unequalled power, miraculous might, firm in the strength of patience is the Buddha; a great ruler is the Jina, free from imperfections. The ignorant cannot bear or understand such things as these.
60. Always returning, he preaches the law to those whose course of life is conditioned, he, the Lord of the law, the Lord of all the world, the great Lord, the Chief among the leaders of the world.
61. Fully aware of the circumstances or places of all beings he indicates their duties, so multlfarious, and considering the variety of their dispositions he inculcates the law with thousands of arguments.
62. He, the Tathagata, who is fully aware of the course of all beings and individuals, preaches a multifarious law, while pointing to this superior enlightenment.

◆ ◆ ◆ ◆ ◆

5
PARABLES OF PLANTS AND A BLIND MAN

Parable of the plants and the rain, to show the impartiality and equal care of the Lord for all creatures; another parable of the blind man to show that the ultimate goal is to reach all-knowingness.

Thereupon the Lord addressed the venerable Maha-Kasyapa and the other senior great disciples, and said: Very well, very well, Kasyapa; you have done very well to proclaim the real qualities of the Tathagata. They are the real qualities of the Tathagata, Kasyapa, but he has many more, innumerable, incalculable, the end of which it would be difficult to reach, even were one to continue enumerating them for immeasurable Aeons. The Tathagata, Kasyapa, is the master of the law, the king, lord, and master of all laws. And whatever law for any case has been instituted by the Tathagata, remains unchanged. All laws, Kasyapa, have been aptly instituted by the Tathagata. In his Tathagata-wisdom he has instituted them in such a manner that all those laws finally lead to the stage those who know all. The Tathagata also distinctly knows the meaning of all laws. The Tathagata, the Arhat, etc., is possessed of the faculty of penetrating all laws, possessed of the highest perfection of knowledge, so that he is able to decide all laws, able to display the knowledge of the all-knowing, impart the knowledge of the all-knowing, and lay down the rules of the knowledge of the all-knowing.

It is a case, Kasyapa, similar to that of a great cloud big with rain, coming up in this wide universe over all grasses, shrubs, herbs, trees of various species and kind, families of plants of different, names growing on earth, on hills, or in mountain caves, a cloud covering the wide universe to pour down its rain everywhere and at the same time. Then, Kasyapa, the grasses, shrubs, herbs, and wild trees in this universe, such as have young and tender stalks, twigs, leaves, and foliage, and such as have middle-sized stalks, twigs, leaves, and foliage, and such as have the same fully developed, all those grasses, shrubs, herbs, and wild trees, smaller and greater other trees will each, according to its faculty and power, suck the humid element from the water emitted by that great cloud, and by that water which, all of one essence, has been abundantly poured down by the cloud, they will each, according to its germ, acquire a regular development, growth, shooting up, and bigness; and so they will produce blossoms and fruits, and will receive, each severally, their names. Rooted in one and the same soil, all those families of plants and germs are drenched and vivified by water of one essence throughout.

In the same manner, Kasyapa, does the Tathagata, the Arhat, etc., appear in the world. Like unto a great cloud coming up, the Tathagata appears and sends forth his call to the whole world, including gods, men, and demons. And even as a great cloud, Kasyapa, extending over the whole universe, in like manner, Kasyapa, the Tathagata, the Arhat, etc., before the face of the world, including gods, men, and demons, lifts his voice and utters these words: I am the Tathagata, O ye gods and men! the Arhat, the perfectly enlightened one; having reached the shore myself, I carry others to the shore; being free, I make free; being comforted, I comfort; being perfectly at rest, I lead others to rest. By my perfect wisdom I know both this world and the next, such as they really are. I am all-knowing, all-seeing. Come to me, ye gods and men! hear the law. I am he who indicates the path; who shows the path, as knowing the path, being acquainted with the path. Then, Kasyapa, many hundred thousand myriads of kotis of beings come to hear the law of the Tathagata; and the Tathagata, who knows the difference as to the faculties and the energy of those beings, produces various Dharmaparyayas, tells many tales, amusing, agreeable, both instructive and pleasant, tales by means of which all beings not only become pleased with the law in this present life, but also after death will reach happy states, where they are to enjoy many pleasures and hear the law. By listening to the law they will be freed from hindrances and in due course apply themselves to the law of the all-knowing, according to their faculty, power, and strength.

Even as the great cloud, Kasyapa, after expanding over the whole universe, pours out the same water and recreates by it all grasses, shrubs, herbs, and trees; even as all these grasses, shrubs, herbs, and trees, according to their faculty, power, and strength, suck in the water and thereby attain the full development assigned to their kind; in like manner, Kasyapa, is the law preached by the Tathagata, the Arhat, etc., of one and the same essence, that is to say, the essence of it is deliverance, the final aim being absence of passion, annihilation, knowledge of the all-knowing. As to that, Kasyapa, it must be understood that the beings who hear the law when it is preached by the Tathagata, who keep it in their memory and apply themselves to it, do not know, nor perceive, nor understand their own self. For, Kasyapa, the Tathagata only really knows who, how, and of what kind those beings are; what, how, and whereby they are meditating; what, how, and whereby they are contemplating; what, why, and whereby they are attaining. No one but the Tathagata, Kasyapa, is there present, seeing all intuitively, and seeing the state of those beings in different stages, as of the lowest, highest, and mean grasses, shrubs, herbs, and trees. I am he, Kasyapa, who, knowing the law which is of but one essence, viz., the essence of deliverance, the law ever peaceful, ending in Nirvana, law of eternal rest, having but one stage and placed in voidness who knowing this do not on a sudden reveal to all the knowledge of the all-knowing, since I pay regard to the dispositions of all beings.

You are astonished, Kasyapa, that you cannot fathom the mystery expounded by the Tathagata. It is, Kasyapa, because the mystery expounded by the Tathagatas, the Arhats, etc., is difficult to be understood.

And on that occasion, the more fully to explain the same subject, the Lord uttered the following stanzas:

1. I am the Dharmaraja, born in the world as the destroyer of existence. I declare the law to all beings after discriminating their dispositions.

2. Superior men of wise understanding guard the word, guard the mystery, and do not reveal it to living beings.
3. That science is difficult to be understood; the simple, if hearing it on a sudden, would be perplexed; they would in their ignorance fall out of the way and go astray.
4. I speak according to their reach and faculty; by means of various meanings I accommodate my view.
5. It is, Kasyapa, as if a cloud rising above the horizon shrouds all space in darkness and covers the earth.
6. That great rain-cloud, big with water, is wreathed with flashes of lightning and rouses with its thundering call all creatures.
7. By warding off the sunbeams, it cools the region; and gradually lowering so as to come in reach of hands, it begins pouring down its water all around.
8. And so, flashing on every side, it pours out an abundant mass of water equally, and refreshes this earth.
9. And all herbs which have sprung up on the face of the earth, all grasses, shrubs, forest trees, other trees small and great;
10. The various field-fruits and whatever is green; all plants on hills, in caves, and thickets;
11. All those grasses, shrubs, and trees are vivified by the cloud that both refreshes the thirsty earth and waters the herbs.
12. Grasses and shrubs absorb the water of one essence which issues from the cloud according to their faculty and reach.
13. And all trees, great, small, and mean, drink that water according to their growth and faculty, and grow lustily.
14. The great plants whose trunk, stalk, bark, twigs, pith, and leaves are moistened by the water from the cloud develop their blossoms and fruits.
15. They yield their products, each according to its own faculty, reach, and the particular nature of the germ; still the water emitted from the cloud is of but one essence.
16. In the same way, Kasyapa, the Buddha comes into the world like a rain-cloud, and, once born, he, the world's Lord, speaks and shows the real course of life.

17. And the great Seer, honoured in the world, including the gods, speaks thus: I am the Tathagata, the highest of men, the Jina; I have appeared in this world like a cloud.
18. I shall refresh all beings whose bodies are withered, who are clogged to the triple world. I shall bring to felicity those that are pining away with toils, give them pleasures and final rest.
19. Hearken to me, ye hosts of gods and men; I approach to behold me: I am the Tathagata, the Lord, who has no superior, who appears in this world to save.
20. To thousands of kotis of living beings I preach a pure and most bright law that has but one scope, to wit, deliverance and rest.
21. I preach with ever the same voice, constantly taking enlightenment as my text. For this is equal for all; no partiality is in it, neither hatred nor affection.
22. I am inexorable, bear no love nor hatred towards anyone, and proclaim the law to all creatures without distinction, to the one as well as the other.
23. Whether walking, standing, or sitting, I am exclusively occupied with this task of proclaiming the law. I never get tired of sitting on the chair I have ascended.
24. I recreate the whole world like a cloud shedding its water without distinction; I have the same feelings for respectable people as for the low; for moral persons as for the immoral;
25. For the depraved as for those who observe the rules of good conduct; for those who hold sectarian views and unsound tenets, for those whose views are sound and correct.
26. I preach the law to the inferior, in mental culture as well as to persons of superior understanding and extraordinary faculties; inaccessible to weariness, I spread in season the rain of the law.
27. After hearing me, each according to his faculty, the several beings find their determined place in various situations, amongst gods, men, beautiful beings, amongst Indras, Brahmas, or the monarchs, rulers of the universe.

28. Hear, now, I am going to explain what is meant by those plants of different size, some of them being low in the world, others middle-sized and great.
29. Small plants are called the men who walk in the knowledge of the law, which is free from evil after the attaining of Nirvana, who possess the six transcendent faculties and the triple science.
30. Mean plants are called the men who, dwelling in mountain caverns, covet the state of a Pratyeka Buddha, and whose intelligence is moderately purified.
31. Those who aspire to become leading men thinking, I will become a Buddha, a chief of gods and men, and who practise exertion and meditation, are called the highest plants.
32. But the sons of Sugata, who sedulously practise benevolence and a peaceful conduct, who have arrived at certainty about their being leading men, these are called trees.
33. Those who move forward the wheel that never rolls back, and with manly strength stand firm in the exercise of miraculous power, releasing many kotis of beings, those are called great trees.
34. Yet it is one and the same law which is preached by the Jina, like the water emitted by the cloud is one and the same; different only are the faculties as described, just as the plants on the face of the earth.
35. By this parable thou mayst understand the skilfulness of the Tathagata, how he preaches one law, the various developments whereof may be likened to drops of rain.
36. I also pour out rain: the rain of the law by which this whole world is refreshed; and each according to his faculty takes to heart this well-spoken law that is one in its essence.
37. Even as all grasses and shrubs, as well as plants of middle size, trees and great trees at the time of rain look bright in all quarters;
38. So it is the very nature of the law to promote the everlasting weal of the world; by the law the whole world is recreated, and as the plants when refreshed expand their blossoms, the world does the same when refreshed.

39. The plants that in their growth remain middle-sized, are Arhats stopping when they have overcome frailties, and the Pratyeka Buddhas who, living in woody thickets, accomplish this well-spoken law.
40. But the many Bodhisattvas who, thoughtful and wise, go their way all over the triple world, striving after supreme enlightenment, they continue increasing in growth like trees.
41. Those who, endowed with magical powers and being adepts in the four degrees of meditation, feel delight at hearing of complete voidness and emit thousands of rays, they are called the great trees on earth.
42. So then, Kasyapa, is the preaching of the law, like the water poured out by the cloud everywhere alike; by which plants and men thrive, endless and eternal blossoms are produced.
43. I reveal the law which has its cause in itself; at due time I show Buddha-enlightenment; this is my supreme skilfulness and that of all leaders of the world.
44. What I here say is true in the highest sense of the word; all my disciples attain Nirvana; by following the sublime path of enlightenment all my disciples shall become Buddhas.

And further, Kasyapa, the Tathagata, in his educating, creatures, is equal, i.e., impartial and not unequal, i.e. partial. As the light of the sun and moon, Kasyapa, shines upon all the world, upon the virtuous and the wicked, upon high and low, upon the fragrant and the ill-smelling; as their beams are sent down upon everything equally, without inequality partiality; so, too, Kasyapa, the intellectual light of the knowledge of the omniscient, the Tathagatas, the Arhats, etc., the preaching of the true law proceeds equally in respect to all beings in the five states of existence, to all who according to their particular disposition are devoted to the great vehicle, or to the vehicle of the Pratyeka Buddhas, or to the vehicle of the disciples. Nor is there any deficiency or excess in the brightness of the Tathagata-knowledge up to one's becoming fully acquainted with the law. There are not three vehicles, Kasyapa; there are but beings who act differently; therefore it is declared that there are three vehicles.

When the Lord had thus spoken, the venerable Maha-Kasyapa said to him: Lord, if there are not three vehicles, for what reason then is the designation of disciples, Sravakas, Buddhas, and Bodhisattvas kept up in the present times?

On this speech the Lord answered the venerable Maha-Kasyapa as follows: It is, Kasyapa, as if a potter made different vessels out of the same clay. Some of those pots are to contain sugar, others ghee, others curds and milk; others, of inferior quality, are vessels of impurity. There is no diversity in the clay used; no, the diversity of the pots is only due to the substances which are put into each of them. **In like manner, Kasyapa, is there but one vehicle, the Buddha-vehicle; there is no second vehicle, no third.**

The Lord having thus spoken, the venerable Maha-Kasyapa said: Lord, if the beings are of different disposition, will there be for those who have left the triple world one Nirvana, or two, or three? The Lord replied: Nirvana, Kasyapa, is a consequence of understanding that all things are equal. Hence there is but one Nirvana, not two, not three. Therefore, Kasyapa, I will tell thee a parable, for men of good understanding will generally readily enough catch the meaning of what is taught under the shape of a parable.

It is a case, Kasyapa, similar to that of a certain blind-born man, who says: There are no handsome or ugly shapes; there are no men able to see handsome or ugly shapes; there exists no sun nor moon; there are no asterisms nor planets; there are no men able to see planets. But other persons say to the blind-born: There are handsome and ugly shapes; there are men able to see handsome and ugly shapes; there is a sun and moon; there are asterisms and planets; there are men able to see planets. But the blind-born does not believe them, nor accept what they say. Now there is a physician who knows all diseases. He sees that blind-born man and makes to himself this reflection: The disease of this man originates in his sinful actions in former times. All diseases possible to arise are fourfold: rheumatical, cholerical, phlegmatical, and caused by a complication of the corrupted humours. The physician, after thinking again and again on a means to cure the disease, makes to himself this reflection: Surely, with the drugs in common use it is impossible to cure this disease, but there are in the Himalaya, the king of mountains, four herbs, to wit: first, one called Possessed-of-all-sorts-of-colours-and-flavours; second, Delivering-from-all-diseases; third, Delivering-from-all-poisons; fourth, Procuring-happiness-to-those-standing-in-the-right-place.

As the physician feels compassion for the blind-born man he contrives some device to get to the Himalaya, the king of mountains. There he goes up and down and across to search. In doing so he finds the four herbs. One he gives after chewing it with the teeth; another after pounding; another after having it mixed with another drug and boiled; another after having it mixed with a raw drug; another after piercing with a lancet somewhere a vein; another after singeing it in fire; another after combining it with various other substances so as to enter in a compound potion, food, etc. Owing to these means being applied the blind-born recovers his eyesight, and in consequence of that recovery he sees outwardly and inwardly, far and near, the shine of sun and moon, the asterisms, planets, and all phenomena.

Then he says: O how foolish was I that I did not believe what they told me, nor accepted what they affirmed. Now I see all; I am delivered from my blindness and have recovered my eyesight; there is none in the world who could surpass me. And at the same moment Seers of the five transcendent faculties, strong in the divine sight and hearing, in the knowledge of others' minds, in the memory of former abodes, in magical science and intuition, speak to the man thus: Good man, thou hast just recovered thine eyesight, nothing more, and dost not know yet anything. Whence comes this conceitedness to thee? Thou hast no wisdom, nor art, thou a clever man. Further they say to him: Good man, when sitting in the interior of thy room, thou canst not see nor distinguish forms outside, nor discern which beings are animated with kind feelings and which with hostile feelings; thou canst not distinguish nor hear at the distance of five yojanas the voice of a man or the sound of a drum, conch trumpet, and the like; thou canst not even walk as far as a kos without lifting up thy feet; thou hast been produced and developed in thy mother's womb without remembering the fact; how then wouldst thou be clever, and how canst thou say: I see all? Good man, thou takest darkness for light, and takest light for darkness.

Whereupon the Seers are asked by the man: By what means and by what good work shall I acquire such wisdom and with your favour acquire those good qualities, or virtues? And the Seers say to that man: If that be thy wish, go and live in the wilderness or take thine abode in mountain caves, to meditate on the law and cast off evil passions. So shalt thou become endowed with the virtues of an ascetic and acquire the transcendent faculties. The man catches their meaning and becomes an ascetic. Living in the wilderness, the mind intent upon one sole object, he shakes off worldly desires, and acquires the five transcendent faculties. After that acquisition he reflects thus: Formerly I did not do the right thing; hence no good accrued to me. Now, however, I can go whither my mind prompts me; formerly I was ignorant, of little understanding, in fact, a blind man.

Such, Kasyapa, is the parable I have invented to make thee understand my meaning. The moral to be drawn from it is as follows. The word 'blind-born,' Kasyapa, is a designation for the creatures staying in the whirl of the world with its six states; the creatures who do not know the true law and are heaping up the thick darkness of evil passions. Those are blind from ignorance, and in consequence of it they build up conceptions; in consequence of the latter name-and-form, and so forth, up to the genesis of this whole huge mass of evils.

So the creatures blind from ignorance remain in the whirl of life, but the Tathagata, who is out of the triple world; feels compassion, prompted by which, like a father for his dear and only son, he appears in the triple world and sees with his eye of wisdom that the creatures are revolving in the circle of the mundane whirl, and are toiling without finding the right means to escape from the rotation. And on seeing this he comes to the conclusion: Yon beings, according to the good works they have done in former states, have feeble aversions and strong attachments; or feeble attachments and strong aversions; some have little wisdom, others are clever; some have soundly developed views, others have unsound views. To all of them the Tathagata skilfully shows three vehicles.

The Seers in the parable, those possessing the five transcendent faculties and clear-sight, are the Bodhisattvas who produce enlightened thought, and by the acquirement of acquiescence in the eternal law awake us to supreme, perfect enlightenment.

The great physician in the parable is the Tathagata. To the blind-born may be likened the creatures blind with infatuation. Attachment, aversion, and infatuation are likened to rheum, bile, and phlegm. The sixty-two false theories also must be looked upon as such—i.e. as doshas, humours and corrupted humours of the body, faults and corruptions. The four herbs are like vanity or voidness causelessness or purposelessness, unfixedness, arid reaching Nirvana. Just as by using different drugs different diseases are healed, so by developing the idea of vanity or voidness, purposelessness, unfixedness, which are the principles of emancipation, is ignorance suppressed; the suppression of ignorance is succeeded by the suppression of conceptions or fancies; and so forth, up to the suppression of the whole huge mass of evils. Arid thus one's mind will dwell no more on good nor on evil.

To the man who recovers his eyesight is likened the votary of the vehicle of the disciples and of Pratyeka Buddhas. He rends the ties of evil passion in the whirl of the world; freed from those ties he is released from the triple world with its six states of existence. Therefore the votary of the vehicle of the disciples may think and speak thus: There are no more laws to be penetrated; I have reached Nirvana, Then the Tathagata preaches to him: How can he who has not penetrated all laws have reached Nirvana? The Lord rouses him to enlightenment, and the disciple, when the consciousness of enlightenment has been awakened in him, no longer stays in the mundane whirl, but at the same time has not yet reached Nirvana. As he has arrived at true insight, he looks upon this triple world in every direction as void, resembling the produce of magic, similar to a dream, a mirage, an echo. He sees that all laws, and phenomena, are unborn and undestroyed, not bound and not loose, not dark and not bright. He who views the profound laws in such a light sees, as if he were not seeing, the whole triple world full of beings of contrary and omnifarious fancies and dispositions.

And on that occasion, in order to more amply explain the same subject, the Lord uttered the following stanzas:

45. As the rays of the sun and moon descend alike on all men, good and bad, without deficiency in one case or surplus in the other;
46. So the wisdom of the Tathagata shines like the sun and moon, leading all beings without partiality.
47. As the potter, making clay vessels, produces from the same clay pots for sugar, milk, ghee, or water;
48. Some for impurities, others for curdled milk, the clay used by the artificer for the vessels being of but one sort;
49. As a vessel is made to receive all its distinguishing qualities according to the quality of the substance laid into it, so the Tathagatas, on account of the diversity of taste,
50. Mention a diversity of vehicles, though the Buddha-vehicle be the only indisputable one. He who ignores the rotation of mundane existence, has no perception of blessed rest;
51. But he who understands that all laws are void and without reality and without individual character penetrates the enlightenment of the perfectly enlightened Lords in its very essence.
52. One who occupies a middle position of wisdom is called a Pratyekajina (i.e. Pratyeka Buddha); one lacking the insight of voidness is termed a disciple.
53. But after understanding all laws one is called a perfectly enlightened one; such a one is assiduous in preaching the law to living beings by means of hundreds of devices.
54. It is as if some blind-born man, because he sees no sun, moon, planets, and stars, in his blind ignorance should say: There are no visible things at all.
55. But a great physician taking compassion on the blind man, goes to the Himalaya, where seeking across, up and down,

56. He fetches from the mountain four plants; the herb of-all-colours-flavours-and-cases, and others. These he intends to apply.
57. He applies them in this manner: one he gives to the blind man after chewing it, another after pounding, again another by introducing it with the point of a needle into the man's body.
58. The man having got his eyesight, sees the sun, moon, planets, and stars, and arrives at the conclusion that it was from sheer ignorance that he spoke thus as he had formerly done.
59. In the same way do people of great ignorance, blind from their birth, move in the turmoil of the world, because they do not know the wheel of causes and effects. the path of toils.
60. In the world so blinded by ignorance appears the highest of those who know all, the Tathagata, the great physician, of compassionate nature.
61. As an able teacher he shows the true law; he reveals supreme Buddha-enlightenment to him who is most advanced.
62. To those of middling wisdom the Leader preaches a middling enlightenment; again another enlightenment he recommends to him who is afraid of the mundane whirl.
63. The disciple who by his discrimination has escaped from the triple world thinks he has reached pure, blest Nirvana, but it is only by knowing all laws and the universal laws that the immortal Nirvana is reached.
64. In that case it is as if the great Seers, moved by compassion, said to him: Thou art mistaken; do not be proud of thy knowledge.
65. When thou art in the interior of thy room, thou canst not perceive what is going on without, fool as thou art.
66. Thou who, when staying within, dost not perceive even now what people outside are doing or not doing, how wouldst thou be wise, fool as thou art?

67. Thou art not able to hear a sound at a distance of but five yojanas, far less at a greater distance.
68. Thou canst not discern who are malevolent or benevolent towards thee. Whence then comes that pride to thee?
69. If thou hast to walk so far as a kos, thou canst not go without a beaten track; and what happened to thee when in thy mother's womb thou hast immediately forgotten.
70. In this world he is called all-knowing who possesses the five transcendent faculties, but when thou who knowest nothing pretendest to be all-knowing, it is an effect of infatuation.
71. If thou art desirous of omniscience, direct thy attention to transcendent wisdom; then betake thy self to the wilderness and meditate on the pure law; by it thou shalt acquire the transcendent faculties.
72. The man catches the meaning, goes to the wilderness, meditates with the greatest attention, and, as he is endowed with good qualities, ere long I acquires the five transcendent faculties.
73. Similarly all disciples fancy having reached Nirvana, but the Jina instructs them by saying: This is at temporary repose, no final rest.
74. It is an artifice of the Buddhas to enunciate this dogma. There is no real Nirvana without all-knowingness; try to reach this.
75. The boundless knowledge of the three paths of time, the six utmost perfections, Paramitas, voidness, the absence of purpose or object, the absence of finiteness;
76. The idea of enlightenment and the other laws leading to Nirvana, both such as are mixed with imperfection and such as are exempt from it, such as are tranquil and comparable to ethereal space;
77. The four Brahmaviharas and the four Sangrahas, as well as the laws sanctioned by eminent sages for the education of creatures;
78. He who knows these things and that all phenomena have the nature of illusion and dreams, that they are pithless as the stem of the plantain, and similar to an echo;

79. And who knows that the triple world throughout is of that nature, not fast and not loose, he knows rest.
80. He who considers all laws to be alike, void, devoid of particularity and individuality, not derived from an intelligent cause; nay, who discerns that nothingness is law;
81. Such a one has great wisdom and sees the whole of the law entirely. There are no three vehicles by any means; there is but one vehicle in this world.
82. All laws or the laws of all are alike, equal, for all, and ever alike. Knowing this, one understands immortal, blest Nirvana.

◆ ◆ ◆ ◆ ◆

6

FUTURE DESTINY

Several predictions as proof of the power of the Sugata to look into the future.

After pronouncing these stanzas the Lord addressed the assembly of monks: I announce to you, monks, I make known to you that the monk Kasyapa, my disciple, here present, shall do homage to thirty thousand kotis of Buddhas; shall respect, honour, and worship them; and shall keep the true law of those Lords and Buddhas. In his last bodily existence in the world Avabhasa (i.e. lustre), in the Aeon Mahavyuha (i.e., great division) he shall be a Tathagata, an Arhat, etc., etc., by the name of Rasmiprabhasa, i.e., beaming with rays, His lifetime shall last twelve intermediate kalpas, and his true law twenty intermediate kalpas; the counterfeit of his true law shall last as many intermediate kalpas. His Buddha-field will be pure, clean, devoid of stones, grit, gravel; of pits and precipices; devoid of gutters and dirty pools; even, pretty, beautiful, and pleasant to see; consisting of lapis lazuli, adorned with jewel-trees, and looking like a checkerboard with eight compartments set off with gold threads. It will be strewed with flowers, and many hundred thousand Bodhisattvas are to appear in it. As to disciples, there will be innumerable hundred thousands of myriads of kotis of them. Neither Mara the evil one, nor his host will be discoverable in it, though Mara and his followers shall afterwards be there; for they will apply themselves to receive the true law under the command of that very Lord Rasmiprabhasa.

And on that occasion the Lord uttered the following stanzas:

1. With my Buddha-eye, monks, I see that the senior Kasyapa here shall become a Buddha at a future epoch, in an incalculable Aeon, after he shall have paid homage to the most high of men.
2. This Kasyapa shall see fully thirty thousand kotis of Jinas, under whom he shall lead a spiritual life for the sake of Buddha-knowledge.
3. After having paid homage to those highest of men and acquired that supreme knowledge, he shall in his last bodily existence be a Lord of the world, a matchless, great Seer.
4. And his field will be magnificent, excellent, pure, goodly, beautiful, pretty, nice, ever delightful, and set off with gold threads.
5. That field, monks, appearing like a board divided into eight compartments, will have several jewel-trees, one in each compartment, from which issues a delicious odour.
6. It will be adorned with plenty of flowers, and embellished with variegated blossoms; in it are no pits nor precipices; it is even, goodly, beautiful.
7. There will be found hundreds of kotis of Bodhisattvas, subdued of mind and of great magical power, mighty keepers of Sutrantas of great extension.
8. As to disciples, faultless, princes of the law, standing in their last period of life, their number can ,never be known, even if one should go on counting for Aeons, and that with the aid of divine knowledge.
9. He himself shall stay twelve intermediate kalpas, and his true law twenty complete Aeons; the counterfeit is to continue as many Aeons, in the domain of Rasmiprabhasa.

Thereupon the venerable senior Maha-Maudgalyayana, the venerable Subhuti, and the venerable Maha-Katyayana, their bodies trembling, gazed up to the Lord with unblenching eyes, and at the same moment severally uttered, in mental concert, the following stanzas:

10. O hallowed one Arhat, great hero, Sakya lion, most high of men! out of compassion to us speak the Buddha-word.

11. The highest of men, the Jina, he who knows the fatal term, will, as it were, sprinkle us with nectar by predicting our destiny also.
12. It is as if a certain man, in time of famine, comes and gets good food, but to whom, when the food is already in his hands, they say that he should wait.
13. Similarly it was with us, who after minding the lower vehicle, at the calamitous conjuncture of a bad time, were longing for Buddha-knowledge.
14. But the perfectly enlightened great Seer has not yet favoured us with a prediction of our destiny, as if he would say: Do not eat the food that has been put into your hand.
15. Quite so, O hero, we were longing as we heard the exalted voice and thought: Then shall we be at rest, when we shall have received a prediction.
16. Utter a prediction, O great hero, so benevolent and merciful! let there be an end of our feeling of poverty!

And the Lord, who in his mind apprehended the thoughts arising in the minds of those great senior disciples, again addressed the assembly of monks: This great disciple of mine, monks, the senior Subhuti, shall likewise pay homage to thirty hundred thousand myriads of kotis of Buddhas; shall show them respect, honour, reverence, veneration, and worship. Under them shall he lead a spiritual life and achieve enlightenment. After the performance of such duties shall he, in his last bodily existence, become a Tathagata in the world, an Arhat, etc., etc., by the name of Sasiketu.

His Buddha-field will be called Ratnasambhava and his epoch Ratnaprabhasa. And that Buddha-field will be even, beautiful, crystalline, variegated with jewel-trees, devoid of pits and precipices, devoid of sewers, nice, covered with flowers. And there will men have their abode in palaces, or towers, given them for their use. In it will be many disciples, innumerable, so that it would be impossible to terminate the calculation. Many hundred thousand myriads of kotis of Bodhisattvas also will be there. The lifetime of that Lord is to last twelve intermediate kalpas; his true law is to continue twenty intermediate kalpas, and its counterfeit as many. That Lord will, while standing poised in the firmament, preach the law to the monks, and educate many thousands of Bodhisattvas and disciples.

And on that occasion the Lord uttered the following stanzas:

17. I have something to announce, monks, something to make known; listen then to me: The senior Subhuti, my disciple, shall in days to come be a Buddha.
18. After having seen of most mighty Buddhas thirty myriads of kotis in full, he shall enter upon the straight course to obtain this knowledge.
19. In his last bodily existence shall the hero, possessed of the thirty-two distinctive signs, become a great Seer, similar to a column of gold, beneficial and bounteous to the world.
20. The field where that friend of the world shall save myriads of kotis of living beings will be most beautiful, pretty, and delightful to people at large.
21. In it will be many Bodhisattvas to turn the wheel that never rolls back or never deviates; endowed with keen faculties they will, under that Jina, be the ornaments of the Buddha-field.
22. His disciples are so numerous as to pass calculation and measure; gifted with the six transcendent faculties, the triple science and magic power; firm in the eight emancipations.
23. His magic power, while he reveals supreme enlightenment, is inconceivable. Gods and men, as numerous as the sands of the Ganges, will always reverentially salute him with joined hands.
24. He shall stay twelve intermediate kalpas; the true law of that most high of men is to last twenty intermediate kalpas and the counterfeit of it as many.

Again the Lord addressed the assembly of monks: I announce to you, monks, I make known that the senior Maha-Katyayana here present, my disciple, shall pay homage to eight thousand kotis of Buddhas; shall show them respect, honour, reverence, veneration, and worship; at the expiration of those Tathagatas he shall build Stupas, a thousand yojanas in height, fifty yojanas in circumference, and consisting of seven precious substances, gold, silver, lapis lazuli, crystal, red pearl, emerald, and, seventhly, coral. Those Stupas he shall worship with flowers, incense, perfumed wreaths, ointments, powder, robes, umbrellas, banners, flags, triumphal streamers. Afterwards he shall again pay a similar homage to twenty kotis of Buddhas; show them respect, honour, reverence, veneration, and worship. Then in his last bodily existence, his last corporeal appearance, he shall be a Tathagata in the world, an Arhat, etc., etc., named Jambunada-prabhasa, i.e. gold-shine, endowed with science and conduct, etc. His Buddha-field will be thoroughly pure, even, nice, pretty, beautiful, crystalline, variegated with jewel-trees, interlaced with gold threads, strewed with flowers, free from beings of the brute creation, hell, and the host of demons, replete with numerous men and gods, adorned with many hundred thou-sand disciples and many hundred thousand Bodhisattvas. The measure of his lifetime shall be twelve intermediate kalpas; his true law shall continue twenty intermediate kalpas and its counterfeit as many.

And on that occasion the Lord uttered the following stanzas:

25. Listen all to me, ye monks, since I am going to utter an infallible word. Katyayana here, the senior, my disciple, shall render worship to the Leaders.
26. He shall show veneration of various kinds and in many ways to the Leaders, after whose expiration he shall build Stupas, worshipping them with flowers and perfumes.
27. In his last bodily existence he shall be a Jina, in a thoroughly pure field, and after acquiring full knowledge he shall preach to a thousand kotis of living beings.
28. He shall be a mighty Buddha and illuminator, highly honoured in this world, including the gods, under the name of Jambunada-prabhasa, and save kotis of gods and men.
29. Many Bodhisattvas as well as disciples, beyond measure and calculation, will in that field adorn the reign of that Buddha, all of them freed from existence and exempt from existence.

Again the Lord addressed the complete assembly of monks: I announce to you, monks, I make known, that the senior Maha-Maudgalyayana here present, my disciple, shall propitiate twenty-eight thousand Buddhas and pay those Lords homage of various kinds; he shall show them respect, etc., and after their expiration build Stupas consisting of seven precious substances, to wit, gold, silver, lapis lazuli, crystal, red pearl, emerald, and, seventhly, coral; Stupas a thousand yojanas in height and five hundred yojanas in circumference, which Stupas he shall worship in different ways, with flowers, incense, perfumed wreaths, ointments, powder, robes, umbrellas, banners, flags, and triumphal streamers.

Afterwards he shall again pay a similar worship to twenty hundred thousand kotis of Buddhas; he shall show respect, etc., and in his last bodily exist-ence become in the world a Tathagata, etc., named Tamalapatra-chandanagandha, endowed with science and conduct, etc. The field of that Buddha will be called Manobhirama; his period Ratipratipurna. And that Buddha-field well be even, nice, pretty, beautiful, crystalline, variegated with jewel-trees, strewn with detached flowers, replete with gods and men, frequented by hundred thousands of Seers, that is to say, disciples and Bodhisattvas. The measure of his lifetime shall be twenty-four intermediate kalpas; his true law is to last forty intermediate kalpas and its counterfeit as many.

And on that occasion the Lord uttered the following stanzas:

30. The scion of the Mudgala-race, my disciple here, after leaving human existence shall see twenty thousand mighty Jinas and eight thousand more of these faultless beings.
31. Under them he shall follow a course of duty, trying to reach Buddha-knowledge; he shall pay homage in various ways to those Leaders and to the most high of men.
32. After keeping their true law, of wide reach and sublime, for thousands of kotis of Aeons, he shall at the expiration to those Sugatas worship their Stupas.
33. In honour of those most high Jinas, those mighty beings so beneficial to the world, he shall erect Stupas consisting of precious substances, and decorated with triumphal streamers, worshipping them with flowers, perfumes, and the sounds of music.
34. At the period of his last bodily existence he shall, in a nice and beautiful field, be a Buddha bounteous and compassio-

nate to the world, under the name of Tamalapatra-chandanagandha.

35. The measure of that Sugata's life shall be fully twenty-four intermediate kalpas, during which he shall be assiduous in declaring the Buddha-rule to men and gods.
36. That Jina shall have many thousands of kotis of disciples, innumerable as the sands of the Ganges, gifted with the six transcendent faculties and the triple science, and possessed of magic power, under the command of that Sugata.
37. Under the reign of that Sugata there shall also appear numerous Bodhisattvas, many thousands of them, unable to slide back, or to deviate, developing zeal, of extensive knowledge and studious habits.
38. After that Jina's expiration his true law shall measure in time twenty-four intermediate kalpas in full; its counterfeit shall have the same measure.
39. These are my five mighty disciples whom I have destined to supreme enlightenment and to become in future self-born Ginas; now hear from me their course.

◆ ◆ ◆ ◆ ◆

7

IN ANCIENT TIMES

The Lord remembers the past, the turning of the wheel by Tathagata Mahabhijnajnanabhibhu, and the history of his 16 sons.

Of yore, monks, in the past, incalculable, more than incalculable, inconceivable, immense, measurless Aeons since, nay, at a period, an epoch far beyond, there appeared in the world a Tathagata, etc., named Mahabhijnananabhibhu, endowed with science and conduct, a Sugata, etc., etc., in the sphere Sambhava (i.e. origin, genesis), in the period Maharupa. You ask, monks, how long ago is it that the Tathagata was born? Well, suppose some man was to reduce to powder the whole mass of the earth element as much as is to be found in this whole universe; that after taking one atom of dust from this world he is to walk a thousand worlds farther in easterly direction to deposit that single atom; that after taking a second atom of dust and walking a thousand worlds farther he deposits that second atom, and proceeding in this way at last gets the whole of the earth element deposited in eastern direction. Now, monks, what do you think of it, is it possible by calculation to find the end or limit of these worlds? They answered: Certainly not, Lord; certainly not, Sugata.

The Lord said: On the contrary, monks, some arithmetician or master of arithmetic might, indeed, be able by calculation to find the end or limit of the worlds, both those where the atoms have been deposited and where they have not, but it is impossible by applying the rules of arithmetic to find the limit of those hundred thousands of myriads of Aeons; so long, so inconceivable, so immense is the number of Aeons which have elapsed since the expiration of that Lord, the Tathagata Mahabhijnajanabhibhu. Yet, monks, I perfectly remember that Tathagata who has been extinct for so long a time, as if he had reached extinction to-day or yesterday, because of my possessing the mighty knowledge and sight of the Tathagata.

And on that occasion the Lord pronounced the following stanzas:

1. I remember the great Seer Abhijnajnanabhibhu, the most high of men, who existed many kotis of Aeons ago as the superior Jina of the period.
2. If, for example, some men after reducing this universe to atoms of dust took one atom to deposit it a thousand regions farther on;
3. If he deposited a second, a third atom, and so proceeded until he had done with the whole mass of dust, so that this world were empty and the mass of dust exhausted;
4. To that immense mass of the dust of these worlds, entirely reduced to atoms, I liken the number of Aeons past.
5. So immense is the number of kotis of Aeons past since that extinct Sugata; the whole of existing atoms is no adequate expression of it; so many are the Aeons which have expired since.
6. That Leader who has expired so long ago, those disciples and Bodhisattvas, I remember all of them as if it were to-day or yesterday. Such is the knowledge of the Tathagatas.
7. So endless, monks, is the knowledge of the Tathagata; I know what has taken place many hundreds of Aeons ago, by my precise and faultless memory.

To proceed, monks, the measure of the lifetime of the Tathagata Mahabhijnajnanabhibhu, the Arhat, etc., was fifty-four hundred thousand myriads of kotis of Aeons.

In the beginning when the Lord had not yet reached supreme, perfect enlightenment and had just occupied the summit of the terrace of enlightenment, he discomfited and defeated the whole host of Mara, after which he thought: I am to reach perfect enlightenment. But those laws of perfect enlightenment had not yet dawned upon him. He stayed on the terrace of enlightenment at the foot of the tree of enlightenment during one intermediate kalpa. He stayed there a second, a third intermediate kalpa, but did not yet attain supreme, perfect enlightenment. He remained a fourth, a fifth, a sixth, a seventh, an eighth, a ninth, a tenth inter-mediate kalpa on the terrace of enlightenment at the foot of the tree of enlightenment, continuing sitting cross-legged without in the meanwhile rising. He stayed, the mind motionless, the body unstirring and untrembling, but those laws had not yet dawned upon him.

Now, monks, while the Lord was just on the summit of the terrace of enlightenment, the gods of Paradise, Trayastrimsas, prepared him a magnificent royal throne, a hundred yojanas high, on occupying which the Lord attained supreme, perfect enlightenment; and no sooner had the Lord occupied the seat of enlightenment than the Brahmakayika gods scattered a rain of flowers all around the seat of enlightenment over a distance of a hundred yojanas; in the sky they let loose storms by which the flowers, withered, were swept away. From the beginning of the rain of flowers, while the Lord was sitting on the seat of enlightenment, it poured without interruption during fully ten intermediate kalpas, covering the Lord. That rain of flowers having once begun falling continued to the moment of the Lord's complete Nirvana. The angels belonging to the division of the four guardians of the cardinal points made the celestial drums of the gods resound; they made them resound without interruption in honour of the Lord who had attained the summit of the terrace of enlightenment. Thereafter, during fully ten intermediate kalpas, they made uninterruptedly resound those celestial musical instruments up to the moment of the complete extinction of the Lord.

Again, monks, after the lapse of ten intermediate kalpas the Lord Mahabhijnajnanabhibhu, the Tathagata, etc., reached supreme, perfect enlightenment. Immediately on knowing his having become enlightened the sixteen sons born to that Lord when a prince royal, the eldest of whom was named Jnanakara—which sixteen young princes, monks, had severally toys to play with, variegated and pretty—those sixteen princes, I repeat, monks, left their toys, their amusements, and since they knew that the Lord Mahabhijnajnanabhibhu, the Tathagata, etc., had attained supreme, perfect knowledge, went, surrounded and attended by their weeping mothers and nurses, along with the noble, rich king Chakravartin, many ministers, and hundred thousands of myriads of kotis of living beings, to the place where the Lord Mahabhijnajnanabhibhu, the Tathigata, etc., was seated on the summit of the terrace of enlightenment. They went up to the Lord in order to honour, respect, worship, revere, and venerate him, saluted his feet with their heads, made three turns round him keeping him to the right, lifted up their joined hands, and praised the Lord, face to face, with the following stanzas:

8. Thou art the great physician, having no superior, rendered perfect in eadle is Aeons. Thy benign wish of saving all mortals from darkness has to-day been fulfilled.
9. Most difficult things hast thou achieved during the ten intermediate kalpas now past; thou hast been sitting all that time without once moving thy body, hand, foot, or any other part.
10. Thy mind also was tranquil and steady, motionless, never to be shaken; thou knewest no distraction; thou art completely quiet and faultless.
11. Joy with thee! that thou so happily and safely, without any hurt, hast reached supreme enlightenment. How great a fortune is ours! we congratulate ourselves, O Lion amongst kings!
12. These unhappy creatures, vexed in all ways, deprived of eyes, as it were, and joyless, do not find the road leading to the end of toils, nor develop energy for the sake of deliverance.
13. Dangers are for a long time on the increase, and the laws, or phenomena, things, are deprived of the possession of a celestial body; the word of the Jina is not being heard; the whole world is plunged in thick darkness.
14. But to-day, or now, hast thou, Majesty of the world, reached this hallowed, high, and faultless spot; we as well as the world are obliged to thee, and approach to seek our refuge with thee, O Protector!

When, O monks, those sixteen princes in the condition of boys, childlike and young, had with such stanzas celebrated the

Lord Mahabhijnajnanabhibhu, the Tathagata, etc., they urged the Lord to move on the wheel of the law: Preach the law, O Lord; preach the law, O Sugata, for the weal of the public, the happiness of the public, out of compassion for the world; for the benefit, weal, and happiness of the people generally, both of gods and men. And on that occasion they uttered the following stanzas:

15. Preach the law, O thou who art marked with a hundred auspicious signs, O Leader, O incomparable great Seer! thou hast attained exalted, sublime knowledge; let it shine in the world, including the gods.
16. Release us as well as these creatures; display the knowledge of the Tathagatas, that we also and, further, these beings may obtain this supreme enlightenment.
17. Thou knowest every course of duty and knowledge; thou knowest the mental and moral disposition and the good works done in a former state; the natural bent of all living beings. Move on the most exalted, sublime wheel!

Then, monks, as the Lord Mahabhijnajnanabhibhu, the Tathagata, etc., reached supreme, perfect enlightenment, fifty hundred thousand myriads of kotis of spheres in each of the ten directions of space were shaken in six different ways and became illumined with a great lustre. And in the intervals between all those spheres, in the dreary places of dark gloom, where even the sun and moon, so powerful, mighty, and splendid, have no advantage of the shining power they are endowed with, have no advantage of the colour and brightness they possess, even in those places a great lustre arose instantly. And the beings who appeared in those intervals behold each other, acknowledge each other, and exclaim: Lo, there are other beings also here appearing! lo there are other beings also here appearing! The palaces and aerial cars of the gods in all those spheres up to the Brahma-world shook in six different ways and became illumined with a great lustre, surpassing the divine majesty of the gods. So then, monks, a great earthquake and a great, sublime lustre arose simultaneously. And the aerial cars of the Brahma-angels to the east, in these fifty hundred thousand myriads of kotis of spheres, began excessively to glitter, glow, and sparkle in splendour and glory. And those Brahma-angels made this reflection: What may be foreboded by these aerial cars so excessively glittering, glowing, and sparkling in splendour and glory? Thereupon, monks, the Brahma-angels in the fifty hundred thousand myriads of kotis of spheres went all to each other's abodes and communicated the matter to one another. After that, monks, the great Brahma-angel, named Sarvasattvatratri, Saviour of all beings, addressed the numerous host of Brahma-angels in the following stanzas:

18. Our aerial cars to-day, or now, are all bristling with rays in an extraordinary degree, and blazing in beautiful splendour and brilliancy. What may be the cause of it?

19. Come, let us investigate the matter, what divine being has to-day sprung into existence, whose power, such as was never seen before, here now appears?

20. Or should it be the Buddha, the king of kings, who to-day has been born somewhere in the world, and whose birth is announced by such a token that all the points of the horizon are now blazing in splendour?

Thereupon, monks, the great Brahma-angels in the fifty hundred thousand myriads of kotis of spheres mounted all together their own divine aerial cars, took with them divine bags, as large as Mount Sumeru, with celestial flowers, and went through the four quarters successively until they arrived at the western quarter, where those great Brahma-angels, O monks, stationed in the western quarter, saw the Lord Mahabhijnajnanabhibhu, the Tathagata, etc., on the summit of the exalted terrace of enlightenment, seated on the royal throne at the foot of the tree of enlightenment, surrounded and attended by gods, Nagas, goblins, Gandharvas, demons, Garudas, Kinnaras, great serpents, men, and beings not human, while his sons, the sixteen young princes, were urging him to move forward the wheel of the law. On seeing which the Brahma-angels came up to the Lord, saluted his feet with their heads, walked many hundred thousand times round him from left to right, strewing flowers and overwhelming both him and the tree of enlightenment, over a distance of ten yojanas, with those flower-bags as large as Mount Sumeru. After that they presented to the Lord their aerial cars with the words: Accept, O Lord, these aerial cars out of compassion to us; use, O Sugata, those cars out of compassion to us.

On that occasion, monks, after presenting their own cars to the Lord, the Brahma-angels celebrated the Lord, face to face, with the following seasonable stanzas:

21. A wonderful, matchless Jina, so beneficial and merciful, has arisen in the world. Thou art born a protector, a ruler and teacher, a master; to-day all quarters are blessed.

22. We have come as far as fully fifty thousand kotis of worlds from here to humbly salute the Jina by surrendering our lofty aerial cars all together.

23. We possess these variegated and bright cars, owing to previous works; accept them to oblige us, and make use of them to thine heart's content, O Knower of the world!

After the great Brahma-angels, monks, had celebrated the Lord Mahabhijnajnanabhibhu, the Tathagata, etc., face to face, with these seasonable stanzas, they besought him, saying: May the Lord move forward the wheel of the law! May the Lord preach final rest! May the Lord release all beings! Be favourable, O Lord, to this world! Preach the law, O Lord, to this world, including gods, Maras, and Brahma-angels; to all people, including ascetics and Brahmans, gods, men, and demons! It will tend to the weal of the public, to the happiness of the public; out of mercy to the world, for the benefit and happiness of the people at large, both gods and men.

Thereupon, monks, those fifty hundred thousand myriads of kotis of Brahma-angels addressed the Lord, with one voice, in common chorus, with the following stanzas:

24. Show the law, O Lord; show it, O most high of men! Show the power of thy kindness; save the tormented beings.

25. Rare is the light of the world like the blosson of the glamerated fig-tree. Thou hast arisen, O great Hero; we pray to thee, the Tathagata.

And the Lord, O monks, silently intimated his assent to the Brahma-angels.

Somewhat later, monks, the aerial cars of the Brahma-angels in the south-eastern quarter in the fifty, hundred thousand myriads of spheres began excessively to glitter, glow, and sparkle in splendour and glory. And those Brahma-angels made this reflection: What may be foreboded by these aerial cars so excessively glittering, glowing, and sparkling in splendour and glory? Thereupon, monks, the Brahma-angels in the fifty hundred thousand myriads of kotis of spheres went all to each other's abodes and communicated the matter to one another. After that, monks, the great Brahma-angel, named Adhimatra-karunika, i.e. exceedingly compassionate, addressed the numerous host of Brahma-angels with the following stanzas:

26. What foretoken is it we see today or now, friends? Who or what is foreboded by the celestial cars shining with such uncommon glory?
27. May, perhaps, some blessed divine being have come hither, by whose power all these aerial cars are illumined?
28. Or may the Buddha, the most high of men, have appeared in this world, that by his power these celestial cars are in such a condition as we see them?
29. Let us all together go and search; be the cause of it; such a foretoken, never seen before.
30. Come, let us go and visit kotis of fields, along the four quarters; a Buddha will certainly now have made his appearance in this world.

Thereupon, monks, the great Brahma-angels in the fifty hundred thousand myriads of kotis of spheres mounted all together their own divine aerial cars took with them divine bags, as large as Mount Sumeru, with celestial flowers, and went through the four quarters successively until they arrived at the north-western quarter, where those great Brahma-angels, stationed in the north-western quarter, saw the Lord Mahabhijnajnanabhibhu [etc., as above till compassion to us].

On that occasion, monks, after presenting their own cars to the Lord the Brahma-angels celebrated the Lord, face to face, with the following seasonable stanzas:

31. Homage to thee, matchless great Seer, chief god of gods, whose voice is sweet as the lark's. Leader in the world, including. the gods, I salute thee, who art so benign and bounteous to the world.

32. How wonoerful, O Lord, is it that after so long a time thou appearest in the world. Eighty hundred complete Aeons this world of the living was without Buddha.

33. It was deprived of the most high of men; hell was prevailing and the celestial bodies constantly went on waning during eighty hundred complete Aeans.

34. But now he has appeared, owing to our good works, who is our eye, refuge, resting-place, protection, father, and kinsman; he, the benign and bounteous one, the King of the law.

After the great Brahma-angels, monks, had celebrated the Lord Mahabhijnajnanabhibhu, the Tathagata, etc., face to face, with these seasonable stanzas, they besought him: May the Lord move forward the wheel of the law! [as above till both gods and men.]

Thereupon, monks, those fifty hundred thousand myriads of kotis of Brahma-angels addressed the Lord, with one voice, in common chorus, with the following stanzas:

35. Move forward the exalted wheel, O great ascetic! reveal the law in all directions; deliver all beings oppressed with suffering; produce amongst mortals gladness and joy!

36. Let them by hearing the law partake of enlightenment and reach divine places. Let all shake off their demon body and be peaceful, meek, and at ease.

And the Lord, O monks, silently intimated his assent to these Brahma-angels also.

Somewhat later, monks, the aerial cars of the Brahma-angels in the southern quarter [etc., as above till to one another]. After that, monks, the great Brahma-angel, named Sudharma, addressed the numerous host of Brahma-angels in stanzas:

37. It cannot be without cause or reason, friends, that to-day, or now, all these celestial cars are so brilliant; this bespeaks

some portent somewhere in the world. Come, let us go and investigate the matter.

38. No such portent has appeared in hundreds of Aeans past. Either some god has been born or a Buddha has arisen in this world.

Thereupon, monks, the great Brahma-angels in the fifty hundred thousand myriads of kotis of spheres mounted [etc., as above till compassion to us].

On that occasion, monks, after presenting their own cars to the Lord, the Brahma-angels celebrated the Lord, face to face, with the following seasonable stanzas:

39. Most rare and precious is the sight of the Leaders. Be welcome, thou dispeller of worldly defilement. It is after a long time that thou now appearest in the world; after hundreds of complete Aeons one now beholds thee.

40. Refresh the thirsty creatures, O Lord of the world! Now first thou art seen; it is not easy to behold thee. As rare or precious as the flowers of the glomerated fig-tree is thine appearance, O Lord.

41. By thy power these aerial cars of ours are so uncommonly illumined now, O Leader. To show us thy favour accept them, O thou whose look pierces everywhere!

After the great Brahma-angels, monks, had celebrated the Lord Mahabhijnajnanabhibhu, the Tathagata, etc., face to face, with these seasonable stanzas, they besought him: May the Lord move forward the wheel of the law! [as above till gods and men.]

Thereupon, monks, those fifty hundred thousand myriads of kotis of Brahma-angels addressed the Lord, with one voice, in common chorus, with the following stanzas:

42. Preach the law, O Lord and Leader! move forward the wheel of the law, make the drum of the law resound, and blow the conch-trumpet of the law.

43. Shed the rain of the true law over this world and proclaim the sweet-sounding good word; manifest the law required, save myriads of kotis of beings.

And the Lord, monks, silently intimated his assent to the Brahma-angels.

Repetition; the same occurred in the south-west, in the west, in the north-west, in the north, in the north-east, in the nadir.

Then, monks, the aerial cars of the Brahma-angels in the nadir, in those fifty hundred thousand myriads of kotis of spheres [etc., as above till to one another] After that, monks, the great Brahma-angel, named Sikhin, addressed the numerous host of Brahma-angels with the following stanzas:

44. What may be the cause, O friends, that our cars are so bright with splendour, colour, and light? What may be the reason of their being so exceedingly glorious?
45. We have seen nothing like this before nor heard of it from others. These (cars) are now bright with splendour and exceedingly glorious; what may be the cause of it?
46. Should it be some god who has been be-stowed upon the world in recompense of good works, and whose grandeur thus comes to light? Or is perhaps a Buddha born in the world?

Thereupon, monks, the great Brahma-angels in the fifty hundred thousand myriads of kotis of spheres mounted all together their own divine aerial cars, took with them divine bags, as large as Mount Sumeru, with celestial flowers, and went through the four quarters successively until they arrived at the zenith, where those great Brahma-angels, stationed at the zenith, saw the Lord Mahabhijnajnanabhibhu [etc., as above till compassion to us].

On that occasion, monks, after presenting their own cars to the Lord, the Brahma-angels celebrated the Lord, face to face, with the following seasonable stanzas:

47. How goodly is the sight of the Buddhas, the mighty Lords of the world; those Buddhas who are to deliver all beings in this triple world.
48. The all-seeing Masters of the world send their looks' in all directions of the horizon, and by opening the gate of immortality they make people reach the safe shore.
49. An inconceivable number of Aeons now past were void, and all quarters wrapt in darkness, as the chief Jinas did not appear.

50. The dreary hells, the brute creation and demo answer on the increase; thousands of kotis of living beings fell into the state of ghosts.
51. The heavenly bodies were on the wane; after their disappearance they entered upon evil ways; their course became wrong because they did not hear the law of the Buddhas.
52. All creatures lacked dutiful behaviour, purity, good state, and understanding; their happiness was lost, and the consciousness of happiness was gone.
53. They did not observe the rules of morality; were firmly rooted in the false law; not being led by the Lord of the world, they were precipitated into a false course.
54. Hail! thou art come at last, O Light of the world! thou, born to be bounteous towards all beings.
55. Hail! thou hast safely arrived at supreme Buddha-knowledge; we feel thankful before thee, and so does the world, including the gods.
56. By thy power, O mighty Lord, our aerial cars are glittering; to thee we present them, great Hero; deign to accept them, great Solitary.
57. Out of grace to us, O Leader, make use of them, so that we, as well as all other beings, may attain supreme enlightenment.

After the great Brahma-angels, O monks, had celebrated the Lord Mahabhijnajnanabhibhu, the Tathagata, etc., face to face, with seasonable stanzas, they besought him: May the Lord move forward the wheel of the law! [etc., as above till both and men.]

Thereupon, monks, those fifty hundred thousand myriads of kotis of Brahma-angels addressed the Lord, with one voice, in common chorus, with the following two stanzas:

58. Move forward the exalted, unsurpassed wheel! beat the drum of immortality! release all beings from hundreds of evils, and show the path of Nirvana.
59. Expound the law we pray for; show thy favour to us and this world. Let us hear thy sweet and lovely voice

which thou hast exercised during thousands of kotis of Mons.

Now, monks, the Lord Mahabhijnajnanabhibhu, the Tathagata, etc., being acquainted with the prayer of the hundred thousand myriads of kotis of Brahma-angels and of the sixteen princes, his sons, commenced at that juncture to turn the wheel that has three turns and twelve parts, the wheel never moved by any ascetic, Brahman, god, demon, nor by anyone else. His preaching consisted in this: This is pain; this is the origin of pain; this is the suppression of pain; this is the treatment leading to suppression of pain. He moreover extensively set forth how the series of causes and effects is evolved, and said: It is thus, monks.

From ignorance proceed conceptions or fancies; from conceptions or fancies proceeds understanding; from under- standing name and form; from name and form the six senses; from the six senses proceeds contact; from contact sensation; from sensation proceeds longing; from longing proceeds striving; from striving as cause issues existence; from existence birth; from birth old age, death, mourning, lamentation, sorrow, dismay, and despondency. So originates this whole mass of misery. From the suppression of ignorance results the suppression of conceptions; from the suppression of conceptions results that of understanding; from the suppression of understanding results that of name and form; from the suppression of name and form results that of the six senses; from the suppression of the six senses results that of contact; from the suppression of contact results that of sensation; from the suppression of sensation results that of longing; from the suppression of longing results that of striving; from the suppression of striving results that of existence; from the suppression of existence results that of birth; from the suppression of birth results that of old age, death, mourning, lamentation, sorrow, dismay, and despondency. In this manner the whole mass of misery is suppressed.

And while this wheel of the law, monks, was being moved onward by the Lord Mahabhijnajnanabhibhu, the Tathagata, etc., in presence or the world, including the gods, demons, and Brahma-angels; of the assemblage, including ascetics and Brahmins; then, at that time, on that occasion, the minds of sixty hundred thousand myriads of kotis of living beings were without effort freed from imperfections and became all possessed of the triple science, of the sixfold transcendent wisdom, of the emancipations and meditations. In due course, monks, the Lord Mahabhijnajnanabhibhu, the Tathagata, etc., again gave a second exposition of the law; likewise a third and a fourth exposition. And at each exposition, monks, the minds of hundred thousands of myriads of kotis of beings, like the sands of the river Ganges, were without effort freed from imperfections. Afterwards, monks, the congregation of disciples of that Lord was so numerous as to surpass all calculation.

Meanwhile, monks, the sixteen princes, the youths, had, full of faith, left home to lead the vagrant life of mendicants, and had all of them become novices, clever, bright, intelligent, pious, followers of the course of duty under many hundred thousand Buddhas, and striving after supreme, perfect enlightenment. These sixteen novices, monks, said to the Lord Mahabhijnajnanabhibhu, the Tathagata, etc., the following: O Lord, these many hundred thousand myriads of kotis of disciples of the Tathagata have become very mighty, very powerful, very potent, owing to the Lord's teaching of the law. Deign, O Lord, to teach us also, for mercy's sake, the law with a view to supreme, perfect enlightenment, so that we also may follow the teaching of the Tathagata. We want, O Lord, to see the knowledge of the Tathagata; the Lord can himself testify to this, for thou, O Lord, who knowest the disposition of all beings, also knowest ours.

Then, monks, on seeing that those princes, the youths, had chosen the vagrant life of mendicants and become novices, the half of the whole retinue of the king chakravartin, to the number of eighty hundred thousand myriads of kotis of living beings, chose the vagrant life of mendicants.

Subsequently, monks, the Lord Mahabhijnajnanabhibhu, the Tathagata, etc., viewing the prayer of those novices at the lapse of twenty thousand Aeons, amply and completely revealed the Dharmaparyaya called 'the Lotus of the True Law,' a text of great extent, serving to instruct Bodhisattvas and proper for all Buddhas, in presence of all the four classes of auditors.

In course of time, monks, those sixteen novices grasped, kept, and fully penetrated the Lord's teaching.

Subsequently, monks, the Lord Mahabhijnajnanabhibhu, the Tathagata, etc., foretold those sixteen novices their future destiny to supreme, perfect, enlightenment. And while the Lord Mahabhijnajnanabhibhu, the Tathagata, etc., was propounding the Dharmaparyaya of the Lotus of the True Law, the disciples as well as the sixteen novices were full, of faith, and many hundred thousand myriads of kotis of beings acquired perfect certainty.

Thereupon, monks, after propounding the Dharmaparyaya of the Lotus of the True Law during eight thousand Aeons without interruption, the Lord Mahabhijnajnanabhibhu, the Tathagata, etc., entered the monastery to retire for the purpose of meditation, and in that retirement, monks, the Tathagata continued in the monastery during eighty-four thousand kotis of Aeons.

Now, monks, when the sixteen novices perceived that the Lord was absorbed, they sat down on the seats, the royal thrones which had been prepared for each of them, and amply expounded, during eighty-four hundred thousand myriads of kotis, the Dharmaparyaya of the Lotus of the True Law to the four classes. By doing this, monks, each of those novices, as Bodhisattvas fully developed, instructed, excited, stimulated, edified, confirmed in respect to supreme, perfect enlightenment 60 × 60 hundred thousand myriads of kotis of living beings, equal to the sands of the river Ganges.

Now, monks, at the lapse of eighty-four thousand Aeons the Lord Mahabhijnajnanabhibhu, the Tathigata, etc., rose from his meditation, in possession of memory and consciousness, whereafter he went up to the seat of the law, designed for him, in order to occupy it.

As soon as the Lord had occupied the seat of the law, monks, he cast his looks over the whole circle of the audience and addressed the congregation of monks: They are wonderfully gifted, monks, they are prodigiously gifted, these sixteen novices, wise, servitors to many hundred thousand myriads of kotis of Buddhas: observers of the course of duty, who have received Buddha-knowledge, transmitted Buddha-knowledge, expounded Buddha-knowledge. Honour these sixteen novices, monks, again and again; and all, be they devoted to the vehicle of the disciples, the vehicle of the Pratyekabuddhas, or the vehicle of the Bodhisattvas, who shall not reject nor repudiate the preaching of these young men of good family, O monks, shall quickly gain supreme, perfect enlightenment, and obtain Tathagata-knowledge.

In the sequel also, monks, have these young men of good family repeatedly revealed this Dharmaparyaya of the Lotus of the True Law under the mastership of that Lord. And the 60 × 60 hundred thousand myriads of kotis of living beings, equal to the sands of the river Ganges, who by each of the sixteen novices, the Bodhisattvas Mahasattvas, in the quality of Bodhisattva, had been roused to enlightenment, all those beings followed the example of the sixteen novices in choosing along with them the vagrant life of mendicants, in their several existences; they enjoyed their sight and heard the law from their mouth. They propitiated forty kotis of Buddhas, and some are doing so up to this day.

I announce to you, monks, I declare to you: Those sixteen princes, the youths, who as novices under the mastership of the Lord were interpreters of the law, have all reached supreme, perfect enlightenment, and all of them are staying, existing, living even now, in the several directions of space, in different Buddha-fields, preaching the law to many hundred thousand myriads of kotis of disciples and Bodhisattvas, to wit: In the east, monks, in the world Abhirati the Tathagata named Akshobhya, the Arhat, etc., and the Tathagata Meruklita, the Arhat, etc. In the south-east, monks, is the Tathagata Simhaghosha, etc., and the Tathagata Simhadhva, etc. In the south, monks, is the Tathagata named Akasapratishthita, etc., and the Tathagata named Nityaparinirvrita, etc. In the south-west, monks, is the Tathagata named Indradhvaja, etc., and the Tathagata named Brahmadhvaja, etc. In the west, monks, is the Tathagata named Amitayus, etc., and the Tathagata named Sarvalokadhatupadravodvegapratyuttima, etc. In the north-west, monks, is the Tathagata named Tamalapatrakandanagandhabhi, etc., and the Tathagata Merukalpa, etc. In the north, monks, is the Tathagata named Meghasvarapradipa, etc., and the Tathagata named Meghasvararaja, etc. In the north-east, monks, is the Tathagata named Sarvalokabhayaji-tachchambhitatvavidhvamsanakara, the Arhat, etc., and, the sixteenth, myself, Sakyamuni, the Tathagata, the Arhat, etc., who have attained supreme, perfect enlightenment in the centre of this Saha world.

Further, monks, those beings who have heard the law from us when we were novices, those many hundred thousand myriads of kotis of beings, numerous as the sands of the river Ganges, whom we have severally initiated in supreme, perfect enlightenment, they are up to this day standing on the stage of disciples and matured for supreme, perfect enlightenment. In regular turn they are to attain supreme, perfect enlightenment, for it is difficult, monks, to penetrate the knowledge of the Tathagatas. And which are those beings, monks, who, innumerable, incalculable like the sands of the Ganges, those hundred thousands of myriads of kotis of living beings, whom I, when I was a Bodhisattva under the mastership of that Lord, have taught the law of omniscience? Yourselves, monks, were at that time those beings.

And those who shall be my disciples in future, when I shall have attained complete Nirvana, shall learn the course of duty of Bodhisattvas, without conceiving the idea of their being Bodhisattvas. And, monks, all who shall have the idea of complete Nirvana, shall reach it. It should be added, monks, as I stay under different names in other worlds, they shall there be born again seeking after the knowledge of the Tathagatas, and there they shall anew hear this dogma: The complete Nirvana of the Tathagatas is but one; there is no other, no second Nirvana of the Tathagatas. Herein, monks, one has to see a device of the Tathagatas and a direction for the preaching of the law. When the Tathagata, monks, knows that the moment of his complete extinction has arrived, and sees that the assemblage is pure, strong in faith, penetrated with the law of voidness, devoted to meditation, devoted to great meditation, then, monks, the Tathagata, because the time has arrived, calls together all Bodhisattvas and all disciples to teach them thus: There is, O monks, in this world no second vehicle at all, no second Nirvana, far less a third. It is an able device of the Tathagata, monks, that on seeing creatures far advanced on the path of perdition, delighting in the low and plunged in the mud of sensual desires, the Tathagata teaches them that Nirvana to which they are attached.

By way of example, monks, suppose there is some dense forest five hundred yojanas in extent which has been reached by a great company of men. They have a guide to lead them on their journey to the Isle of Jewels, which guide, being able, clever, sagacious, well acquainted with the difficult passages of the forest, is to bring the whole company out of the forest. Meanwhile that great troop of men, tired, weary, afraid, and anxious, say: 'Verily, M aster, guide, and leader, know that we are tired, weary, afraid, and anxious; let us return; this dense forest stretches so far.' The guide, who is a man of able devices, on seeing those people desirous of returning, thinks within himself: It ought not to be that these poor creatures should not reach that great Isle of Jewels. Therefore out of pity for them he makes use of an artifice. In the middle of that forest he produces a magic city more than a hundred or two hundred yojanas in extent. Thereafter he says to those men: Be not afraid, sirs, do not return; there you see a populous place where you may take repose and perform all you have to do; there stay in the enjoyment of happy rest. Let him who after reposing there wants to do so, proceed to the great Isle of Jewels.

Then, monks, the men who are in the forest are struck with astonishment, and think: Weare out of the forest; we have reached the place of happy rest; let us stay here. They enter that magic city, in the meaning that they have arrived at the place of their destination, that they are saved and in the enjoyment of rest. They think: We are at rest, we are refreshed. After a while, when the guide perceives that their fatigue is gone, he causes the magic city to disappear, and says to them: Come, sirs, there you see the great Isle of Jewels quite near; as to this great city, it has been produced by me for no other purpose but to give you some repose.'

In the same manner, monks, is the Tathagata, the Arhat, etc., your guide, and the guide of all other beings. Indeed, monks, the Tathagata, etc., reflects thus: Great is this forest of evils which must be crossed, left, shunned. It ought not to be that these beings, after hearing the Buddha-knowledge, should suddenly turn back and not proceed to the end because they think: This Buddha-knowledge is attended with too many difficulties to be gone through to the end. Under those circumstances the Tathagata, knowing the creatures to be feeble of character, does as the guide who produces the magic city in order that those people may have repose, and after their having taken repose, he tells them that the city is one produced by magic. In the same manner, monks, the Tathagata, etc., to give a repose to the creatures, very skilfully teaches and proclaims two stages of Nirvana, the stage of the disciples and that of the Pratyeka Buddhas. And, monks, when the creatures are there halting, then the Tathagata, etc., himself, pronounces these words: You have not accomplished your task, monks; you have not finished what you had to do. But behold, monks! the Buddha-knowledge is near; behold and be convinced: what to you seems Nirvana, that is not Nirvana. Nay, monks, it is an able device of the Tathagatas, etc., that they expound three vehicles.

In order to explain this same subject more in detail, the Lord on that occasion uttered the following stanzas:

60. The Leader of the world, Abhijnajnanabhibhu, having occupied the terrace of enlightenment, continued ten complete intermediate kalpas without gaining enlightenment, though he saw the things in their very essence.
61. Then the gods, Nagas, demons, and goblins, zealous to honour the Jina, sent down a rain of flowers on the spot where the Leader awakened to enlightenment.
62. And high in the sky they beat the cymbals to worship and honour the Jina, and they were vexed that the Jina delayed so long in coming to the highest place.

63. After the lapse of ten intermediate kalpas the Lord Anabhibhu attained enlightenment; then all gods, men, serpents, and demons were glad and overjoyed.
64. The sixteen sons of the Leader of men, those heroes, being at the time young princes, rich in virtues, came along with thousands of kotis of living beings to honour the eminent chiefs of men.
65. And after saluting the feet of the Leader they prayed: Reveal the law and refresh us as well as this world with thy good word, O Lion amongst kings.
66. After a long time thou art seen again in the ten points of this world; thou appearest, great Leader, while the aerial cars of the Brahma-angels are stirring to reveal a token to living beings.
67. In the eastern quarter fifty thousand kotis of fields have been shaken, and the lofty angelic cars in them have become excessively brilliant.
68. The Brahma-angels on perceiving this foretoken went and approached the Chief of the Leaders of the world, and, covering him with flowers, presented all of them their cars to him.
69. They prayed him to move forward the wheel of the law, and celebrated him with stanzas and songs. But the king of kings was silent, for he thought: The time has not yet arrived for me to proclaim the law.
70. Likewise in the south, west, north, the nadir, zenith, and in the intermediate points of the compass there were thousands of kotis of Brahma-angels.
71. Unremittingly covering the Lord with flowers they saluted the feet of the Leader, presented all their aerial cars, celebrated him, and again prayed:
72. Move forward the wheel, thou whose sight is infinite! Rarely art thou met in the course of many kotis of Aeons. Display the benevolence thou hast observed in so many former generations; open the gate of immortality.
73. On hearing their prayer, he whose sight is infinite exposed the multifarious law and the four Truths, extensively. All

existences said he spring successively from their antecedents.

74. Starting from ignorance, the Seer proceeded to speak of death, endless woe; all those evils spring from birth. Know likewise that death is the lot of mankind.

75. No sooner had he expounded the multifarious, different, endless laws, than eighty myriads of kotis of creatures who had heard them quickly attained the stage of disciples.

76. On a second occasion the Jina expounded many laws, and beings like the sands of the Ganges became instantly purified and disciples.

77. From that moment the assembly of that Leader of the world was innumerable; no man would be able to reach the term of its number, even were he to go on counting for myriads of kotis of Aeons.

78. Those sixteen princes also, his own dear sons, who had become mendicants and novices, said to the Jina: Expound, O Chief, the superior law;

79. That we may become sages, knowers of the world, such as thyself art, O supreme of all Jinas, and that all these beings may become such as thyself art, O hero, O clear-sighted one.

80. And the Jina, considering the wish of his sons, the young princes, explained the highest superior enlightenment by means of many myriads of kotis of illustrations.

81. Demonstrating with thousands of arguments and elucidating the knowledge of transcendent wisdom, the Lord of the world indicated the veritable course of duty such as was followed by the wise Bodhisattvas.

82. This very Sutra of great extension, this good Lotus of the True Law, was by the Lord delivered in many thousands of stanzas, so numerous as to equal the sands of the Ganges.

83. After delivering this Sutra, the Jina entered the monastery for the purpose of becoming absorbed in meditation; during eighty-four complete Aeans the Lord of the world continued meditating, sitting on the same seat.

84. Those novices, perceiving that the Chief remained in the monastery without coming out of it, imparted to many kotis of creatures that Buddha-knowledge, which is free from imperfections and blissful.
85. On the seats which they had made to be prepared, one for each, they expounded this very Sutra under the mastership of the Sugata of that period. A service of the same kind they render to me.
86. Innumerable as the sands of sixty thousand rivers like the Ganges were the beings then taught; each of the sons of the Sugata converted or trained endless beings.
87. After the Jina's complete Nirvana they commenced a wandering life and saw kotis of Buddhas; along with those pupils they rendered homage to the most exalted amongst men.
88. Having observed the extensive and sublime course of duty and reached enlightenment in the ten points of space, those sixteen sons of the Jina became themselves Jinas, two by two, in each point of the horizon.
89. And all those who had been their pupils became disciples of those Jinas, and gradually obtained possession of enlightenment by various means.
90. I myself was one of their number, and you have all been taught by me. Therefore you are my disciples now also, and I lead you all to enlightenment by my devices.
91. This is the cause dating from old, this is the motive of my expounding the law, that I lead you to superior enlightenment. This being the case, monks, you need not be afraid.
92. It is as if there were a forest dreadful, terrific, barren, without a place of refuge or shelter, replete with wild beasts, deprived of water, frightful for persons of no experience.
93. Suppose further that many thousand men have come to the forest, that waste track of wilderness which is fully five hundred yojanas in extent.
94. And he who is to act as their guide through that rough and horrible forest is a rich man, thoughtful, intelligent, wise, well instructed, and undaunted.

95. And those beings, numbering many kotis, feel tired, and say to the guide: We are tired, Master; we are not able to go on; we should like now to return.
96. But he, the dexterous and clever guide, is searching in his mind for some apt device. Alas! he thinks, by going back these foolish men will be deprived of the possession of the jewels.
97. Therefore let me by dint of magic power now produce a great city adorned with thousands of kotis of buildings and embellished by monasteries and parks.
98. Let me produce ponds and canals; a city adorned with gardens and flowers, provided with walls and gates, and inhabited by an infinite number of men and women.
99. After creating that city he speaks to them in this manner: Do not fear, and be cheerful; you have reached a most excellent city; enter it and do your business, speedily.
100. Be joyful and at ease; you have reached the limit of the whole forest. It is to give them a time for repose that he speaks these words, and, in fact, they recover from their weariness.
101. As he perceives that they have sufficiently reposed, he collects them and addresses them again: , Come, hear what I have to tell you: this city have I produced by magic.
102. On seeing you fatigued, I have, lest you should go back, made use of this device; now strain your energy to reach the Isle.
103. In the same manner, monks, I am the guide, the conductor of thousands of kotis of living beings; in the same manner I see creatures toiling and unable to break the shell of the egg of evils.
104. Then I reflect on this matter: These beings have enjoyed repose, have been tranquillised; now I will remind them of the misery of all things and I say: At the stage of Arhat you shall reach your aim.
105. At that time, when you shall have attained that state, and when I see all of you have become Arhats, then will I call you all together and explain to you how the law really is.

106. It is an artifice of the Leaders, when they, the great Seers, show three vehicles, for there is but one vehicle, no second; it is only to help creatures that two vehicles are spoken of.

107. Therefore I now tell you, monks: Rouse to the utmost your lofty energy for the sake of the knowledge of the all-knowing; as yet, you have not come so far as to possess complete Nirvana.

108. But when you shall have attained the knowledge of the all-knowing and the ten powers proper to Jinas, you shall become Buddhas marked by the thirty-two characteristic signs and have rest for ever.

109. Such is the teaching of the Leaders: in order to give quiet they speak of repose, but when they see that the creatures have had a repose, they, knowing this to be no final resting-place, initiate them in the knowledge of the all-knowing.

◆ ◆ ◆ ◆ ◆

8

FUTURE OF THE FIVE HUNDRED MONKS

Prophecy regarding 500 Arhats.

On hearing from the Lord that display of skilfulness and the instruction by means of mysterious speech; on hearing the announcement of the future destiny of the great Disciples, as well as the foregoing tale concerning ancient devotion and the leadership of the Lord, the venerable Purna, son of Maitrayani, was filled with wonder and amazement, thrilled with pure-heartedness, a feeling of delight and joy. He rose from his seat, full of delight and joy, full of great respect for the law, and while prostrating himself before the Lord's feet, made within himself the following reflection : Wonderful, O Lord; wonderful, O Sugata; it is an extremely difficult thing that the Tathagatas, etc., perform, the conforming to this world, composed of so many elements, and preaching the law to all creatures with many proofs of their skilfulness, and skilfully releasing them when attached to this or that. What could we do, O Lord, in such a case? None but the Tathagata knows our inclination and our ancient course. Then, after saluting with his head the Lord's feet, Purna went and stood apart, gazing up to the Lord with unmoved eyes and so showing his veneration.

And the Lord, regarding the mental disposition of the venerable Purna, son of Maitrayani, addressed the entire assembly of monks in this strain: Ye monks, see this disciple, Purna, son of Maitrayani, whom I have designated as the foremost of preachers in this assembly, praised for his many virtues, and who has applied himself in various ways to comprehend the true law. He is the man to excite, arouse, and stimulate the four classes of the audience; unwearied in the preaching of the law; as capable to preach the law as to oblige his fellow-followers of the course of duty. The Tathagata excepted, monks, there is none able to equal Purna, son of Maitrayani, either essentially or in accessories. Now, monks, do you suppose that he keeps my true law only? No, monks, you must not think so. For I remember, monks, that in the past, in the times of the ninety-nine Buddhas, the same Purna kept the true law under the mastership of those Buddhas. Even as he is now with me, so he has, in all periods, been the foremost of the preachers of the law; has in all periods been a consummate knower of Voidness; has in all periods acquired the four distinctive qualifications of an Arhat; has in all periods reached mastership in the transcendent wisdom of the Bodhisattvas. He has been a strongly convinced preacher of the law, exempt from doubt, and quite pure. Under the mastership of those Buddhas he has during his whole existence observed a spiritual life, and everywhere they termed him 'the Disciple.' By this means he has promoted the interest of innumerable, incalculable hundred thousands of myriads of kotis of beings, and brought innumerable and incalculable beings to full ripeness for supreme and perfect enlightenment. In all periods he has assisted the creatures in the function of a Buddha, and in all periods he has purified his own Buddha-field, always striving to bring creatures to ripeness. He was also, monks, the foremost among the preachers of the law under the seven Tathagatas, the first of whom is Vipasyin and the seventh myself.

And as to the Buddhas, monks, who have in future to appear in this Bhadra-kalpa, to the number of a thousand less four, under the mastership of them also shall this same Purna, son of Maitrayani, be the foremost among the preachers of the law and the keeper of the true law. Thus he shall keep the true law of innumerable and incalculable Lords and Buddhas in future, promote the interest of innumerable and incalculable beings, and bring innumerable and incalculable beings to full ripeness for supreme and perfect enlightenment. Constantly and assiduously he shall be instant in purifying his own Buddha-field and bringing creatures to ripeness. After completing such a Bodhisattva-course, at the end of innumerable, incalculable Aeons, he shall reach supreme and perfect enlightenment; he shall in the world be the Tathagata called Dharmaprabhasa, an Arhat, etc., endowed with science and conduct, a Sugata, etc. He shall appear in this very Buddha-field.

Further, monks, at that time the Buddha-field spoken of will look as if formed by thousands of spheres similar to the sands of the river Ganges. It will be even, like the palm of the hand, consist of seven precious substances, be without hills, and filled with high edifices of seven precious substances. There will be cars of the gods stationed in the sky; the gods will behold men, and men will behold the gods. Moreover, monks, at that time that Buddha-field shall be exempt from places of punishment and from womankind, as all beings shall be born by apparitional birth. They shall lead a spiritual life, have ideal bodies, be self-lighting, magical, moving in the firmament, strenuous, of good memory, wise, possessed of gold-coloured bodies, and adorned with the thirty-two characteristics of a great man. And at that time, monks, the beings in that Buddha-field will have two things to feed upon, viz., the delight in the law and the delight in meditation. There will be an immense, incalculable number of hundred thousands of myriads of kotis of Bodhisattvas; all endowed with great transcendent wisdom, accomplished in the four distinctive qualifications of an Arhat, able in instructing creatures. He that Buddha will have a number of disciples, beyond all calculation, mighty in magic, powerful, masters in the meditation of the eight emancipations. So immense are the good qualities that Buddha-field will be possessed of. And that Aeon shall be called Ratnavabhasa, i.e., radiant with gems, and that world Suvisuddha, i.e., very pure. His lifetime shall last immense, incalculable Aeons; and after the complete extinction of that Lord Dharmaprabhasa, the Tathagata, etc., his true law shall last long, and his world shall be full of Stupas made of precious substances. Such inconceivable good qualities, monks, shall the Buddha-field of that Lord be possessed of.

So spoke the Lord, and thereafter he, the Sugata, the Master, added the following stanzas:

1. Listen to me, monks, and hear how my son has achieved his course of duty, and how he, well-trained and skilful, has observed the course of enlightenment.

2. Viewing these beings to be lowly-disposed and to be startled at the lofty vehicle, the Bodhisattvas become disciples and exercise Pratyeka-buddhaship.
3. By many hundreds of able devices they bring numerous Bodhisattvas to full ripeness and declare: We are but disciples, indeed, and we are far away from the highest and supreme enlightenment.
4. It is by learning from them this course of duty that koiis of beings arrive at full ripeness, who at first, lowly-disposed and somewhat lazy, in course of time all become Buddhas.
5. They follow a course in ignorance thinking: We, disciples, are of little use, indeed! In despondency they descend into all places of existence successively, and so clear their own field.
6. They show in their own persons that they are not free from affection, hatred, and infatuation; and on perceiving other beings clinging to heretical views, they go so fat as to accommodate themselves to those views.
7. By following such a course my numerous disciples skilfully save creatures; simple people would go mad, if they were taught the whole course of life or story,
8. Purna here, monks, my disciple, has formerly fulfilled his course of duty under thousands of kotis of Buddhas, he has got possession of this true law by seeking after Buddha-knowledge.
9. And at all periods has he been the foremost of the disciples, learned, a brilliant orator, free from hesitation; he has, indeed, always been able to excite to gladness and at all times ready to perform the Buddha-task.
10. He has always been accomplished in the sublime transcendent faculties and endowed with the distinctive qualifications of an Arhat; he knew the faculties and range of other beings, and has always preached the perfectly pure law.
11. By exposing the most eminent of true laws ; he has brought thousands of kotis of beings to full ripeness for this supreme, foremost vehicle, whilst purifying his own excellent field.

12. In future also he shall likewise honour thousands of kotis of Buddhas, acquire knowledge of the most eminent of good laws, and clean his own field.
13. Always free from timidity he shall preach the law with thousands of kotis of able devices, and bring many beings to full ripeness for the knowledge of the all-knowing that is free from imperfections.
14. After having paid homage to the Chiefs of men and always kept the most eminent of laws, he shall in the world be a Buddha self-born, widely renowned everywhere by the name of Dharmaprabhasa.
15. And his field shall always be very pure and always set off with seven precious substances; his Aeon shall be called Ratnavibhasa, and his world Suvisuddha.
16. That world shall be pervaded with many thousand kotis of Bodhisattvas, accomplished masters in the great transcendent sciences, pure in every respect, and endowed with magical power.
17. At that period the Chief shall also have an assemblage or thousands of kotis of disciples, endowed with magical power, adepts at the meditation of the eight emancipations, and accomplished in the (four) distinctive qualifications of an Arhat.
18. And all beings in that Buddha-field shall be pure and lead a spiritual life. Springing into existence by apparitional birth, they shall all be gold-coloured and display the thirty-two characteristic signs.
19. They shall know no other food but pleasure in the law and delight in knowledge. No womankind shall be there, nor fear of the places of punishments or of dismal states.
20. Such shall be the excellent field of Purna, who is possessed of all good qualities; it shall abound with all goodly things, a small part only of which has here been mentioned.

Then this thought arose in the mind of those twelve hundred self-controlled Arhats: We are struck with wonder and amazement. How if the Tathagata would predict to us severally our future destiny as the Lord has done to those other great disciples? And the Lord apprehending in his own mind what was going on in the minds of these great disciples addressed the venerable Maha-Kasyapa: Those twelve hundred self-controlled hearers whom I am now beholding from face to face, to all those twelve hundred self-controlled hearers, Kasyapa, I will presently foretell their destiny. Amongst them, Kasyapa, the monk Kaundinya, a great disciple, shall, after sixty-two hundred thousand myriads of kotis of Buddhas, become a Tathagata, an Arhat, etc., under the name of Samantaprabhasa, endowed with science and conduct, a Sugata, etc. etc.; but of those twelve hundred, Kasyapa, five hundred shall become Tathagatas of the same name. Thereafter shall all those five hundred great disciples reach supreme and perfect enlightenment, all bearing the name of Samantaprabhasa; Gaya-Kasyapa, Nadi- Kasyapa, Uruvilva-Kasyapa, Kala, Kalodayin, Aniruddha, Kapphilla, Vakkula, Chunda, Svagata, and the rest of the five hundred self-controlled Arhats.

And on that occasion the Lord uttered the following stanzas:

21. The scion of the Kundina family, my disciple here, shall in future be a Tathagata, a Lord of the world, after the lapse of an endless period; he shall educate hundreds of kotis of living beings.
22. After seeing many endless Buddhas, he shall in future, after the lapse of an endless period, become the Jina Samantaprabhasa, whose field shall be thoroughly pure.
23. Brilliant, gifted with the powers of a Buddha, with a voice far resounding in all quarters, waited upon by thousands of kotis of beings, he shall preach supreme and eminent enlightenment.
24. There shall be most zealous Bodhisattvas, mounted on lofty aireal cars, and moving, meditative, pure in morals, and assiduous in doing good.
25. After hearing the law from the highest of men, they shall invariably go to other fields, to salute thousands of Buddhas and show them great honour.
26. But ere long they shall return to the field of the Leader called Prabhasa, the Tathagata, So great shall be the power of their course of duty.

27. The measure of the lifetime of that Sugata shall be sixty thousand Aeans, and, after the complete extinction of that mighty one, his true law shall remain twice as long in the world.

28. And the counterfeit of it shall continue three times as long. When the true law of that holy one shall he exhausted, men and gods shall be vexed.

29. There shall appear a complete number of five hundred Chiefs, supreme amongst men, who shall bear the same name with that Jina, Samantaprabha, and follow one another in regular succession.

39. All shall have like divisions, magical powers, Buddha-fields, and hosts of followers. Their true law also shall be the same and stand equally long.

31. All shall have in this world, including the gods, the same voice as Samantaprabhasa, the highest of men, such as I have mentioned before.

32. Moved by benevolence and compassion they shall in succession foretell each other's destiny, with the words: This is to be my immediate successor, and he is to command the world as I do at present.

33. Thus, Kasyapa, keep now in view here these self-controlled Arhats, no less than five hundred in number, as well as my other disciples, and speak of this matter to the other disciples.

On hearing from the Lord the announcement of their own future destiny, the five hundred Arhats, contented, satisfied, in high spirits and ecstasy, filled with cheerfulness, joy, and delight, went up to the place where the Lord was sitting, reverentially saluted with their heads his feet, and spoke thus: We confess our fault, O Lord, in having continually and constantly persuaded ourselves that we had arrived at final Nirvana, as persons who are dull, inept, ignorant of the rules. For, O Lord, whereas we should have thoroughly penetrated the knowledge of the Tathagatas, we were content with such a trifling degree of knowledge.

It is, O Lord, as if some man having come to a friend's house got drunk or fell asleep, and that friend bound a priceless gem within his garment, with the thought: Let this gem be his. After a while, O Lord, that man rises from his seat and travels further; he goes to some other country, where he is befallen by incessant difficulties, and has great trouble to find food and clothing. By dint of great exertion he is hardly able to obtain a bit of food, with which however he is contented and satisfied. The old friend of that man, O Lord, who bound within the man's garment that priceless gem, happens to see him again and says: How is it, good friend, that thou hast such difficulty in seeking food and clothing, while I, in order that thou shouldst live in ease, good friend, have bound within thy garment a priceless gem, quite sufficient to fulfil all thy wishes? I have given thee that gem, my good friend, the very gem I have bound within thy garment. Still thou art deliberating: What has been bound? by whom? for what reason and purpose? It is something foolish, my good friend, to be contented, when thou hast with so much difficulty to procure food and clothing. Go, my good friend, betake thyself with this gem, to some great city, exchange the gem for money, and with that money do all that can be done with money.

In the same manner, O Lord, has the Tathagata formerly, when he still followed the course of duty of a Bodhisattva, raised in us also ideas of omniscience, but we, O Lord, did not perceive, nor know it. We fancied, O Lord, that on the stage of Arhat we had reached Nirvana. We live in difficulty, O Lord, because we content ourselves with such a trifling degree of knowledge. But as our strong aspiration after the knowledge of the all-knowing has never ceased, the Tathagata teaches us the right: 'Have no such idea of Nirvana, monks; there are in your intelligence roots of goodness which of yore I have fully developed. In this you have to see an able device of mine that from the expressions used by me, in preaching the law, you fancy Nirvana to take place at this moment: And after having taught us the right in such a way, the Lord now predicts our future destiny to supreme and perfect knowledge.

And on that occasion the five hundred self-controlled Arhats, Ajnata-Kaundinya and the rest, uttered the following stanzas:

34. We are rejoicing and delighted to hear this unsurpassed word of comfort that we are destined to the highest, supreme enlightenment. Homage be to thee, O Lord of unlimited sight!
35. We confess our fault before thee; we were so childish, nescient, ignorant that we were fully contented with a small part of Nirvana, under the mastership of the Sugata.
36. This is a case like that of a certain man who enters the house of a friend, which friend, being rich and wealthy, gives him much food, both hard and soft.
37. After satiating him with nourishment, he gives him a jewel of great value. He ties it with a knot within the upper robe and feels satisfaction at having given that jewel.
38. The other man, unaware of it, goes forth and from that place travels to another town. There he is befallen with misfortune and, as a miserable beggar, seeks his food in affliction.
39. He is contented with the pittance he gets by begging without caring for dainty food; as to that jewel, he has forgotten it; he has not the slightest remembrance of its having been tied in his upper robe.
40. Under these circumstances he is seen by his old friend who at home gave him that jewel. This friend properly reprimands him and shows him the jewel within his robe.
41. At this sight the man feels extremely happy. The value of the jewel is such that he becomes a very rich man, of great power, and in possession of all that the five senses can enjoy.
42. In the same manner, O Lord, we were unaware of our former aspiration, the aspiration laid in us by the Tathagata himself in previous existences from time immemorial.
43. And we were living in this world, O Lord, with dull understanding and in ignorance, under the mastership of the Sugata ; for we were contented with a little of Nirvana; we required nothing higher, nor even cared for it.

44. But the Friend of the world has taught us better: 'This is no blessed Rest at all; the full knowledge of the highest men, that is blessed Rest, that is supreme beatitude.
45. After hearing this sublime, grand, splendid, and matchless prediction, O Lord, we are greatly elated with joy, when thinking of the prediction we shall have to make to each other in regular succession.

◆ ◆ ◆ ◆ ◆

9

MORE PROPHECIES

The future destiny of Ananda, Rahula, and the two thousand monks.

On that occasion the venerable Ananda made this reflection: Should we also receive a similar prediction? Thus thinking, pondering, wishing, he rose from his seat, prostrated himself at the Lord's feet and uttered the following words. And the venerable Rahula also, in whom rose the same thought and the same wish as in Ananda, prostrated himself at the Lord's feet, and uttered these words: 'Let it be our turn also, O Lord; let it be our turn also, O Sugata. The Lord is our father and procreator, our refuge and protection. For in this world, including men, gods, and demons, O Lord, we are particularly distinguished, as people say: These are the Lord's sons, the Lord's attendants; these are the keepers of the law-treasure of the Lord. Therefore, Lord, it would seem meet (Pratirupa), were the Lord ere long to predict our destiny to supreme and perfect enlightenment.

Two thousand other monks, and more, both such as were still under training and such as were not, likewise rose from their seats, put their upper robes upon one shoulder, stretched their joined hands towards the Lord and remained gazing up to him, all preoccupied with the same thought, of this very Buddha-knowledge: Should we also receive a prediction of our destiny to supreme and perfect enlightenment.

Then the Lord addressed the venerable Ananda in these words: Thou, Ananda, shalt in future become a Tathagata by the name of Sagaravaradharabuddhivikriditabhjna, an Arhat, etc., endowed with science and conduet, etc. After having honoured, respected, venerated, and worshipped sixty-two kotis of Buddhas, kept in memory the true law of those Buddhas and received this command, thou shalt arrive at supreme and perfect enlightenment, and bring to full ripeness for supreme, perfect enlightenment twenty hundred thousand myriads of kotis of Bodhisattvas similar to the sands of twenty Ganges. And thy Buddha-field shall consist of lapis lazuli and be superabundant. The sphere shall be named Anavanamita-vaijayanta and the Aeon Manojnasabdabhigajita. The lifetime of that Lord Sagara-varadharabuddhivikriditabhjna, the Tathagata, etc., shall measure an immense number of Aeons, Aeons the term of which is not to be found by calculation. So many hundred thousand myriads of kotis of incalculable Aeons shall last the lifetime of that Lord. Twice as long, Ananda, after the complete extinction of that Lord, shall his true law stand, and twice as long again shall continue its counterfeit. And further, Ananda, many hundred thousand myriads of kotis of Buddhas, similar to the sands of the river Ganges, shall in all directions of space speak the praise of that Tathagata Sagaravaradharabuddhivikriditabhijna, the Arhat, etc.

1. I announce to you, congregated monks, that Ananda-Bhadra, the keeper of my law, shall in future become a Jina, after having worshipped sixty kotis of Sugatas.
2. He shall be widely renowned by the name of Sagarabuddhidharin Abhijnaprapta, in a beautiful, thoroughly clear field, termed Anavanata Vaijayantt, i.e. triumphal banner unlowered.
3. There shall be Bodhisattvas like the sands of the Ganges and even more, whom he shall bring to; full ripeness; he shall be a Jina endowed with great magical power, whose word shall widely resound in all quarters of the world.
4. The duration of his life shall be immense. He shall always be benign and merciful to the world. After the complete extinction of that Jina and mighty saint, his true law shall stand twice as long.
5. The counterfeit shall continue twice as long under the rule of that Jina. Then also shall beings like grains of sand of

the Ganges produce in this world what is the cause of Buddha-enlightenment:

In that assembly were eight thousand Bodhisattvas who had newly entered the vehicle. To them this thought presented itself: Never before did we have such a sublime prediction to Bodhisattvas, far less to disciples. What may be the cause of it? what the motive? The Lord, who apprehended in his mind what was going on in the minds of those Bodhisattvas, addressed them in these words: Young men of good family, I and Ananda have in the same moment, the same instant conceived the idea of supreme and perfect enlightenment in the presence of the Tathagata Dharmagahanabhyudgataraja, the Arhat, etc. At that period, young men of good family, Ananda constantly and assiduously applied himself to great learning, whereas I was applying myself to strenuous labour. Hence I sooner arrived at supreme and perfect enlightenment, whilst Ananda-Bhadra was the keeper of the law-treasure of the Lords Buddhas; that is to say, young men of good family, he made a vow to bring Bodhisattvas to full development.

When the venerable Ananda heard from the Lord the announcement of his own destiny to supreme and perfect enlightenment, when he learned the good qualities of his Buddha-field and its divisions, when he heard of the vow he had made in the past, he felt pleased, exultant, ravished, joyous, filled, with cheerfulness and delight. And at that juncture he remembered the true law of many hundred thousand myriads of kotis of Buddhas and his own vow of yore.

And on that occasion the venerable Ananda uttered the following stanzas:

6. Wonderful, boundless are the Jinas who remind us of the law preached by the extinct Jinas and mighty saints. Now I remember it as if it had happened to-day or yesterday.
7. I am freed from all doubts; I am ready for enlightenment. Such is my skilfulness, as I am the servitor, and keep the true law for the sake of enlightenment.

Thereupon the Lord addressed the venerable Rahula-Bhadra in these words: Thou, Rahula, shalt be in future a Tathagata of the name of Saptaratna-padmavikrantagamin, an Arhat, etc., endowed with science and conduct, etc. After having honoured, respected, venerated, worshipped a number of Tathagatas, etc., equal to the atoms of ten worlds, thou shalt always be the eldest son of those Lords Buddhas, just as thou art mine at present. And, Rahula, the measure of the lifetime of that Lord Saptaratna-padmavikrantagamin, the Tathagata, etc., and the abundance of all sorts of good qualities belonging to him shall be exactly the same as of the Lord Sagaravaradharabuddhivikriditabhijna, the Tathagata, etc.; likewise shall the divisions of the Buddha-field and its qualities be the same as those possessed by that Lord. And, Rahula, thou shalt be the eldest son of that Tathagata Sagaravaradharabuddhivikriditabhijna, the Arhat, etc. Afterwards thou shalt arrive at supreme and perfect enlightenment.

8. Rahula here, my own eldest son, who was born to me when I was a prince royal, he, my son, after my reaching enlightenment, is a great Seer, an heir to the law.

9. The great number of kotis of Buddhas which he shall see in future, is immense. To all these Jinas he shall be a son, striving after enlightenment.

10. Unknown is this course of duty to Rahula, but I know his former vow. He glorifies the Friend of the world by saying: I am, forsooth, the Tathagata's son.

11. Innumerable myriads of kotis of good qualities, the measure of which is never to be found, appertain to this Rahula, my son; for it has been said: He exists by reason of enlightenment.

The Lord now again regarded those two thousand disciples, both such as were still under training and such as were not, who were looking up to him with serene, mild, placid minds. And the Lord then addressed the venerable Ananda: Seest thou, Ananda, these two thousand disciples, both such as are still under training and such as are not? 'I do, Lord; I do, Sugata.' The Lord proceeded: All these two thousand monks, Ananda, shall simultaneously accomplish the course of Bodhisattvas, and after honouring, respecting, venerating, worshipping Buddhas as numerous as the atoms of fifty worlds, and after acquiring the true law, they shall, in their last bodily existence, attain supreme and perfect enlightenment at the same time, the same moment, the same instant, the same juncture in all directions of space, in different worlds, each in his own Buddha-field. They shall become Tathagatas, Arhats, etc., by the name of Ratnaketurajas. Their lifetime shall last a complete Aeon. The division and good qualities of their Buddha-fields shall be equal; equal also shall be the number of the congregation of their disciples and Bodhisattvas; equal also shall be their complete extinction, and their true law shall continue an equal time.

And on that occasion the Lord uttered the following stanzas:

12. These two thousand disciples, Ananda, who here are standing before me, to them, the sages, I now predict that in future they shall become Tathagatas.

13. After having paid eminent worship to the Buddhas, by means of infinite comparisons and examples, they shall, when standing in their last bodily existence, reach my extreme enlightenment.

14. They shall all, under the same name, in every direction, at the same moment and instant, and sitting at the foot of the most exalted tree, become Buddhas, after they shall have reached the knowledge.

15. All shall bear the same name of Ketus of the Ratna, by which they shall be widely famed in this world. Their excellent fields shall be equal, and equal the congregation of disciples and Bodhisattvas.

16. Strong in magic power, they shall all simultaneously, in every direction of space, reveal the law in this world and all at once become extinct; their true law shall last equally long.

And the disciples, both such as were still under training and such as were not, on hearing from the Lord, face to face, the prediction concerning each of them, were pleased, exultant, ravished, joyous, filled with cheerfulness and delight, and addressed the Lord with the following stanzas:

17. We are satisfied, O Light of the world, to hear this prediction; we are pleased, O Tathagata, as if sprinkled with nectar.
18. We have no doubt, no uncertainty that we shall become supreme amongst men; to-day we have obtained felicity, because we have heard that prediction.

◆ ◆ ◆ ◆ ◆

10

THE PREACHER

Pious preachers of the law will come, honour them, they will be protected.

The Lord addressed the eighty thousand Bodhisattvas Mahasattvas by turning to Bhaishajyaraja as their representative. Seest thou, Bhaishajyaraja, in this assembly the many gods, Nagas, goblins, Gandharvas, demons, Garudas, Kinnaras, great serpents, men, and beings not human, monks, nuns, male and female lay devotees, votaries of the vehicle of disciples, votaries of the vehicle of PratyekaBuddhas, and those of the vehicle of Bodhisattvas, who have heard this Dharmaparyaya from the mouth of the Tathagata? 'I do, Lord; I do Sugata.' The Lord proceeded: Well, Bhaishajyaraja, all those Bodhisattvas Mahasattvas who in this assembly have heard, were it but a single stanza a single verse or word, or who even by a single rising thought have joyfully accepted this Sutra, to all of them, Bhaishajyaraja, among the four classes of my audience I predict their destiny to supreme and perfect enlightenment. And all whosoever, Bhaishajyaraja, who, after the complete extinction of the Tathagata, shall hear this Dharmaparyaya and after hearing, were it but a single stanza, joyfully accept it, even with a single rising thought, to those also, Bhaishajyaraja, be they young men or young ladies of good family, I predict their destiny to supreme and perfect enlightenment. Those young men or ladies of good family, Bhaishajyaraja, shall be worshippers of many hundred thousand myriads of kotis of Buddhas. Those young men or ladies of good family, Bhaishajyaraja, shall have made a vow under hundred thousands of myriads of kotis of Buddhas. They must be considered as being reborn amongst the people of Jambudvipa, out of compassion to all creatures. Those who shall take, read, make known, recite, copy, and after copying always keep in memory and from time to time regard were it but a single stanza of this Dharmaparyaya; who by that book shall feel veneration for the Tathagatas, treat them with the respect due to Masters, honour, revere, worship them; who shall worship that book with flowers, incense, perfumed garlands, ointment, powder, clothes, umbrellas, flags, banners, music, etc., and with acts of reverence such as bowing and joining hands; in short, Bhaishajyaraja, any young men or young ladies of good family who shall keep or joyfully accept were it but a single stanza of this Dharmaparyaya, to all of them, Bhaishajyaraja, I predict their being destined to supreme and perfect enlightenment.

Should some man or woman, Bhaishajyaraja, happen to ask: How now have those creatures to be who in future are to become Tathagatas, Arhats, etc.? then that man or woman should be referred to the example of that young man or young lady of good family. 'Whoever is able to keep, recite, or teach, were it but a single stanza of four lines, and whoever shows respect for this Dharmaparyaya, that young man or young lady of good family shall in future become a Tathagata, etc.; be persuaded of it. For, Bhaishajyaraja, such a young man or young lady of good family must be considered to be a Tathagata, and by the whole world, including the gods, honour should be done to such a Tathagata who keeps were it but a single stanza of this Dharmaparyaya, and far more, of course, to one who grasps, keeps, comprehends, makes known, copies, and after copying always retains in his memory this Dharmaparyaya entirely and completely, and who honours that book with flowers, incense, petfumed garlands, ointment, powder, clothes, umbrellas, flags, banners, music, joined hands, reverential bows and salutations. Such a young man or young lady of good family, Bhaishajyaraja, must be held to be accomplished in supreme and perfect enlightenment; must be held to be the like of a Tathagata, who out of compassion and for the benefit of the world, by virtue of a former vow, makes his appearance here in Jambudvipa, in order to make this Dharmaparyaya generally known. Whosoever, after leaving his own lofty conception of the law and the lofty Buddha-field occupied by him, in order to make generally known this Dharmaparyaya, after my complete Nirvana, may be deemed to have appeared in the predicament of a Tathagata, such a one, Bhaishajyaraja, be it a young man or a young lady of good family, must be held to perform the function of the Tathagata, to be a deputy of the Tathagata. As such, Bhaishajyaraja, should be acknowledged the young man or the young lady of good family, who communicates this Dharmaparyaya, after the complete Nirvana of the Tathagata, were it but in secret or by stealth or to one single creature that he communicated or told it.

Again, Bhaishajyaraja, if some creature vicious, wicked, and cruelminded should in the current Age speak something injurious in the face of the Tathagata, and if some should utter a single harsh word, founded or unfounded, to those irreproachable preachers of the law and keepers of this Sutranta, whether lay devotees or clergymen, I declare that the latter sin is the graver. For, Bhaishajyaraja, such a young man or young lady of good family must be held to be adorned with the apparel of the Tathagata. He carries the Tathagata on his shoulder, Bhaishajyaraja, who after having copied this Dharmaparyaya and made a volume of it, carries it on his shoulder. Such a one, wherever he goes, must be saluted by all beings with joined hands, must be honoured, respected, worshipped, venerated, revered by gods and men with flowers, incense, perfumed garlands, ointment, powder, clothes, umbrellas, flags, banners, musical instruments, with food, soft and hard, with nourishment and drink, with vehicles, with heaps of choice and gorgeous jewels. That preacher of the law must be honoured by heaps of gorgeous jewels being presented to that preacher of the law. For it may be that by his expounding this Dharmaparyaya, were it only once, innumerable, incalculable beings who hear it shall soon become accomplished in supreme and perfect enlightenment.

And on that occasion the Lord uttered the following stanzas:

1. He who wishes to be established in Buddhahood and aspires to the knowledge of the Self-born, must honour those who keep this doctrine.

2. And he who is desirous of omniscience and thinks: How shall I soonest reach it? must try to know this Sutra by heart, or at least honour one who knows it.
3. He has been sent by the Lord of the world to convert or catechise men, he who out of compassion for mankind recites this Sutra.
4. After giving up a good position, that great man has come hither, he who out of compassion for mankind keeps this Sutra in memory.
5. It is by force of his position, that in the last times he is seen preaching this unsurpassed Sutra.
6. That preacher of the law must be honoured with divine and human flowers and all sorts of perfumes; be decked with divine cloth and strewed with jewels.
7. One should always reverentially salute him with joined hands, as if he were the Chief of Jinas or the Self-born, he who in these most dreadful, last days keeps this Sutra of the Extinct Buddha.
8. One should give food, hard and soft, nourishment and drink, lodging in a convent, kotis of robes to honour the son of Jina, when he has propounded, be it but once, this Sutra.
9. He performs the task of the Tathagatas and has been sent by me to the world of men, he who in the last days shall copy, keep, or hear this Sutra.
10. The man who in wickedness of heart or with frowning brow should at any time of a whole Aeon utter something injurious in my presence, commits a great sin.
11. But one who reviles and abuses those guardians of this Sutranta, when they are expounding this Sutra, I say that he commits a still greater sin.
12. The man who, striving for superior enlightenment, shall in a complete Aeon praise me in my face with joined hands, with many myriads of kotis of stanzas,
13. Shall thence derive a great merit, since he has glorified me in gladness of heart. But a still greater merit shall he acquire who pronounces the praise of those preachers.

14. One who shall during eighteen thousand kotis of Aeons pay worship to those objects of veneration with words, visible things, flavours, with divine scents and divine kinds of touch,
15. If such a one, by his paying that worship to the objects of veneration during eighteen thousand kotis of Aeons, happens to hear this Sutra, were it only once, he shall obtain an amazingly great advantage.

I announce to thee, Bhaishajyaraja, I declare to thee, that many are the Dharmaparyayas which I have propounded, am propounding, and shall propound. And among all those Dharmaparyayas, Bhaishajyaraja, it is this which is apt to meet with no acceptance with everybody, to find no belief with everybody. This, indeed, Bhaishajyaraja, is the transcendent spiritual esoteric lore of the law, preserved by the power of the Tathagatas, but never divulged; it is an article of creed not yet made known. By the majority of people, Bhaishajyaraja, this Dharmaparyaya is rejected during the lifetime of the Tathagata; in far higher degree such will be the case after his complete extinction.

Nevertheless, Bhaishajyaraja, one has to consider those young men or young ladies of good family to be invested with the robes of the Tathagata; to be regarded and blessed by the Tathagatas living in other worlds, that they shall have the force of individual persuasion, the force that is rooted in virtue, and the force of a pious vow. They shall dwell apart in the convents of the Tathagata, Bhaishajyaraja, and shall have their heads stroked by the hand of the Tathagata, those young men and young ladies of good family, who after the complete extinction of the Tathagata shall believe, read, write, honour this Dharmaparyaya and recite it to others.

Again, Bhaishajyaraja, on any spot of the earth where this Dharmaparyaya is expounded, preached, written, studied, or recited in chorus, on that spot, Bhaishajyaraja, one should build a Tathagata-shrine, magnificent, consisting of precious substances, high, and spacious; but it is not necessary to depose in it relics of the Tathagata. For the body of the Tathagata is, so to say, collectively deposited there. Any spot of the earth where this Dharmaparyaya is expounded or taught or recited or rehearsed in chorus or written or kept in a volume, must be honoured, respected, revered, worshipped as if it were a Stupa, with all sorts of flowers, incense, perfumes, garlands, ointment, powder, clothes, umbrellas, flags, banners, triumphal streamers, with all kinds of song, music, dancing, musical instruments, castanets, and shouts in chorus. And those, Bhaishajyaraja, who approach a Tathagata-shrine to salute or see it, must be held to be near supreme and perfect enlightenment. For, Bhaishajyaraja, there are many laymen as well as priests who observe the course of a Bodhisattva without, however, coming so far as to see, hear, write or worship this Dharmaparyaya. So long as they do not hear this Dharmaparyaya, they are not yet proficient in the course of a Bodhisattva. But those who hear this Dharmaparyaya and thereupon accept, penetrate, understand, comprehend it, are at the time near supreme, perfect enlightenment, so to say, immediately near it.

It is a case, Bhaishajyaraja, similar to that of a certain man, who in need and in quest of water, in order to get water, causes a well to be dug in an arid tract of land. So long as he sees that the sand being dug out is dry and white, he thinks: the water is still far off. After some time he sees that the sand being dug out is moist, mixed with water, muddy, with trickling drops, and that the working men who are engaged in digging the well are bespattered with mire and mud. On seeing that foretoken, Bhaishajyaraja, the man will be convinced and certain that water is near. In the same manner, Bhaishajyaraja, will these Bodhisattvas Mahasattvas be far away from supreme and perfect enlightenment so long as they do not hear, nor catch, nor penetrate, nor fathom, nor mind this Dharmaparyaya. But when the Bodhisattvas Mahasattvas shall hear, catch, penetrate, study, and mind this Dharmaparyaya, then, Bhaishajyaraja, they will be, so to say, immediately near supreme, perfect enlightenment. From this Dharmaparyaya, Bhaishajyaraja, will accrue to creatures supreme and perfect enlightenment. For this Dharmaparyaya contains an explanation of the highest mystery, the secret article of the law which the Tathagatas, etc., have revealed for the perfecting of the Bhaishajyaraja Mahasattvas. Any Bodhisattva, Bhaishajyaraja, who is startled, feels anxiety, gets frightened at this Dharmaparyaya, may be held, Bhaishajyaraja, to have but newly entered the vehicle. If, however, a votary of the vehicle of the disciples is startled, feels anxiety, gets frightened at this Dharmaparyaya, such a person, devoted to the vehicle of the disciples, Bhaishajyaraja, may be deemed a conceited man.

Any Bodhisattva Mahasattva, Bhaishajyaraja, who after the complete extinction of the Tathagata, in the last times, the last period shall set forth this Dharmaparyaya to the four classes of hearers, should do so, Bhaishajyaraja, after having entered the abode of the Tathagata, after having put on the robe of the Tathagata, and occupied the pulpit of the Tathagata. And what is the abode of the Tathagata, Bhaishajyaraja? It is the abiding in charity or kindness to all beings; that is the abode of the Tathagata, Bhaishajyaraja, which the young man of good family has to enter. And what is the robe of the Tathagata, Bhaishajyaraja? It is the apparel of sublime forbearance; that is the robe of the Tathagata, Bhaishajyaraja, which the young man of good family has to put on. What is the pulpit of the Tathagata, Bhaishajyaraja? It is the entering into the voidness or complete abstraction of all laws or things; that is the pulpit, Bhaishajyaraja, on which the young man of good family has to sit in order to set forth this Dharmaparyaya to the four classes of hearers. A Bodhisattva ought to propound this Dharmaparyaya with unshrinking mind, before the face of the congregated Bodhisattvas, the four classes of hearers, who are striving for the vehicle of Bodhisattvas, and I, staying in another world, Bhaishajyaraja, will by means of fictious creatures make the minds of the whole congregation favourably disposed to that young man of good family, and I will send fictious monks, nuns, male and female lay devotees in order to hear the sermon of the preacher, who are unable to gainsay or contradict him. If afterwards he shall have retired to the forest, I will send thither many gods, Nagas, goblins, Gandharvas, demons, Garudas, Kinnaras, and great serpents to hear him preach, while I, staying in another world, Bhaishajyaraja, will show my face to that young man of good family, and the words and syllables of this Dharmaparyaya which he happens to have forgotten will I again suggest to him when he repeats his lesson.

And on that occasion the Lord uttered the following stanzas:

16. Let one listen to this exalted Sutra, avoiding all distractedness; for rare is the occasion given for hearing it, and rare also the belief in it.
17. It is a case similar to that of a certain man who in want of water goes to dig a well in an arid tract of land, and sees how again and again only dry sand is being dug up.
18. On seeing which he thinks: the water is far off; a token of its being far off is the dry white sand which appears in digging.
19. But when he afterwards sees again and again the sand moist and smooth, he gets the conviction that water cannot be very far off.
20. So, too, are those men far from Buddha-knowledge who have not heard this Sutra and have failed to repeatedly meditate on it.
21. But those who have heard and oft meditated on this profound king amongst Sutras, this authoritative book for disciples,
22. Are wise and near Buddha-knowledge, even as from the moisture of sand may be inferred that water is near.
23. After entering the abode of the Jina, putting on his robe and sitting down on my seat, the preacher should, undaunted, expound this Sutra.
24. The strength of charity or kindness is my abode; the apparel of forbearence is my robe; and voidness or complete abstraction is my seat; let the preacher take his stand on this and preach.
25. Where clods, sticks, pikes, or abusive words and threats fall to the lot of the preacher, let him be patient, thinking of me.
26. My body has existed entire in thousands of kotis of regions; during a number of kotis of Aeons beyond comprehension I teach the law to creatures.
27. To that courageous man who shall proclaim this Sutra after my complete extinction I will also send many creations.

28. Monks, nuns, lay devotees, male and female, will honour him as well as the classes of the audience.
29. And should there be some to attack him with clods, sticks, injurious words, threats, taunts, then the creations shall defend him.
30. And when he shall stay alone, engaged in study, in a lonely place, in the forest or the hills,
31. Then will I show him my luminous body and enable him to remember the lesson he forgot.
32. While he is living lonely in the wilderness, I will send him gods and goblins in great number to keep him company.
33. Such are the advantages he is to enjoy; whether he is preaching to the four classes, or living, a solitary, in mountain caverns and studying his lesson, he will see me.
34. His readiness of speech knows no impediment; he understands the manifold requisites of exegesis; he satisfies thousands of kotis of beings because he is, so to say, inspired or blessed by the Buddha.
35. And the creatures who are entrusted to his care shall very soon all become Bodhisattvas, and by cultivating his intimacy they shall behold Buddhas as numerous as the sands of the Ganges.

◆ ◆ ◆ ◆ ◆

11

THE STUPA

Display of the miraculous power of Sakyamuni shown in the appearance of a stupa, how Sakyamuni in a former birth strove to acquire the Lotus, etc.

Then there arose a Stupa, consisting of seven precious substances, from the place of the earth opposite the Lord, the assembly being in the middle, a Stupa five hundred yojanas in height and proportionate in circumference. After its rising, the Stupa, a meteoric phenomenon, stood in the sky sparkling, beautiful, nicely decorated with five thousand successive terraces of flowers, adorned with many thousands of arches, embellished by thousands of banners and triumphal streamers, hung with thousands of jewel-garlands and with hourplates and bells, and emitting the scent of Xanthochymus and sandal, which scent filled this whole world. Its row of umbrellas rose so far on high as to touch the abodes of the four guardians of the horizon and the gods. It consisted of seven precious substances, gold, silver, lapis lazuli, Musaragalva, emerald, red coral, and Karketana-stone. This Stupa of precious substances once formed, the gods of paradise strewed and covered it with Mandarava and great Mandara flowers. And from that Stupa of precious substances there issued this voice: Excellent, excellent, Lord Sakyamuni! thou hast well expounded this Dharmaparyaya of the Lotus of the True Law. So it is, Lord; so it is, Sugata.

At the sight of that great Stupa of precious substances, that meteoric phenomenon in the sky, the four classes of hearers were filled with gladness, delight, satisfaction and joy. Instantly they rose from their seats, stretched out their joined hands, and remained standing in that position. Then the Bodhisattva

Mahasattva Mahapratibhana, perceiving the world, including gods, men, and demons, filled with curiosity, said to the Lord: O Lord, what is the cause, what is the reason of so magnificent a Stupa of precious substances appearing in the world? Who is it, O Lord, who causes that sound to go out from the magnificent Stupa of precious substances?

Thus asked, the Lord spake to Mahapratibhana, the Bodhisattva Mahasattva, as follows: In this great Stupa of precious substances, Mahapratibhana, the proper body of the Tathagata is contained condensed; his is the Stupa; it is he who causes this sound to go out. In the point of space below, Mahapratibhana, there, are innumerable thousands of worlds. Further on is the world called Ratnavisuddha, there is the Tathagata named Prabhutaratna, the Arhat, etc. This Lord of yore made this vow: Formerly, when following the course of a Bodhisattva, I have not arrived at supreme, perfect enlightenment before I had heard this Dharmaparyaya of the Lotus of the True Law, serving for the instruction of Bodhisattvas. But from the moment that I had heard, this Dharmaparyaya of the Lotus of the True Law, I have become fully ripe for supreme, perfect enlightenment.

Now, Mahapratibhana, that Lord Prabhutaratna, the Tathagata, etc., at the juncture of time when his complete extinction was to take place, announced in presence of the world, including the gods: After my complete extinction, monks, one Stupa must be made of precious substances of this frame or form of the proper body of the Tathagata; the other Stupas, again, should be made in dedication for in referencel to me. Thereupon, Mahapratibhana, the Lord Prabhutaratna, the Tathagata, etc., pronounced this blessing: Let my Stupa here, this Stupa of my proper bodily frame or form, arise wherever in any Buddhafield in the ten directions of space, in all worlds, the Dharmaparyaya of the Lotus of the True Law is propounded, and let it stand in the sky above the assembled congregation when this Dharmaparyaya of the Lotus of the True Law is being preached by some Lord Buddha or another, and let this Stupa of the frame or form of my proper body give a shout of applause to those Buddhas while preaching this Dharmaparyaya of the Lotus of the True Law. It is that Stupa, Mahapratibhana, of the relics of the Lord Prabhutaratna, the Tathagata, etc., which, while I was preaching this Dharmaparyaya of the Lotus of the True Law in this Saha-world, arose above this assembled congregation and, standing as a meteor in the sky, gave its applause.

Then said Mahapratibhana, the Bodhisattva Mahasattva, to the Lord: Show us, O Lord, through thy power the frame of the aforementioned Tathagata. Whereon the Lord spake to the Bodhisattva Mahasattva Mahapratibhana as follows: This Lord Prabhutaratna, Mahapratibhana, has made a grave and pious vow. That vow consisted in this: When the Lords, the Buddhas, being in other Buddha-fields, shall preach this Dharmaparyaya of the Lotus of the True Law, then let this Stupa of the frame of my proper body be near the Tathagata to hear from him this Dharmaparyaya of the Lotus of the True Law. And when those Lords, those Buddhas wish to uncover the frame of my proper body and show it to the four classes of hearers, let then the Tathagata-frames, made by the Tathagatas in all quarters, in different Buddha-fields, from their own proper body, and preaching the law to creatures, under different names in several Buddha-fields, let all those Tathagata-frames, made from the proper body, united together, along with this Stupa containing the frame of my own body, be opened and shown to the four classes of hearers. Therefore, Mahapratibhana, have I made many Tathagata-frames which in all quarters, in several Buddha-fields in thousands of worlds. preach the law to creatures. All those ought to be brought hither.

Thereupon the Bodhisattva Mahasattva Mahapratibhana said to the Lord: Then, O Lord, shall we reverentially salute all those bodily emanations of the Tathagata and created by the Tathagata.

And instantly the Lord darted from the circle of hair on his brow a ray, which was no sooner darted than the Lords, the Buddhas stationed in the east in fifty hundred thousand myriads of kotis of worlds. equal to the sands of the river Ganges, became all visible, and the Buddha-fields there, consisting of crystal, became visible, variegated with jewel trees, decorated with strings of fine cloth, replete with many hundred thousands of

Bodhisattvas, covered with canopies, decked with a network of seven precious substances and gold. And in those fields appeared the Lords, the Buddhas, teaching with sweet and gentle voice the law to creatures; and those Buddha-fields seemed replete-with hundred thousands of Bodhisattvas. So, too, it was in the south-east; so in the south; so in the south-west; so in the west; so in the north-west; so in the north; so in the north-east; so in the nadir; so in the zenith; so in the ten directions of space; in each direction were to be seen many hundred thousand myriads of kotis of Buddha-fields, similar to the sands of the river Ganges, in many worlds similar to the sands of the river Ganges, Lords Buddhas in many hundred thousand myriads of kotis of Buddha-fields.

Those Tathagatas, etc., in the ten directions of space then addressed each his own troop of Bodhisattvas: We shall have to go, young men of good family, to the Saha-world near the Lord Sakyamuni, the Tathagata, etc., to humbly salute the Stupa of the relics of Prabhataratna, the Tathagata, etc. Thereupon those Lords, those Buddhas resorted with their own satellites, each with one or two, to this Saha-world. At that period this all-embracing world was adorned with jewel trees; it consisted of lapis lazuli, was covered with a network of seven precious substances and gold, smoking with the odorous incense of magnificent jewels, everywhere strewn with Mandarava and great Mandarava flowers, decorated with a network of little bells, showing a checker board divided by gold threads into eight compartments, devoid of villages, towns, boroughs, provinces, kingdoms, and royal capitals, without Kala-mountain, without the mountains Muchlinda and great Muchlinda, without a mount Sumeru, without a Muchlinda (i.e. horizon) and great Muchlinda (i.e, extended horizon), without other principal mountains, without great oceans, without rivers and great rivers, without bodies of gods, men, and demons, without hells, without brute creation, without a kingdom of Yama. For it must be understood that at that period all beings in any of the six states of existence in this world had been removed to other worlds, with the exception of those who were assembled at that congregation. Then it was that those Lords, those Buddhas, attendetl by one or two satellites, arrived at this Saha-world and went one after the other to occupy their place close to the foot of a jewel tree. Each of the jewel trees was five hundred yojanas in height, had boughs, leaves, foliage, and circumference in proportion, and was provided with blossoms and fruits. At the foot of each jewel tree stood prepared a throne, five yojanas in height, and adorned with magnificent jewels. Each Tathagata went to occupy his throne and sat on it cross-legged. And so all the Tathagatas of the whole sphere sat cross-Iegged at the foot of the jewel trees.

At that moment the whole sphere was replete with Tathagatas, but the beings produced from the proper body of the Lord Sakyamuni had not yet arrived, not even from a single point of the horizon. Then the Lord Sakyamuni, the Tathagata, etc., proceeded to make room for those Tathagata-frames that were arriving one after the other. On every side in the eight directions of space appeared twenty hundred thousand myriads of kotis of Buddha-fields of lapis lazuli, decked with a network of seven precious substances and gold, decorated with a fringe of little bells, strewn with Mandarava and great Mandarava flowers, covered with heavenly awnings, hung with wreaths of heavenly flowers, smoking with heavenly odorous incense. All those twenty hundred thousand myriads of kotis of Buddha-fields were without villages, towns, boroughs, etc., without Kala-mountain, etc., without great oceans, etc., without bodies of gods, etc. All those Buddha-fields were so arranged by him as to form one Buddha-field, one soil, even, lovely, set off with trees of seven precious substances, trees five hundred yojanas in height and circumference, provided with boughs, flowers, and fruits in proportion. At the foot of each tree stood prepared a throne, five yojanas in height and width, consisting of celestial gems, glittering and beautiful. The Tathagatas arriving one after the other occupied the throne near the foot of each tree, and sat cross-legged. In like manner the Tathagata Sakyamuni prepared twenty hundred thousand myriads of kotis of other worlds, in every direction of space, in order to give room to the Tathagatas who were arriving one after the other. These twenty hundred thousand myriads of kotis of worlds in every direction of space were likewise so made by him as to be without villages, towns, etc. [as above]. They were without bodies of gods, etc., [as above];

all those beings had been removed to other worlds. These Buddha-fields also were of lapis lazuli, etc., [as above]. All those jewel trees measured five hundred yojanas, and near them were thrones, artificially made and measuring five yojanas. Then those Tathagatas sat down cross-legged, each on a throne at the foot of a jewel tree.

At that moment the Tathagatas produced by the Lord Sakyamuni, who in the east were preaching the law to creatures in hundred thousands of myriads of kotis of Buddha-fields, similar to the sands of the river Ganges, all arrived from the ten points of space and sat down in the eight quarters. Thereupon thirty kotis of worlds in each directiqn were occupied by those Tathagatas from all the eight quarters. Then, seated on their thrones, those Tathagatas deputed their satellites into the presence of the Lord Sakyamuni, and after giving them bags with jewel flowers enjoined them thus: Go, young men of good family, to the Gridhrakuta mountain, where the Lord Sakyamuni, the Tathagata, etc., is; salute him reverentially and ask, in our name, after the state of health, well-being, lustiness, and comfort both of himself and the crowd of Bodhisattvas and disciples. Strew him with this heap of jewels and speak thus: Would the Lord Tathagata deign to open this great Stupa, of jewels? It was in this manner that all those Tathagatas deputed their satellites.

And when the Lord Sakyamuni, the Tathagata, perceived that his creations, none wanting, had arrived; perceived that they were severally seated, on their thrones, and perceived that the satellites of those Tathagatas, etc., were present, he, in consideration of the wish expressed by those Tathagatas, etc., rose from his seat and stood in the sky, as a meteor. And all the four classes of the assembly rose from their seats, stretched out their joined hands, and stood gazing up to the face of the Lord. The Lord then, with the right forefinger, unlocked the middle of the great Stupa of jewels, which showed like a meteor, and so severed the two parts. Even as the double doors of a great city gate separate when the bolt is removed, so the Lord opened the great Stupa, which showed like a meteor, by unlocking it in the middle with the right forefinger. The great Stupa of jewels had no sooner been opened than the Lord Prabhutaratna, the Tathagata, etc., was seen sitting cross-legged on his throne, with emaciated limbs and faint body, as if absorbed in abstract meditation, and he pronounced these words: Excellent, excellent, Lord Sakyamuni; thou hast well expounded this Dharmaparyaya of the Lotus of the True Law. I repeat, thou hast well expounded this Dharmaparyaya of the Lotus of the True Law, Lord Sakyamuni, to the four classes of the assembly. I myself, Lord, have come hither to hear the Dharmaparyaya of the Lotus of the True Law.

Now the four classes of the assembly, on perceiving the Lord Prabhutaratna, the Tathagata, etc., who had been extinct for many hundred thousand myriads of kotis of Aeons, speaking in this way, were filled with wonder and amazement. Instantly they covered the Lord Prabhutaratna, the Tathagata, etc., and the Lord Sakyamuni, the Tathagata, etc., with heaps of divine and human flowers. And then the Lord Prabhutaratna, the Tathagata, etc., ceded to the Lord Sakyamuni, the Tathagata, etc., the half of the seat on that very throne within that same great Stupa of jewels and said: Let the Lord Sakyamuni, the Tathagata, etc., sit down here. Whereon the Lord Sakyamuni, the Tathagata, etc., sat down upon that half-seat together with the other Tathagata, so that both Tathagatas were seen as meteors in the sky, sitting on the throne in the middle of the great Stupa of jewels.

And in the minds of those four classes of the assembly rose this thought: We are far off from the two Tathagatas; therefore let us also, through the power of the Tathagata, rise up to the sky. As the Lord apprehended in his mind what was going on in the minds of those four classes of the assembly, he instantly, by magic power, established the four classes as meteors in the sky. Thereupon the Lord Sakyamuni, the Tathagata, addressed the four classes: Who amongst you, monks, will endeavour to expound this Dharmaparyaya of the Lotus of the True Law in this Saha-world? The fatal term, the time of death, is now at hand; the Tathagata longs for complete extinction, monks, after entrusting to you this Dharmaparyaya of the Lotus of the True Law.

And on that occasion the Lord uttered the following stanzas:

1. Here you see, monks, the great Seer, the extinct Chief, within the Stupa of jewels, who now has come to hear the law. Who would not call up his energy for the law's sake?
2. Albeit completely extinct for many kotis of Aeons, he yet now comes to hear the law; for the law's sake he moves hither and thither; very rare (and very precious) is a law like this.
3. This Leader practised a vow when he was in a former existence; even after his complete extinction he wanders through this whole world in all ten points of space.
4. And all these you here see are my proper bodies, by thousands of kotis, like the sands of the Ganges; they have appeared that the law may be fulfilled and in order to see this extinct Master.
5. After laying out for each his peculiar field, as well as having created all disciples, men and gods, in order to preserve the true law, as long as the reign of the law shall last,
6. I have by magic power cleared many worlds, destined as seats for those Buddhas, and transported all creatures.
7. It has always been my anxious care how this line of the low might be manifested. So you see Buddhas here in immense number staying at the foot of trees like a great multitude of lotuses.
8. Many kotis of bases of trees are brightened by the Leaders sitting on the thrones which are perpetually occupied by them and brightened as darkness is by fire,
9. A delicious fragrance spreads from the Leaders of the world over all quarters, a fragrance by which; when the wind is blowing, all these creatures are intoxicated.
10. Let him who after my extinction shall keep this Dharmaparyaya quickly pronounce his declaration in the presence of the Lords of the world.
11. The Seer Prabhataratna who, though completely extinct, is awake, will hear the lion's roar of him who shall take this resolution.

12. Myself, in the second place, as well as the many Chiefs who have flocked hither by kotis, will hear that resolution from the son of Jina, who is to exert himself to expound this law.
13. And thereby shall I always be honoured as well as Prabhataratna, the self-born Jina, who perpetually wanders through the quarters and intermediate quarters in order to hear such a law as this.
14. And these other Lords of the world here present, by whom this soil is so variegated and splendid, to them also will accrue ample and manifold honour from this Sutra being preached.
15. Here on this seat you see me, together with the Lord next to me, in the middle of the Stupa; likewise many other Lords of the world here present, in many hundreds of fields.
16. Ye, young men of good family, mind, for mercy's sake towards all beings, that it is a very difficult task to which the Chief urges you.
17. One might expound many thousands of Sutras, like to the sands of the Ganges, without overmuch difficulty.
18. One who after grasping the Sumeru in the fist were to hurl it a distance of kotis of fields, would do nothing very difficult.
19. Nor would it be so very difficult if one could shake this whole universe by the thumb to hurl it a distance of kotis of fields.
20. Nor would one who, after taking stand on the limit of the existing world, were to expound the law and thousands of other Sutras, do something so very difficult.
21. But to keep and preach this Sutra in the dreadful period succeeding the extinction of the Chief of the world, that is difficult.
22. To throw down the totality of ether-element after compressing it in one fist, and to leave it behind after having thrown it away, is not difficult.

23. But to copy a Sutra like this in the period after my extinction, that is difficult.
24. To collect the whole earth-element at a nail's end cast it away, and then walk off to the Brahma-world.
25. Is not difficult, nor would it require a strength surpassing everybody's strength to do this work of difficulty.
26. Something more difficult than that will he do who in the last days after my extinction shall pronounce this Sutra, were it but a single moment.
27. It will not be difficult for him to walk in the midst of the conflagration at the time of the end of the world, even if he carries with him a load of hay.
28. More difficult it will be to keep this Sutra after my extinction and teach it to a single creature.
29. One may keep the eighty-four thousand divisions of the law and expound them, with the instructions and such as they have been set forth, to kotis of living beings;
30. This is not so difficult; nor is it, to train at the present time monks, and confirm my disciples in the five parts, of transcendent knowledge.
31. But more difficult is it to keep this Sutra, believe in it, adhere to it, or expound it again and again..
32. Even he who confirms many thousands of kotis of Arhats, blest with the possession of the six transcendent faculties, Abhijnas, like sands of the Ganges,
33. Performs something not so difficult by far as the excellent man does who after my extinction shall keep my sublime law.
34. I have often, in thousands of worlds, preached the law, and to-day also I preach it with the view that Buddha-knowledge may be obtained.
35. This Sutra is declared the principal of all Sutras; he who keeps in his memory this Sutra, keeps the body of the Jina.
36. Speak, O young men of good family, while the Tathagata is still in your presence, who amongst you is to exert himself in later times to keep the Sutra.

37. Not only I myself shall be pleased, but the Lords of the world in general, if one would keep for a moment this Sutra so difficult to keep.
38. Such a one shall ever be praised by all the Lords of the world, famed as an eminent hero, and quick in arriving at transcendent wisdom.
39. He shall be entrusted with the leadership amongst the sons of the Tathagatas, he who, after having reached the stage of meekness, shall keep this Sutra.
40. He shall be the eye of the world, including gods and men, who shall speak this Sutra after the extinction of the Chief of men.
41. He is to be venerated by all beings, the wise man who in the last times shall preach this Sutra were it but a single moment.

Thereupon the Lord addressed the whole company of Bodhisattvas and the world, including gods and I demons, and said: Of yore, monks, in times past I have, unwearied and without repose, sought after the Sutra of the Lotus of the True Law, during immense, immeasurable Aeons; many Aeons before have been a king, during many thousands of Aeons. Having once taken the strong resolution to arrive at supreme, perfect enlightenment, my mind did not swerve from its aim. I exerted myself to fulfil the six Perfections (Paramitas), bestowing immense aims: gold, money, gems, pearls, lapis lazuli, conch-shells, stones, coral, gold and silver, emerald, Musaragalva, red pearls; villages, towns, boroughs, provinces, kingdoms, royal capitals; wives, sons, daughters, slaves, male and female; elephants. horses, cars, up to the sacrifice of life and body, of limbs and members, hands, feet, head. And never did the thought of self-complacency rise in me. In those days the life of men lasted long, so that for a time of many hundred thousand years I was exercising the rule of a King of the Law for the sake of duty, not for the sake of enjoyment. After installing in government the eldest prince royal, I went in quest of the best law in the four quarters, and had promulgated with sound of bell the following proclamation: He who procures for me the best law or points out what is useful, to him will I become a servant.

At that time there lived a Seer; he told me: Noble king, there is a Sutra, called the Lotus of the True Law, which is an exposition of the best law. If thou consent to become my servant, I will teach thee that law. And I, glad, content, exulting and ravished at the words I heard from the Seer, became his pupil, and said: I will do for thee the work of a servant. And so having agreed upon becoming the servant of the Seer, I performed the duties of a servitor, such as fetching grass, fuel, water, bulbs, roots, fruit, etc. I held also the office of a doorkeeper. When I had done such kind of work at daytime, I at night kept his feet while he was lying on his couch, and never did I feel fatigue of body or mind. In such occupations I passed a full millennium.

And for the fuller elucidation of this matter the Lord on that occasion uttered the following stanzas:

42. I have a remembrance of past ages when I was Dharmika, the King of the Law, and exercised the royal sway for duty's sake, not for love's sake, in the interest of the best law.
43. I let go out in all directions this proclamation: I will become a servant to him who shall explain Dharma. At that time there was a far-seeing Sage, a revealer of the Sutra called the True Law.
44. He said to me: If thou wish to know Dharma, become my servant; then I will explain it to thee. As I heard these words I rejoiced and carefully performed such work as a servant ought to do.
45. I never felt any bodily nor mental weariness since I had become a servant for the sake of the true law. I did my best for real truth's sake, not with a view to win honour or enjoy pleasure.
46. That king meanwhile, strenuously and without engaging in other pursuits, roamed in every direction during thousands of kotis of complete Aeons without being able to obtain the Sutra called Dharma.

Now, monks, what is your opinion? that it was another who at that time, at that juncture was the king? No, you must certainly not hold that view. For it was myself, who at that time, at that juncture was the king. What then, monks, is your opinion?

that it was another who at that time, at that juncture was the Seer? No, you must certainly not hold that view. For it was this Devadatta himself the monk, who at that time, at that juncture was the Seer. Indeed, monks, Devadatta was my good friend. By the aid of Devadatta have I accomplished the six perfect virtues, Paramitas. Noble kindness, noble compassion, noble sympathy, noble indifference, the thirty-two signs of a great man, the eighty lesser marks, the gold-coloured tinge, the ten powers, the fourfold absence of hesitation, the four articles of sociability, the eighteen uncommon properties, magical power, ability to save beings in all directions of space,—all this have I got after having come to Devadatta. I announce to you, monks, I declare to you: This Devadatta, the monk, shall in an age to come, after immense, innumerable Aeons, become a Tathagata named Devaraja (i.e. King of the gods), an Arhat, etc., in the world Devasopana (i.e. Stairs of the gods). The lifetime of that Tathagata Devaraja, monks, shall measure twenty intermediate kalpas. He shall preach the law in extension, and beings equal to the sands of the river Ganges shall through him forsake all evils and realise Arhatship. Several beings shall also elevate their minds to Pratyeka-buddhaship, whereas beings equal to the sands of the river Ganges shall elevate their minds to supreme, perfect enlightenment, and become endowed with unflinching patience. Further, monks, after the complete extinction of the Tathagata Devaraja, his true law shall stay twenty intermediate kalpas. His body shall not be seen divided into different parts and relics; it shall remain as one mass within a Stupa of seven precious substances, which Stupa is to be sixty hundred yojanas in height and forty yojanas in extension. All, gods and men, shall do worship to it with flowers, incense, perfumed garlands, unguents, powder, clothes, umbrellas, banners, flags, and celebrate it with stanzas and songs. Those who shall turn round that Stupa from left to right or humbly salute it, shall some of them realise Arhatship, others attain Pratyeka-buddhaship; others, gods and men, in immense number, shall raise their minds to supreme, perfect enlightenment, never to return.

Thereafter the Lord again addressed the assembly of monks: Whosoever in future, monks, be he a young man or a young lady of good family, shall hear this chapter of the Sutra of the Lotus of the True Law, and by doing so be relieved from doubt, become pure-minded, and put reliance on it, to such a one the door of the three states of misfortune shall be shut: he shall not fall so low as to be born in hell, among beasts, or in Yama's kingdom. When born in the Buddha-fields in the ten points of space he shall at each repeated birth hear this very Sutra, and when born amongst gods or men he shall attain an eminent rank. And in the Buddha-field where he is to be born he shall appear by metamorphosis on a lotus of seven precious substances, face to face with the Tathagata.

At that moment a Bodhisattva of the name of Prajnakuta, having come from beneath the Buddha-field of the Tathagata Prabhutaratna, said to the Tathagata Prabhutaratna: Lord, let us resort to our own Buddha-field. But the Lord Sakyamuni, the Tathigata, said to the Bodhisattva Prajnakuta: Wait a while, young man of good family, first have a discussion with my Bodhisattva Manjusri, the prince royal, to settle some point of the law. And at the same moment, lo, Manjusri, the prince royal, rose seated on a centifolious lotus that was large as a carriage yoked with four horses, surrounded and attended by many Bodhisattvas, from the bosom of the sea, from the abode of the Naga-king Sagara (i.e. Ocean). Rising high into the sky he went through the air to the Gridhrakuta mountain to the presence of the Lord. There Manjusri, the prince royal, alighted from his lotus, reverentially saluted the feet of the Lord Sakyamuni and Prabhutaratna, the Tathagata, went up to the Bodhisattva Prajnakuta and, after making the usual complimentary questions as to his health and welfare, seated himself at some distance.

The Bodhisattva Prajnakuta then addressed to Manjusri, the prince royal, the following question: Manjusri, how many beings hast thou educated during thy stay in the sea? Manjusri answered: Many, innumerable, incalculable beings have I educated, so innumerable that words cannot express it, nor thought conceive it. Wait a while, young man of good family, thou shalt presently see a token. No sooner had Manjusri, the prince royal, spoken these words than instantaneously many thousands of lotuses rose from the bosom of the sea up to the sky, and on those lotuses were seated many thousands of Bodhisattvas, who flocked through the air to the Gridhrakuta mountain, where they stayed, appearing as meteors. All of them had been educated by Manjusri, the prince royal, to supreme, perfect enlightenment. The Bodhisattvas amongst them who had formerly striven after the great vehicle extolled the virtues of the great vehicle and the six perfect virtues, Paramitas. Such as had been disciples extolled the vehicle of disciples. But all acknowledged the voidness of all laws or things, as well as the virtues of the great vehicle. Manjusri, the prince royal, said to the Bodhisattva Prajnakuta: Young man of good family, while I was staying in the bosom of the great ocean I have by all means educated creatures, and here thou seest the result. Whereupon the Bodhisattva Prjnakuta questioned Manjusri, the prince royal, in chanting the following stanzas:

47. O thou blessed one, who from thy wisdom art called the Sage, by whose power is it that thou to-day, or now, hast educated those innumerable beings? Tell it me upon my question, O thou god amongst men.
48. What law hast thou preached, or what Sutra, in showing the path of enlightenment, so that those who are there with you have conceived the idea of enlightenment? that, once having gained a safe ford, they have been decisively established in omniscience?

Manjusri answered: In the bosom of the sea I have expounded the Lotus of the True Law and no other Sutra. Prajnukuta said: That Sutra is profound, subtle, difficult to seize; no other Sutra equals it. Is there any creature able to understand this jewel of a Sutra or to arrive at supreme, perfect enlightenment? Manjusri replied: There is, young man of good family, the daughter of Sagara, the Naga-king, eight years old, very intelligent, of keen faculties, endowed with prudence in acts of body, speech, and mind, who has caught and kept all the teachings, in substance and form, of the Tathagatas, who has acquired in one moment a thousand meditations and proofs of the essence of all laws. She does not swerve from the idea of enlightenment, has great aspirations, applies to other beings the same measure as to herself; she is apt to display all virtues and is never deficient in them. With a bland smile on the face and in the bloom of an extremely handsome appearance she speaks words of kindliness and compassion. She is fit to arrive at supreme, perfect enlightenment.

The Bodhisattva Prajnakuta said: I have seen how the Lord Sakyamuni, the Tathagata, when he was striving after enlightenment, in the state of a Bodhisattva, performed innumerable good works, and during many Aeons never slackened in his arduous task. In the whole universe there is not a single spot so small as a mustard-seed where he has not surrendered his body for the sake of creatures. Afterwards he arrived at enlightenment. Who then would believe that she should have been able to arrive at supreme, perfect knowledge in one moment?

At that very moment appeared the daughter of Sagara, the Naga-king, standing before their face. After reverentially saluting the feet of the Lord she stationed herself at some distance and uttered on that occasion the following stanzas:

49. Spotless, bright, and of unfathomable light is that ethereal body, adorned with the thirty-two characteristic signs, pervading space in all directions.
50. He is possessed of the secondary marks and praised by every being, and accessible to all, like an open market-place.
51. I have obtained enlightenment according to my wish; the Tathagata can bear witness to it; I will extensively reveal the law that releases from sufferance.

Then the venerable Sariputra said to that daughter of Sagara, the Naga-king: Thou hast conceived the idea of enlightenment, young lady of good family, without sliding back, and art gifted with immense wisdom, but supreme, perfect enlightenment is not easily won. It may happen, sister, that a woman displays an unflagging energy, performs good works for many thousands of Aeons, and fulfils the six perfect virtues, Paramitas, but as yet there is no example of her having reached Buddhaship, and that because a woman cannot occupy the five ranks: 1. the rank of Brahma; 2. the rank of Indra; 3. the rank of a chief guardian of the four quarters; 4. the rank of Chakravartin; 5. the rank of a Bodhisattva incapable of sliding back.

Now the daughter of Sagara, the Naga-king, had at the time a gem which in value outweighed the whole universe. That gem the daughter of Sagara, the Naga-king, presented to the Lord, and the Lord graciously accepted it. Then the daughter of Sagara, the Naga-king, said to the Bodhisattva Prajnakuta and the senior priest Sariputra: Has the Lord readily accepted the gem I presented him or has he not? The senior priest answered: As soon as it was presented by thee, so soon it was accepted by the Lord. The daughter of Sagara, the Naga-king, replied: If I were endowed with magic power, brother Sariputra, I should sooner have arrived at supreme, perfect enlightenment, and there would have been none to receive this gem.

At the same instant, before the sight of the whole world and of the senior priest Sariputra, the female sex of the daughter of Sagara, the Naga-king, disappeared; the male sex appeared and she manifested herself as a Bodhisattva, who immediately went to the South to sit down at the foot of a tree made of seven precious substances, in the world Vimala, spotless, where he showed himself enlightened and preaching the law, while filling all directions of space with the radiance of the thirty-two characteristic signs and all secondary marks. All beings in the Saha-world beheld that Lord while he received the homage of all gods, Nagas, goblins, Gandharvas, demons, Garudas, Kinnaras, great serpents, men, and beings not human, and was engaged in preaching the law. And the beings who heard the preaching of that Tathagata became incapable of sliding back in supreme, perfect enlightenment. And that world Vimala and this Saha-world shook in six different ways. Three thousand living beings from the congregational circle of the Lord Sakyamuni gained the acquiescence in the eternal law, whereas three hundred thousand beings obtained the prediction of their future destiny to supreme, perfect enlightenment.

Then the Bodhisattva Prajnakuta and the senior priest Sariputra were silent.

◆ ◆ ◆ ◆ ◆

12

PREDICTION

Prediction to Gautami, Yasodhara and the nuns with them; promise that the disciples and Bodhisattvas will take up the task of preaching after his Nirvana.

Thereafter the Bodhisattva Bhaishjyaraja and the Bodhisattva Mahapratibhana, with a retinue of twenty hundred thousand Bodhisattvas, spoke before the face of the Lord the following words: Let the Lord be at ease in this respect; we will after the extinction of the Tathagata expound this Paryaya to all creatures, though we are aware, O Lord, that at that period there shall be malign beings, having few roots of goodness, conceited, fond of gain and honour, rooted in unholiness, difficult to tame, deprived of good will, and full of unwillingness. Nevertheless, O Lord, we will at that period read, keep, preach, write, honour, respect, venerate, worship this Sutra; with sacrifice of body and life, O Lord, we will divulge this Sutra. Let the Lord be at ease.

Thereupon five hundred monks of the assembly, both such as were under training and such as were not, said to the Lord: We also, O Lord, will exert ourselves to divulge this Dharmaparyaya, though in other worlds. Then all the disciples of the Lord, both such as were under training and such as were not, who had received from the Lord the prediction as to their future supreme enlightenment, all the eight thousand monks raised their joined hands towards the Lord and said: Let the Lord be at ease. We also will divulge this Dharmaparyaya, after the complete extinction of the Lord, in my last days, the last period, though in other worlds. For in this Saha-world, O Lord, the creatures are conceited, possessed of few roots of goodness. always vicious in their thoughts, wicked, and naturally perverse.

Then the noble matron Gautami, the sister of the Lord's mother, along with six hundred nuns, some of them being under training, some being not, rose from her seat, raised the joined hands towards the Lord and remained gazing up to him. Then the Lord addressed the noble matron Gautami: Why dost thou stand so dejected, gazing up to the Tathagata? She replied: I have not been mentioned by the Tathagata, nor have I received from him a prediction of my destiny to supreme, perfect enlightenment. He said: But Gautami, thou hast received a prediction with the prediction regarding the whole assembly. Indeed, Gautami, thou shalt from henceforward, before the face of thirty-eight hundred thousand myriads of kotis of Buddhas be a Bodhisattva and preacher of the law. These six thousand nuns also, partly perfected in discipline, partly not, shall along with others become Bodhisattvas and preachers of the law before the face of the Tathagatas. Afterwards, when thou shalt have completed the course of a Bodhisattva, thou shalt become, under the name of Sarvasattva-priyadarsana, lovely to see for all beings, a Tathagata, an Arhat, etc., endowed with science and conduct, etc., etc. And that Tathagata Sarvasattva-priyadarsana, Gautami, shall give a prediction by regular succession to those six thousand Bodhisattvas concerning their destiny to supreme, perfect enlightenment.

Then the nun Yasodhara, the mother of Rahula, thought thus: The Lord has not mentioned my name. And the Lord comprehending in his own mind what was going on in the mind of the nun Yasodhara said to her: I announce to thee, Yasodhara, I declare to thee: Thou also shalt before the face of ten thousand kotis of Buddhas become a Bodhisattva and preacher of the law, and after regularly completing the course of a Bodhisattva thou shalt become a Tathagata, named Rasmisatasahasra-paripurnadhvaja, an Arhat, etc., endowed with science and conduct, etc., etc., in the world Bhadra; and the lifetime of that Lord Rasmisatasahasra-paripurnadhvaja shall be unlimited.

When the noble matron Gautami, the nun, with her suite of six thousand nuns, and Yasodhara, the nun, with her suite of four thousand nuns, heard from the Lord their future destiny to supreme, perfect enlightenment, they uttered, in wonder and amazement, this stanza:

1. O Lord, thou art the trainer, thou art the leader; thou art the master of the world, including the gods; thou art the giver of comfort, thou who art worshipped by men and gods. Now, indeed, we feel satisfied.

After uttering this stanza the nuns said to the Lord: We also, O Lord, will exert ourselves to divulge this Dharmaparyaya in the last days, though in other worlds.

Thereafter the Lord looked towards the eighty hundred thousand Bodhisattvas who were gifted with magical spells and capable of moving forward the wheel that never rolls back. No sooner were those Bodhisattvas regarded by the Lord than they rose from their seats, raised their joined hands towards the Lord and reflected thus: The Lord invites us to make known the Dharmaparyaya. Agitated by that thought they asked one another: What shall we do, young men of good family, in order that this Dharmaparyaya may in future be made known as the Lord invites us to do? Thereupon those young men of good family, in consequence of their reverence for the Lord and their own pious vow in their previous course, raised a lion's roar before the Lord: We, O Lord, will in future, after the complete extinction of the Lord, go in all directions in order that creatures shall write, keep, meditate, divulge this Dharmaparyaya, by no other's power but the Lord's. And the Lord, staying in another world, shall protect, defend, and guard us.

Then the Bodhisattvas unanimously in a chorus addressed the Lord with the following stanzas:

2. Be at ease, O Lord. After thy complete extinction, in the horrible last period of the world, we will proclaim this sublime Sutra.
3. We will suffer, patiently endure, O Lord, the injuries, threats, blows and threats with sticks at the hands of foolish men.
4. At that dreadful last epoch men will be malign, crooked, wicked, dull, conceited, fancying to have come to the limit when they have not.

5. We do not care but to live in the wilderness and wear a patched cloth; we lead a frugal life;' so will they speak to the ignorant.
6. And persons greedily attached to enjoyments will preach the law to laymen and be honoured as if they possessed the six transcendent qualities.
7. Cruel-minded and wicked men, only occupied with household cares, will enter our retreat in the forest and become our calumniators.
8. The Tirthikas, themselves bent on profit and honour, will say of us that we are so, and—shame on such monks!—they will preach their own fictions.
9. Prompted by greed of profit and honour they will compose Sutras of their own invention and then, in the midst of the assembly, accuse us of plagiarism.
10. To kings, princes, king's peers, as well as to Brahmins and Commoners, and to monks of other confessions,
11. They will speak evil of us and propagate the Tirtha-doctrine. We will endure all that out of reverence for the great Seers.
12. And those fools who will not listen to us, shall sooner or later become enlightened, and therefore will we forbear to the last.
13. In that dreadful, most terrible period of frightful general revolution will many fiendish monks stand up as our revilers.
14. Out of respect for the Chief of the world we will bear it, however difficult it be; girded with the girdle of forbearance will I proclaim this Sutra.
15. I do not care for my body or life, O Lord, but as keepers of thine entrusted deposit we care for enlightenment.
16. The Lord himself knows that in the last period there are to be wicked monks who do not understand mysterious speech.
17. One will have to bear frowning looks, repeated disavowal or concealment: expulsion from the monasteries, many and manifold abuses.

18. Yet mindful of the command of the Lord of the world we will in the last period undauntedly proclaim this Sutra in the midst of the congregation.
19. We will visit towns and villages everywhere, and transmit to those who care for it thine entrusted deposit, O Lord.
20. O Chief of the world, we will deliver thy message; be at ease then, tranquil and quiet, great Seer.
21. Light of the world, thou knowest the disposition of all who have flocked hither from every direction, and thou knowest that we speak a word of truth.

◆ ◆ ◆ ◆ ◆

13

A BODHISATTVA

Vocation of the minister of religion, and practical rules for their conduct in society. A parable that the Buddha will reward those who struggle for his sake.

Manjusri, the prince royal, said to the Lord: It is difficult, Lord, most difficult, what these Bodhisattvas Mahasattvas will attempt out of reverence for the Lord. How are these Bodhisattvas Mahasattvas to promulgate this Dharmaparyaya at the end of time, at the last period? Whereupon the Lord answered Manjusri, the prince royal: A Bodhisattva Mahasattva, Manjusri, he who is to promulgate this Dharmaparyaya at the end of time, at the last period, must be firm in four things. In which things? The Bodhisattva Mahasattva, Manjusri, must be firm in his conduct and proper sphere if he wishes to teach this Dharmaparyaya. And how, Manjusri, is a Bodhisattva Mahasattva firm in his conduct and proper sphere? When the Bodhisattva Mahasattva, Manjusrt, is patient, meek, has reached the stage of meekness; when he is not rash, nor envious; when, moreover, Manjusri, he clings to no law whatever and sees the real Character of the laws, or things; when he is refraining, from investigating and discussing these laws, Manjusri; that is called the conduct of a Bodhisattva Mahasattva. And what is the proper sphere of a Bodhisattva Mahasattva, Manjusri? When the Bodhisattva Mahasattva, Manjusri does not serve, not court, not wait upon kings; does not serve, not court, not wait upon princes; when he does not approach them; when he does not serve, not court, not wait upon persons of another sect, Charakas, Parivrajakas, Ajivakas, Nirgranthas, nor persons passionately fond of fine literature;

when he does not serve, not court, not wait upon adepts at worldly spells, and votaries of a worldly philosophy, nor keep any intercourse with them; when he does not go to see Chandalas, jugglers, vendors of pork, poulterers, deer-hunters, butchers, actors and dancers, wrestlers, nor resort to places whither others flock for amusement and sport; when he keeps no intercourse with them unless from time to time to preach the law to them when they come to him, and that freely; when he does not serve, not court, not wait upon monks, nuns, lay devotees, male and female, who are adherents of the vehicle of disciples, nor keep intercourse with them; when he does not come in contact with them at the place of promenade or in the monastery, unless from time to time to preach the law to them when they come to him, and even that freely. This, Manjusri, is the proper sphere of a Bodhisattva Mahasattva.

Again, Manjusri, the Bodhisattva Mahasattva does not take hold of some favourable opportunity or another to preach the law to females every now and then, nor is he desirous of repeatedly seeing females; nor does he think it proper to visit families and then too often address a girl, virgin, or young wife, nor does he greet them too fondly in return. He does not preach the law to a hermaphrodite, keeps no intercourse with such a person, nor greets too friendly in return. He does not enter a house alone in order to receive alms, unless having the Tathagata in his thoughts. And when he happens to preach the law to females, he does not do so by passionate attachment to the law, far less by passionate attachment to a woman. When he is preaching, he does not display his row of teeth, let alone a quick emotion on his physiognomy. He addresses no novice, male or female, no nun, no monk, no young boy, no young girl, nor enters upon a conversation with them; he shows no great readiness in answering their address, nor cares to give too frequent answers. This, Manjusri, is called the first proper sphere of a Bodhisattva Mahasattva.

Further, Manjusri, a Bodhisattva Mahasattva looks upon all laws, and things, as void; he sees them duly established, remaining unaltered, as they are in reality, not liable to be disturbed, not to be moved backward, unchangeable, existing in the highest sense of the word or in an absolute sense, having the nature of space, escaping explanation and expression by means of common speech, not born, composed and simple, aggregated and isolated, not expressible in words, independently established, manifesting themselves owing to a perversion of perception. In this way then, Manjusri, the Bodhisattva Mahasattva constantly views all laws, and if he abides in this course, he remains in his own sphere. This, Manjusri, is the second proper sphere of a Bodhisattva Mahasattva.

And in order to expound this matter in greater detail, the Lord uttered the following stanzas:

1. The Bodhisattva who, undaunted and unabashed, wishes to set forth this Sutra in the dreadful period hereafter,
2. Must keep to his course of duty and proper sphere; he must be retired and pure, constantly avoid intercourse with kings and princes.
3. Nor should he keep up intercourse with king's servants, nor with Chandalas, jugglers, and Tirthikas in general.
4. He ought not to court conceited men, but catechise such as keep to the religion. He must also avoid such monks as follow the precepts of the Arhat, and immoral men.
5. He must be constant in avoiding a nun who is fond of banter and chatter; he must also avoid notoriously loose female lay devotees.
6. He should shun any intercourse with such female lay devotees as seek their highest happiness in this transient world. This is called the proper conduct of a Bodhisattva.
7. But when one comes to him to question him about the law for the sake of superior enlightenment, he should, at any time, speak freely, always firm and undaunted.
8. He should have no contact with women and hermaphrodites; he should also shun the young wives and girls in families.
9. He must never address them to ask after their health. He must also avoid intercourse with vendors of pork and mutton.

10. With any persons who slay animals of various kind for the sake of profit, and with such as sell meat he should avoid having any intercourse.
11. He must shun the society of whore-mongers, players, musicians, wrestlers, and other people of that sort.
12. He should not frequent whores, nor other sensual persons; he must avoid any exchange of civility with them.
13. And when the sage has to preach for a woman, he should not enter into an apartment with her alone, nor stay to banter.
14. When he has often to enter a village in quest of food, he must have another monk with him or constantly think of the Buddha.
15. Herewith have I shown the first sphere of proper conduct. Wise are they who, keeping this Sutra in memory, live according to it.
16. And when one observes no law at all, low, superior or mean, composed or uncomposed, real or not real;
17. When the wise man does not remark, 'This is a woman,' nor marks, 'This is a man;' when in searching he finds no laws, or things, because they have never existed;
18. This is called the observance of the Bodhisattvas in general. Now listen to me when I set forth what should be their proper sphere.
19. All laws i.e. the laws, the things have been declared to be non-existing, not appearing, not produced, void, immovable, everlasting; this is called the proper sphere of the wise.
20. They have been divided into existing and non-existing, real and unreal, by those who had wrong notions; other laws also, of permanency, of being produced, of birth from something already produced, are wrongly assumed.
21. Let the Bodhisattva be concentrated in mind, attentive, ever firm as the peak of Mount Sumeru, and in such a state of mind look upon all laws, and things, as having the nature of space,
22. Permanently equal to space, without essence, immovable, without substantiality. These, indeed, are the laws, all and for ever. This is called the proper sphere of the wise.

23. The monk observing this rule of conduct given by me may, after my extinction, promulgate this Sutra in the world, and shall feel no depression.
24. Let the sage first, for some time, coerce his thoughts, exercise meditation with complete absorption, and correctly perform all that is required for attaining spiritual insight, and then, after rising from his pious meditation, preach with unquailing mind.
25. The kings of this earth and the princes who listen to, the law protect him. Others also, both laymen and Brahmins, will be found together in his congregation.

Further, Manjusri, the Bodhisattva Mahasattva who, after the complete extinction of the Tathagata at the end of time, the last period, the last five hundred years, when the true law is in a state of decay, is going to propound this Dharmaparyaya, must be in a peaceful state of mind and then preach the law, whether he knows it by heart or has it in a book. In his sermon he will not be too prone to carping at others, not blame other preaching friars, not speak scandal nor propagate scandal. He does not mention by name other monks, adherents of the vehicle of disciples, to propagate scandal. He cherishes even no hostile feelings against them, because he is in a peaceful state. All who come, one after the other, to hear the sermon he receives with benevolence, and preaches the law to them without invidiousness. He refrains from entering upon a dispute; but if he is asked a question, he does not answer in the way of those who follow the vehicle of disciples; on the contrary, he answers as if he had attained Buddha-knowledge.

And on that occasion the Lord uttered the following stanzas:

26. The wise man is always at ease, and in that state he preaches the law, seated on an elevated pulpit which has been prepared for him on a clean and pretty spot.
27. He puts on a clean, nice, red robe, dyed with good colours, and a black woollen garment and a long undergarment;
28. Having duly washed his feet and rubbed his head and face with smooth ointments, he ascends the pulpit, which is

provided with a footbank and covered with pieces of fine cloth of various sorts, and sits down.

29. When he is thus seated on the preacher's pulpit and all who have gathered round him are attentive, he proceeds to deliver many discourses, pleasing by variety, before monks and nuns,

30. Before male and female lay devotees, kings and princes. The wise man always takes care to deliver a sermon diversified in its contents and sweet, free from invidiousness.

31. If occasionally he is asked some question, even after he has commenced, he will explain the matter anew in regular order, and he will explain it in such a way that his hearers gain enlightenment.

32. The wise man is indefatigable; not even the thought of fatigue will rise in him; he knows no listlessness, and so displays to the assembly the strength of charity.

33. Day and night the wise man preaches this sublime law with myriads of kotis of illustrations; he edifies and satisfies his audience without ever requiring anything.

34. Solid food, soft food, nourishment and drink, cloth, couches, robes, medicaments for the sick, all this does not occupy his thoughts, nor does he want anything from the congregation.

35. On the contrary, the wise man is always thinking: How can I and these beings become Buddhas? I will preach this true law, upon which the happiness of all beings depends, for the benefit of the world.

36. The monk who, after my extinction, shall preach in this way, without envy, shall not meet with trouble, impediment, grief or despondency.

37. Nobody shall frighten him, beat or blame him; never shall he be driven away, because he is firm in the strength of forbearance.

38. The wise man who is peaceful, so disposed as I have just said, possesses hundreds of kotis of advantages, so many that one would not be able to enumerate them in hundreds of Aeons.

Again, Manjusri, the Bodhisattva Mahasattva who lives after the extinction of the Tathagata at the end of time when the true law is in decay, the Bodhisattva Mahasattva who keeps this Sutra is not envious, not false, not deceitful; he does not speak disparagingly of other adherents of the vehicle of Bodhisattvas, nor defame, nor humble them. He does not bring forward the shortcomings of other monks, nuns, male and female lay devotees, neither of the adherents of the vehicle of disciples nor of those of the vehicle of Pratyeka Buddhas. He does not say: You young men of good family, you are far off from supreme, perfect enlightenment; you give proof of not having arrived at it; you are too fickle in your doings and not capable of acquiring true knowledge. He does not in this way bring forward the shortcomings of any adherent of the vehicle of the Bodhisattvas. Nor does he show any delight in disputes about the law, or engage in disputes about the law, and he never abandons the strength of charity towards all beings. In respect to all Tathagatas he feels as if they were his fathers, and in respect to all Bodhisattvas as if they were his masters. And as to the Bodhisattvas Mahasattvas in all directions of space, he is assiduous in paying homage to them by good will and respect. When he preaches the law, he preaches no less and no more than the law, without partial predilection for any part of the law, and he does not show greater favour to one than to another, even from love of the law.

Such, Manjusri, is the third quality with which a Bodhisattva Mahasattva is endowed who is to expound this Dharmaparyaya after the extinction of the Tathagata at the end of time when the true law is in decay; who will live at ease and not be annoyed in the exposition of this Dharmaparyaya. And in the synod he will have allies, and he will find auditors at his sermons who will listen to this Dharmaparyaya, believe, accept, keep, read, penetrate, write it and cause it to be written, and who, after it has been written and a volume made of it, will honour, respect, esteem, and worship it.

This said the Lord, and thereafter he, the Sugata, the Master, added the following:

39. The wise man, the preacher, who wishes to expound this Sutra must absolutely renounce falsehood, pride, calumny, and envy.
40. He should never speak a disparaging word of anybody; never engage in a dispute on religious belief; never say to such as are guilty of shortcomings, you will not obtain superior knowledge.
41. He is always sincere, mild, forbearing; as a true son of Sugata he will repeatedly preach the law without any feeling of vexation.
42. 'The Bodhisattvas in all directions of space, who out of compassion for creatures are moving in the world, are my teachers;' thus thinking the wise man respects them as his masters.
43. Cherishing the memory of the Buddhas, the supreme amongst men, he will always feel towards them as if they were his fathers, and by forsaking all idea of pride he will escape hindrance.
44. The wise man who has heard this law, should be constant in observing it. If he earnestly strives after a peaceful life, kotis of beings will surely protect him.

Further, Manjusri, the Bodhisattva Mahasattva, living at the time of destruction of the true law after the extinction of the Tathagata, who is desirous of keeping this Dharmaparyaya, should live as far as possible away from laymen and friars, and lead a life of charity. He must feel affection for all beings who are striving for enlightenment and therefore make this reflection: To be sure, they are greatly perverted in mind, those beings who do not hear, nor perceive, nor understand the skilfulness and the mystery of the Tathagata, who do not inquire for it, nor believe in it, nor even are willing to believe in it. Of course, these beings do not penetrate, nor understand this Dharmaparyaya. Nevertheless will I, who have attained this supreme, perfect knowledge, powerfully bend to it the mind of everyone, whatever may be the position he occupies, and bring about that he accepts, understands, and arrives at full ripeness.

By possessing also this fourth quality, Manjusri, a Bodhisattva Mahasattva, who is to expound the law after the extinction of the Tathagata, will be unmolested, honoured, respected, esteemed, venerated by monks, nuns, and lay devotees, male and female, by kings, princes, ministers, king's officers, by citizens and country people, by Brahmins and laymen; the gods of the sky will, full of faith, follow his track to hear the law, and the angels will follow his track to protect him; whether he is in a village or in a monastery, they will approach him day and night to put questions about the law, and they will be satisfied, charmed with his explanation. For this Dharmaparyaya, Manjusri, has been blessed by all Buddhas. With the past, future, and present Tathagata, Manjusri, this Dharmaparyaya is for ever blessed. Precious in all worlds, Manjusri, is the sound, rumour, or mentioning of this Dharmaparyaya.

It is a case, Manjusri, similar to that of a king, a ruler of armies, who by force has conquered his own kingdom, whereupon other kings, his adversaries, wage war against him. That ruler of armies has soldiers of various description to fight with various enemies. As the king sees those soldiers fighting, he is delighted with their gallantry, enraptured, and in his delight and rapture he makes to his soldiers several donations, such as villages and village grounds, towns and grounds of a town; garments and headgear; hand-ornaments, necklaces, gold threads, earrings, strings of pearls, bullion, gold, gems, pearls, lapis lazuli, conch-shells, stones, corals; he, moreover, gives elephants, horses, cars, foot soldiers, male and female slaves, vehicles, and litters. But to none he makes a present of his crown jewel, because that jewel only fits on the head of a king. Were the king to give away that crown jewel, then that whole royal army, consisting of four divisions, would be astonished and amazed. In the same manner, Manjusri, the Tathagata, the Arhat, etc., exercises the reign of righteousness and of the law in the triple world which he has conquered by the power of his arm and the power of his virtue. His triple world is assailed by Mara, the Evil One. Then the Aryas, the soldiers of the Tathagata, fight with Mara. Then, Manjusri, the king of the law, the lord of the law, expounds to the Aryas, his soldiers, whom he sees fighting, hundred thousands of Sutras in order to encourage the four classes. He gives them the city of Nirvana, the great city of the law; he allures them with that city of Nirvana, but he does not preach to them such a Dharmaparyaya as this. Just as in that case, Manjusri, that king, ruler of armies, astonished at the great valour of his soldiers in battle gives them all his property, at last 'even his crown jewel, and just as that crown jewel has been kept by the king on his head to the last, so, Manjusri, the Tathagata, the Arhat, etc., who as the great king of the law in the triple world exercises his sway with justice, when he sees disciples and Bodhisattvas fighting against the Mara of fancies or the Mara of sinful inclinations, and when he sees that by fighting they have destroyed affection, hatred, and infatuation, overcome the triple world and conquered all Maras, is satisfied, and in his satisfaction he expounds to those noble (arya) soldiers this Dharmaparyaya which meets opposition in all the world, the unbelief of all the world, a Dharmaparyaya never before preached, never before explained. And the Tathagata bestows on all disciples the noble crown jewel, that most exalted crown jewel which brings omniscience to all. For this, Manjusri, is the supreme preaching of the Tathagatas; this is the last Dharmaparyaya of the Tathagatas; this is the most profound discourse on the law, a Dharmaparyaya meeting opposition in all the world. In the same manner, Manjusri, as that king of righteousness and ruler of armies took off the crown jewel which he had kept so long a time and gave it at last to the soldiers, so, Manjusri, the Tathagata now reveals this long-kept mystery of the law exceeding all others, the mystery which must be known by the Tathagatas.

And in order to elucidate this matter more in detail, the Lord on that occasion uttered the following stanzas:

45. Always displaying the strength of charity, always filled with compassion for all creatures, expounding this law, the Sugatas have approved this exalted Sutra.

46. The laymen, as well as the mendicant friars, and the Bodhisattvas who shall live at the end of time, must all show the strength of charity, lest those who hear the law reject it.

47. But I, when I shall have reached enlightenment and be established in Tathagataship, will initiate others, and after

having initiated disciples preach everywhere this superior enlightenment.

48. It is a case like that of a king, ruler of armies, who gives to his soldiers various things, gold, elephants, horses, cars, foot soldiers; he also gives towns and villages, in token of his contentment.
49. In his satisfaction he gives some hand-ornaments, silver and gold thread; pearls, gems, conch-shells, stones, coral; he also gives slaves of various description.
50. But when he is struck with the incomparable daring of one amongst the soldiers, he says: Thou hast admirably done this; and, taking off his crown makes him a present of the jewel.
51. Likewise do I, the Buddha, the king of the law, I who have the force of patience and a large treasure of wisdom, with justice govern the whole world, benign, compassionate, and pitiful.
52. And seeing how the creatures are in trouble, I pronounce thousands of kotis of Sutrantas, when I perceive the heroism of those living beings who by pure-mindedness overcome the sinful inclinations of the world.
53. And the king of the law, the great physician, who expounds hundreds of kotis of Paryayas, when he recognises that creatures are strong, shows them this Sutra, comparable to a crown jewel.
54. This is the last Sutra proclaimed in the world, the most eminent of all my Sutras, which I have always kept and never divulged. Now I am going to make it known; listen all.
55. There are four qualities to be acquired by those who at the period after my extinction desire supreme enlightenment and perform my charge. The qualities are such as follows.
56. The wise man knows no vexation, trouble, sickness; the colour of his skin is not blackish; nor does he dwell in a miserable town.

57. The great Sage has always a pleasant look, deserves to be honoured, as if he were the Tathagata himself, and little angels shall constantly be his attendants.
58. His body can never be hurt by weapons, poison, sticks, or clods, and the month of the man who utters a word of abuse against him shall be closed.
59. He is a friend to all creatures in the world. He goes all over the earth as a light, dissipating the gloom of many kotis of creatures, he who keeps this Sutra after my extinction.
60. In his sleep he sees visions in the shape of Buddha; he sees monks and nuns appearing on thrones and proclaiming the manysided law.
61. He sees in his dream gods and goblins, numerous as the sands of the Ganges, as self as demons and Nagas of many kinds, who lift their joined hands and to whom he expounds the eminent law.
62. He sees in his dream the Tathagata preaching the law to many kotis of beings with lovely voice, the Lord with golden colour.
63. And he stands there with joined hands glorifying the Seer, the highest of men, whilst the Jina, the great physician, is expounding the law to the four classes.
64. And he, glad to have heard the law, joyfully pays his worship, and after having soon reached the knowledge which never slides back, he obtains, in dream, magical spells.
65. And the Lord of the world, perceiving his good intention, announces to him his destiny of becoming a leader amongst men: Young man of good family says he, thou shalt here reach in future supreme, holy knowledge.
66. Thou shalt have a large field and four classes of hearers, even as myself, that respectfully and with joined hands shall hear from thee the vast and faultless law.
67. Again he sees his own person occupied with meditating on the law in mountain caverns; and by meditating he attains the very nature of the law and, on obtaining complete absorption, sees the Jina.

68. And after seeing in his dream the gold-coloured one, him who displays a hundred hallowed signs, he hears the law, whereafter he preaches it in the assembly. Such is his dream.
69. And in his dream he also forsakes his whole realm, harem, and numerous kinsfolk; renouncing all pleasures he leaves home to become an ascetic, and betakes himself to the place of the terrace of enlightenment.
70. There, seated upon a throne at the foot of a tree to seek enlightenment, he will, after the lapse of seven days, arrive at the knowledge of the Tathagatas.
71. On having reached enlightenment he will rise up from that place to move forward the faultless wheel and preach the law during an inconceivable number of thousands of kotis of Aeons.
72. After having revealed perfect enlightenment and led many kotis of beings to perfect rest, he himself will be extinguished like a lamp when the oil is exhausted. So is that vision.
73. Endless, Manjughosha, are the advantages which constantly are his who at the end of time shall expound this Sutra of superior enlightenment that I have perfectly explained.

◆ ◆ ◆ ◆ ◆

14

INNUMERABLE BODHISATTVAS

Splendid phantasmagory of innumerable Bodhisattvas evoked by the power of the Lord.

Out of the multitude of Bodhisattvas Mahasattvas who had flocked from other worlds, Bodhisattvas eight times equal to the sands of the river Ganges then rose from the assembled circle. Their joined hands stretched out towards the Lord to pay him homage, they said to him: If the Lord will allow us, we also would, after the extinction of the Lord, reveal this Dharmaparyaya in this Saha-world; we would read, write, worship it, and wholly devote ourselves to that law. Therefore, O Lord, deign to grant to us also this Dharmaparyaya. And the Lord answered: Nay, young men of good family, why should you occupy yourselves with this task? I have here in this Saha-world thousands of Bodhisattvas equal to the sands of sixty Ganges rivers, forming the train of one Bodhisattva; and of such Bodhisattvas there is a number equal to the sands of sixty Ganges rivers, each of these Bodhisattvas having an equal number in their train, who at the end of time, at the last period after my extinction, shall keep, read, proclaim this Dharmaparyaya.

No sooner had the Lord uttered these words than the Saha-world burst open on every side, and from within the clefts arose many hundred thousand myriads of kotis of Bodhisattvas with gold-coloured bodies and the thirty-two characteristic signs of a great man, who had been staying in the element of ether underneath this great earth, close to this Saha-world. These then on hearing the word of the Lord came up from below the earth. Each of these Bodhisattvas had a train of thousands of Bodhisattvas similar to the sands of sixty Ganges rivers; each had a troop, a great troop, as teacher of a troop. Of such Bodhisattvas Mahasattvas having a troop, a great troop, as teachers of a troop, there were hundred thousands of myriads of kotis equal to the sands of sixty Ganges rivers, who emerged from the gaps of the earth in this Saha-world. Much more there were to be found of Bodhisattvas Mahasattvas having a train of Bodhisattvas similar to the sands of fifty Ganges rivers; much more there were to be found of Bodhisattvas Mahasattvas having a train of Bodhisattvas similar to the sands of forty Ganges rivers; of 30^3, 20, 10, 5, 4, 3, 2, 1 Ganges river; of 1/2′, 1/4′, 1/6′, 1/10′, 1/20′, 1/50′, 1/100′, 1/1000′, 1/100,000′, 1/10,000,000′, 1/100 × 10,000,000′, 1/1000 × 10,000,000′, 1/100×100 ×10,000,000′, 1/100×1000×10,000×10,000,000′, part of the river Ganges. Much more there were to be found of Bodhisattvas Mahasattvas having a train of many hundred thousand myriads of kotis of Bodhisattvas; of one kotis; of one hundred thousand; of one thousand; of 500; of 400; of 300; of 200; of 100; of 50; of 40; of 30; of 20; of 10; of 5, 4, 3, 2. Much more there were to be found of Bodhisattvas Mahasattvas having one follower. Much more there were to be found of Bodhisattvas Mahasattvas standing isolated. They cannot be numbered, counted, calculated, compared, known by occult science, the Bodhisattvas Mahasattvas who emerged from the gaps of the earth to appear in this Saha-world. And after they had successively emerged they went up to the Stupa of precious substances which stood in the sky, where the Lord Prabhutaratna, the extinct Tathagata, was seated along with the Lord Sakyamuni on the throne. Whereafter they saluted the feet of both the Tathagatas, etc., as well as the images of Tathagatas produced by the Lord Sakyamuni from his own body, who all together were seated on thrones at the foot of various jewel trees on every side in all directions, in different worlds. After these Bodhisattvas had many hundred thousand times saluted, and thereon circumambulated the the Tathagatas, etc., from left to right, and celebrated them with various Bodhisattva hymns, they went and kept themselves at a little distance, the joined hands stretched out to honour the Lord Sakyamuni, the Tathagata, etc., and the Lord Prabhutaratna, the Tathagata, etc.

And while those Bodhisattvas Mahasattvas who had emerged from the gaps of the earth were saluting and celebrating the Tathagatas by various Bodhisattva hymns, fifty intermediate kalpas in full rolled away, during which fifty intermediate kalpas the Lord Sakyamuni remained silent, and likewise the four classes of the audience. Then the Lord produced such an effect of magical power that the four classes fancied that it had been no more than one afternoon and they saw this Saha-world assume the appearance of hundred thousands of worlds replete with Bodhisattvas. The four Bodhisattvas Mahasattvas who were the chiefest of that great host of Bodhisattvas, the Bodhisattva Mahasattva called Visisthatacharitra (i.e., of eminent conduct), the Bodhisattva Mahasattva called Anantacharitra (i.e., of endless conduct), the Bodhisattva Mahasattva called Visuddhacharitra (i.e., of correct conduct), and the Bodhisattva Mahasattva called Supratishthitacharitra (i.e., of very steady conduct), these four Bodhisattvas Mahasattvas standing at the head of the great host, the great multitude of Bodhisattvas stretched out the joined hands towards the Lord and addressed him thus: Is the Lord in good health? Does he enjoy well-being and good ease? Are the creatures decorous, docile, obedient, correctly performing their task, so that they give no trouble to the Lord?

And those four Bodhisattvas Mahasattvas addressed the Lord with the two following stanzas:

1. Does the Lord of the world, the illuminator, feel at ease? Dost thou feel free from bodily disease, O Perfect One?
2. The creatures, we hope, will be decorous, docile, performing the orders of the Lord of the world, so as to give no trouble.

And the Lord answered the four Bodhisattvas Mahasattvas who were at the head of that great host, that great multitude of Bodhisattvas: So it is, young men of good family, I am in good health, well-being, and at ease. And these creatures of mine are decorous, docile, obedient, well performing what is ordered; they give no trouble when I correct them; and that, young men of good family, because these creatures, owing to their being already prepared under the ancient, perfectly enlightened Buddhas, have but to see and hear me to put trust in me, to understand and fathom the Buddha-knowledge. And those who fulfilled their duties in the stage of disciples have now been introduced by me into Buddha-knowledge and well instructed in the highest truth.

And at that time the Bodhisattvas Mahasattvas uttered the following stanzas:

3. Excellent, excellent, O great Hero! we are happy to hear that those creatures are decorous, docile, well performing their duty;
4. And that they listen to thy profound knowledge, O Leader, and that after listening to it they have put trust in it and understand it.

This said, the Lord declared his approval to the four Bodhisattvas Mahasattvas who were at the head of that great host, that great multitude of Bodhisattvas Mahasattvas, saying: Well done, young men of good family, well done, that you so congratulate the Tathagata.

And at that moment the following thought arose in the mind of the Bodhisattva Mahasattva Maitreya and the eight hundred thousand myriads of kotis of Bodhisattvas similar to the sands of the river Ganges: We never yet saw so great a host, so great a multitude of Bodhisattvas; we never yet heard of such a multitude, that after issuing from the gaps of the earth has stood in the presence of the Lord to honour, respect, venerate, worship him and greet him with joyful shouts. Whence have these Bodhisattvas Mahasattvas flocked hither?

Then the Bodhisattva Mahasattva Maitreya, feeling within himself doubt and perplexity, and inferring from his own thoughts those of the eight hundred thousand myriads of kotis of Bodhisattvas similar to the sands of the river Ganges, stretched out his joined hands towards the Lord and questioned him about the matter by uttering the following stanzas:

5. Here are many thousand myriads of kotis of Bodhisattvas, numberless, whom we never saw before; tell us, O supreme of men!

6. Whence and how do these mighty persons come? Whence have they come here under the form of great bodies?
7. All are great Seers, wise and strong in memory, whose outward appearance is lovely to see; whence have they come?
8. And each of those Bodhisattvas, O Lord of the world, has an immense train, like the sands of the Ganges.
9. The train of each glorious Bodhisattva is equal to the sands of sixty Ganges in full. All are striving after enlightenment.
10. Of such heroes and mighty possessors of a troop the followers are equal to the sands of sixty Ganges.
11. There are others, still more numerous, with an unlimited train, like the sands of fifty, forty, and thirty Ganges;

12.13. Who have a train equal to the sands of twenty Ganges. Still more numerous are the mighty sons of Buddha, who have each a train equal to the sands of ten, of five Ganges. Whence, O Leader, has such an assembly flocked hither?

14. There are others who have each a train of pupils and companions equal to the sands of four, three, or two Ganges.
15. There are others more numerous yet; it would be impossible to calculate their number in thousands of kotis of Aeons.
16. Equal to a half Ganges, one third, one tenth, one twentieth, is the train of those heroes, those mighty Bodhisattvas.
17. There are yet others who are incalculable; it would be impossible to count them even in hundreds of kotis of Aeons.
18. Many more yet there are, with endless trains; they have in their attendance kotis, and kotis and again kotis, and also half kotis.
19. Other great Seers again, beyond computation, very wise Bodhisattvas are seen in a respectful posture.
20. They have a thousand, a hundred, or fifty attendants; in hundreds of kotis of Aeons one would not be able to count them.
21. The suite of some of these heroes consists of twenty, of ten, five, four, three, or two; those are countless.

22. As to those who are walking alone and come to their rest alone, they have now flocked hither in such numbers as to be beyond computation.
23. Even if one with a magic wand in his hand would try for a number of Aeons equal to the sands of the Ganges to count them, he would not reach the term.
24. Where do all those noble, energetic heroes, those mighty Bodhisattvas, come from?
25. Who has taught them the law or duty and by whom have they been destined to enlightenment? Whose command do they accept? Whose command do they keep?
26. Bursting forth at all points of the horizon through the whole extent of the earth they emerge, those great Sages endowed with magical faculty and wisdom.
27. This world on every side is being perforated, O Seer, by the wise Bodhisattvas, who at this time are emerging.
28. Never before have we seen anything like this. Tell us the name of this world, O Leader.
29. We have repeatedly roamed in all directions of space, but never saw these Bodhisattvas.
30. We never saw a single infant of thine, and now, on a sudden, these appear to us. Tell us their history, O Seer.
31. Hundreds, thousands, ten thousands of Bodhisattvas, all equally filled with curiosity, look up to the highest of men.
32. Explain to us, O incomparable, great hero, who knowest no bounds, where do these heroes, these wise Bodhisattvas, come from?

Meanwhile the Tathagatas, etc., who had flocked from hundred thousands of myriads of kotis of worlds, they, the creations of the Lord Sakyamuni, who were preaching the law to the beings in other worlds; who all around the Lord Sakyamuni, the Tathagata, etc., were seated with crossed legs on magnificent jewel thrones at the foot of jewel trees in every direction of space; as well as the satellites of those Tathagatas were struck with wonder and amazement at the sight of that great host, that great multitude of Bodhisattvas emerging from the gaps of the earth and established in the element of ether, and they the satellites asked each their own Tathagata: Where, O Lord, do so many Bodhisattvas Mahasattvas, so innumerable, so countless, come from? Whereupon those Tathagatas, etc., answered severally to their satellites: Wait awhile, young men of good family; this Bodhisattva Mahasattva here, called Maitreya, has just received from the Lord Sakyamuni a revelation about his destiny to supreme, perfect enlightenment. He has questioned the Lord Sakyamuni, the Tathagata, etc., about the matter, and the Lord Sakyamuni, the Tathagata, etc., is going to explain it; then you may hear.

Thereupon the Lord addressed the Bodhisattva Maitreya: Well done, Ajita, well done; it is a sublime subject, Ajita, about which thou questionest me. Then the Lord addressed the entire host of Bodhisattvas: Be attentive all, young men of good family; be well prepared and steady on your post, you and the entire host of Bodhisattvas; the Tathagata, the Arhat, etc., is now going to exhibit the sight of the knowledge of the Tathagata, young men of good family, the leadership of the Tathagata, the work of the Tathagata, the sport of the Tathagata, the might of the Tathagata, the energy of the Tathagata.

And on that occasion the Lord pronounced the following stanzas:

33. Be attentive all, young men of good family; I am to utter an infallible word; refrain from disputing about it, O sages: the science of the Tathagata is beyond reasoning.

34. Be all steady and thoughtful; continue attentive all. Today you will hear a law as yet unknown, the wonder of the Tathagatas.

35. Never have any doubt, ye sages, for I shall strengthen you, I am the Leader who speaketh infallible truth, and my knowledge is unlimited.

36. Profound are the laws known to the Sugata, above reasoning and beyond argumentation. These laws I am going to reveal; ye, hear which and how they are.

After uttering these stanzas the Lord addressed the Bodhisattva Mahasattva Maitreya: I announce to thee, Ajita, I declare to thee: These Bodhisattvas Mahasattvas, Ajita, so innumerable, incalculable, inconceivable, incomparable, uncountable, whom you never saw before, who just now have issued from the gaps of the earth, these Bodhisattvas Mahasattvas, Ajita, have I roused, excited, animated, fully developed to supreme, perfect enlightenment after my having arrived at supreme, perfect enlightenment in this world. I have, moreover, fully matured, established, confirmed, instructed, perfected these young men of good family in their Bodhisattva-ship. And these Bodhisattvas Mahasattvas, Ajita, occupy in this Saha-world the domain of the ether element below. Only thinking of the lesson they have to study, and devoted to thoroughly comprehend it, these young men of good family have no liking for social gatherings, nor for bustling crowds; they do not put off their tasks, and are strenuous. These young men of good family, Ajita, delight in seclusion, are fond of seclusion. These young men of good family do not dwell in the immediate vicinity of gods and men, they not being fond of bustling crowds. These young men of good family find their luxury in the pleasure of the law, and apply themselves to Buddha-knowledge.

And on that occasion the Lord uttered the following stanzas:

37. These Bodhisattvas, immense, inconceivable and beyond measure, endowed with magic power, wisdom, and learning, have progressed in knowledge, for many kotis of Aeons.
38. It is I who have brought them to maturity for enlightenment, and it is in my field that they have their abode; by me alone have they been brought to maturity; these Bodhisattvas are my sons.
39. All have devoted themselves to a hermit life and are assiduous in shunning places of bustle; they walk detached, these sons of mine, following my precepts in their lofty course.
40. They dwell in the domain of ether, in the lower portion of the field, those heroes who, unwearied, are striving day and night to attain superior knowledge.
41. All strenuous, of good memory, unshaken in the immense strength of their intelligence, those serene sages preach the law, all radiant, as being my sons.

42. Since the time when I reached this superior enlightenment, at the town of Gaya, at the foot of the tree, and put in motion the all-surpassing wheel of the law, I have brought to maturity all of them for superior enlightenment.
43. These words I here speak are faultless, really true; believe me, all of you who hear me: verily, I have reached superior enlightenment, and it is by me alone that all have been brought to maturity.

The Bodhisattva Mahasattva Maitreya and those numerous hundred thousands of myriads of kotis of Bodhisattvas were struck with wonder, amazement, and surprise, and thought: How is it possible that within so short a moment, within the lapse of so short a time so many Bodhisattvas, so countless, have been roused and made fully ripe to reach supreme, perfect enlightenment? Then the Bodhisattva Mahasattva Maitreya asked the Lord: How then, O Lord, has the Tathagata, after he left, when a prince royal, Kapilavastu, the town of the Sakyas, arrived at supreme, perfect enlightenment on the summit of the terrace of enlightenment, not far from the town of Gaya, somewhat more than forty years since, O Lord? How then has the Lord, the Tathagata, within so short a lapse of time, been able to perform the endless task of a Tathagata, to exercise the leadership of a Tathagata, the energy of a Tathagata? How has the Tathagata, within so short a time, been able to rouse and bring to maturity for supreme, perfect enlightenment this host of Bodhisattvas, this multitude of Bodhisattvas, a multitude so great that it would be impossible to count the whole of it, even if one were to continue counting for hundred thousands of myriads of kotis of Aeons? These Bodhisattvas, so innumerable, O Lord, so countless, having long followed a spiritual course of life and planted roots of goodness under many hundred thousands of Buddhas, have in the course of many hundred thousands of Aeons become finally ripe.

It is just as if some man, young and youthful, a young man with black hair and in the prime of youth, twenty-five years of age, would represent centenarians as his sons, and say: ' Here, young men of good family, you see my sons;' and if those centenarians would declare: 'This is the father who begot us.'

Now, Lord, the speech of that man would be incredible, hard to be believed by the public. It is the same case with the Tathagata, who but lately has arrived at supreme, perfect enlightenment, and with these Bodhisattvas Mahasattvas, so immense in number, who for many hundred thousand myriads of kotis of Aeons, having observed a spiritual course of life, have long since come to certainty in regard to Tathagata-knowledge; who are able to plunge in and again rise from the hundred thousand sorts of meditation; who are adepts at the preparatories to noble transcendent wisdom, have accomplished the preparatories to noble transcendent wisdom; who are clever on the Buddha-ground, able in the ecclesiastical Council and in Tathagata duties; who are the wonders and admiration of the world; who are possessed of great vigour, strength, and power. And the Lord says: From the very beginning have I roused, brought to maturity, fully developed them to be fit for this Bodhisattva position. It is I who have displayed this energy and vigour after arriving at supreme, perfect enlightenment. But, O Lord, how can we have faith in the words of the Tathagata, when he says: The Tathagata speaks infallible truth? The Tathagata must know that the Bodhisattvas who have newly entered the vehicle are apt to fall into doubt on this head; after the extinction of the Tathagata those who hear this Dharmaparyaya will not accept, not believe, not trust it. Hence, O Lord, they will design acts tending to the ruin of the law. Therefore, O Lord, deign to explain us this matter, that we may be free from perplexity, and that the Bodhisattvas who in future shall hear it, be they young men of good family or young ladies, may not fall into doubt.

On that occasion the Bodhisattva Mahasattva Maitreya addressed the Lord with the following stanzas:

44. When thou wert born in Kapilavastu, the home of the Sakyas, thou didst leave it and reach enlightenment at the town of Gaya. That is a short time ago, O Lord of the world.

45. And now thou hast so great a crowd of followers, these sages who for many kotis of Aeons have fulfilled their duties, stood firm in magic power, unshaken, well disciplined, accomplished in the might of wisdom;

46. These, who are untainted as the lotus is by water; who today have flocked hither after rending the earth, and are standing all with joined hands, respectful and strong in memory, the sons of the Master of the world.
47. How will these Bodhisattvas believe this great wonder? Expel all doubt, tell the cause, and show how the matter really is.
48. It is as if there were some man, a young man with black hair, twenty years old or somewhat more, who presented as his sons some centenarians,
49. And the latter, covered with wrinkles and grey-haired, declared the young man to be their father. But such a young man never having sons of such appearance, it would be difficult to believe, O Lord of the world, that they were sons to so young a man.
50. In the same manner, O Lord, we are unable to conceive how these numerous Bodhisattvas of good memory and excelling in wisdom, who have been well instructed during thousands of kotis of Aeons;
51. Who are firm, of keen intelligence, lovely and agreeable to sight, free from hesitation in the decisions on law, praised by the Leaders of the world;
52. Who in freedom live in the wood; who unattached in the element of ether constantly display their energy, who are the sons of Sugata striving after this Buddha-ground;
53. How will this be believed when the Leader of the world shall be completely extinct? After hearing it from the Lord's own mouth we shall never more feel any doubt.
54. May Bodhisattvas never come to grief by having doubt on this head. Grant us, O Lord, a truthful account how these Bodhisattvas have been brought to maturity by thee.

◆ ◆ ◆ ◆ ◆

15
THE IMMENSE LIVES OF THE TATHAGATAS

The Buddha explains the innumerability of the Bodhisattvas by revealing the immense duration spread over the past and the future.

Thereupon the Lord addressed the entire host of Bodhisattvas: Trust me, young men of good family, believe in the Tathagata speaking a veracious word. A second time the Lord addressed the Bodhisattvas: Trust me, young gentlemen of good family, believe in the Tathagata speaking a veracious word. A third and last time the Lord addressed the Bodhisattvas: Trust me, young men of good family, believe in the Tathagata speaking a veracious word. Then the entire host of Bodhisattvas with Maitreya, the Bodhisattva Mahasattva at their head, stretched out the joined hands and said to the Lord: Expound this matter, O Lord; expound it, O Sugata; we will believe in the word of the Tathagata. A second time the entire host etc. A third time the entire host, etc.

The Lord, considering that the Bodhisattvas repeated their prayer up to three times, addressed them thus: Listen then, young men of good family. The force of a strong resolve which assumed is such, young men of good family, that this world, including gods, men, and demons, acknowledges: Now has the Lord Sakyamuni, after going out from the home of the Sakyas, arrived at supreme, perfect enlightenment, on the summit of the terrace of enlightenment at the town of Gaya. But, young men of good family, the truth is that many hundred thousand myriads of kotis of Aeons ago I have arrived at supreme, perfect enlightenment. By way of example, young men of good family, let there be the atoms of earth of fifty hundred thousand myriads of kotis of worlds; let there exist some man who takes or of those atoms of dust and then goes in an eastern direction fifty hundred thousand myriads of kotis of worlds further on, there to deposit that atom of dust; let in this manner the man carry away from all those worlds the whole mass of earth, and in the same manner, and by the same act as supposed, deposit all those atoms in an eastern direction. Now, would you think, young men of good family, that anyone should be able to imagine, weigh, count, or determine the number of those worlds? The Lord having thus spoken, the Bodhisattva Mahasattva Maitreya and the entire host of Bodhisattvas replied: They are incalculable, O Lord, those worlds, countless, beyond the range of thought. Not even all the disciples and Pratyekabuddhas, O Lord, with their Arya-knowledge, will be able to imagine, weigh, count, or determine them. For us also, O Lord, who are Bodhisattvas standing on the place from whence there is no turning back, this point lies beyond the sphere of our comprehension; so innumerable, O Lord, are those worlds.

This said, the Lord spoke to those Bodhisattvas Mahasattvas as follows: I announce to you, young men of good family, I declare to you: However numerous be those worlds where that man deposits those atoms of dust and where he does not, there are not, young men of good family, in all those hundred thousands of myriads of kotis of worlds so many dust atoms as there are hundred thousands of myriads of kotis of Aeons since I have arrived at supreme, perfect enlightenment. From the moment, young men of good family, when I began preaching the law to creatures in this Saha-world and in hundred thousands of myriads of kotis of other worlds, and when the other Tathagatas, Arhats, etc., such as the Tathagata Dipankara and the rest whom I have mentioned in the lapse of time preached, from that moment have I, young men of good family, for the complete Nirvana of those Tathagatas, etc., created all that with the express view to skilfully preach the law. Again, young men of good family, the Tathagata, considering the different degrees of faculty and strength of succeeding generations, reveals at each generation his own name, reveals a state in which Nirvana has not yet been reached, and in different ways he satisfies the wants of different creatures through various Dharmaparyayas. This being the case, young men of good family, the Tathagata declares to the creatures, whose dispositions are so various and who possess so few roots of goodness, so many evil propensities: I am young of age, monks; having left my father's home, monks, I have lately arrived at supreme, perfect enlightenment.

When, however, the Tathagata, who so long ago arrived at perfect enlightenment, declares himself to have but lately arrived at perfect enlightenment, he does so in order to lead creatures to full ripeness and make them go in. Therefore have these Dharmaparyayas been revealed; and it is for the education of creatures, young men of good family, that the Tathagata has revealed all Dharmaparyayas. And, young men of good family, the word that the Tathagata delivers on behalf of the education of creatures, either under his own appearance or under another's, either on his own authority or under the mask of another, all that the Tathagata declares, all those Dharmaparyayas spoken by the Tathagata are true. There can be no question of untruth from the part of the Tathagata in this respect. For the Tathagata sees the triple world as it really is: it is not born, it dies not; it is not conceived, it springs not into existence; it moves not in a whirl, it becomes not extinct; it is not real, nor unreal; it is not existing, nor non-existing; it is not such, nor otherwise, nor false.

The Tathagata sees the triple world, not as the ignorant, common people, he seeing things always present to him; indeed, to the Tathagata, in his position, no laws are concealed. In that respect any word that the Tathagata speaks is true, not false. But in order to produce the roots of goodness in the creatures, who follow different pursuits and behave according to different notions, he reveals various Dharmaparyayas with various fundamental principles. The Tathagata then, young men of good family, does what he has to do. The Tathagata who so long ago was perfectly enlightened is unlimited in the duration of his life, he is everlasting. Without being extinct, the Tathagata makes a show of ex-tinction, on behalf of those who have to be educated. And even now, young gentlemen of good family, I have not accomplished my ancient Bodhisattva-course, and the measure of my lifetime is not full. Nay, young men of good family, I shall yet have twice as many hundred thousand myriads of kotis of Aeons before the measure of my lifetime be full.

I announce final extinction, young men of good family, though myself I do not become finally extinct. For in this way, young men of good family, I bring all creatures to maturity, lest creatures in whom goodness is not firmly rooted, who are unholy, miserable, eager of sensual pleasures, blind and obscured by the film of wrong views, should, by too often seeing me, take to thinking: The Tathagata is staying, and fancy that all is a child's play lest they by thinking 'we are near that Tathagata' should fail to exert themselves in order to escape the triple world and not conceive how precious the Tathagata is. Hence, young men of good family, the Tathagata skilfully utters these words: The apparition of the Tathagatas, monks, is precious and rarer or in the course of many hundred thousand myriads of kotis of Aeons creatures may happen to see a Tathagata or not to see him. Therefore and upon that ground, young men of good family, I say: The apparition of the Tathagatas, monks, is precious and rare.

By being more and more convinced of the apparition of the Tathagatas being precious 'or rare' they will feel surprised and sorry, and whilst not seeing the Tathagata they will get a longing to see him. The good roots developing from their earnest thought relating to the Tathagata will lastingly tend to their weal, benefit, and happiness; in consideration of which the Tathagata announces final extinction, though he himself does not become finally extinct, on behalf of the creatures who have to be educated. Such, young men of good family, is the Tathagata's manner of teaching; when the Tathagata speaks in this way, there is from his part no falsehood.

Let us suppose an analogous case, young men of good family. There is some physician, learned, intelligent, prudent, clever in allaying all sorts of diseases. That man has many sons, ten, twenty, thirty, forty, fifty, or a hundred. The physician once being abroad, all his children incur a disease from poison or venom. Overcome with the grievous pains caused by that poison or venom which burns them they lie rolling on the ground. Their father, the physician, comes home from his journey at the time when his sons are suffering from that poison or venom. Some of them have perverted notions, others have right notions, but all suffer the same pain. On seeing their father they cheerfully greet him and say: Hail, dear father, that thou art come back in safety and welfare! Now deliver us from our evil, be it poison or venom; let us live, dear father.

And the physician, seeing his sons befallen with disease, overcome with pain and rolling on the ground, prepares a great remedy, having the required colour, smell, and taste, pounds it on a stone and gives it as a potion to his sons, with these words: Take this great remedy, my sons, which has the required colour, smell, and taste. For by taking this great remedy, my sons, you shall soon be rid of this poison or venom; you shall recover and be healthy. Those amongst the children of the physician that have right notions, after seeing the colour of the remedy, after smelling the smell and tasting the flavour, quickly take it, and in consequence of it are soon totally delivered from their disease.

But the sons who have perverted notions cheerfully greet their father and say: Hail, dear father, that thou art come back in safety and welfare; do heal us. So they speak, but they do not take the remedy offered, and that because, owing to the perverseness of their notions, that remedy does not please them, in colour, smell, nor taste. Then the physician reflects thus: These sons of mine must have become perverted in their notions owing to this poison or venom, as they do not take the remedy nor hail me. Therefore will I by some able device induce these sons to take this remedy. Prompted by this desire he speaks to those sons as follows: I am old, young men of good family, decrepit, advanced in years, and my term of life is near at hand; but be not sorry, young men of good family, do not feel dejected; here have I prepared a great remedy for you; if you want it, you may take it.

Having thus admonished them, he skilfully betakes himself to another part of the country and lets his sick sons know that he has departed life. They are extremely sorry and bewail him extremely: So then he is dead, our father and protector; he who begat us; he, so full of bounty! now are we left without a protector.

Fully aware of their being orphans and of having no refuge, they are continually plunged in sorrow, by which their perverted notions make room for right notions. They acknowledge that remedy possessed of the required colour, smell, and taste to have the required colour, smell, and taste, so that they instantly take it, and by taking it are delivered from their evil.

Then, on knowing that these sons are delivered from evil, the physician shows himself again. Now, young men of good family, what is your opinion? Would anyone charge that physician with falsehood on account of his using that device? No, certainly not, Lord; certainly not, Sugata. He proceeded: In the same manner, young men of good family, I have arrived at supreme, perfect enlightenment since an immense, incalculable number of hundred thousands of myriads of kotis of Aeons, but from time to time I display such able devices to the creatures, with the view of educating them, without there in that respect any falsehood on my part.

In order to set forth this subject more extensively the Lord on that occasion uttered the following stanzas:

1. An inconceivable number of thousands of kotis of Aeons, never to be measured, is it since I reached superior or first enlightenment and never ceased to teach the law.
2. I roused many Bodhisattvas and established them in Buddha-knowledge. I brought myriads of kotis of beings, endless, to full ripeness in many kotis of Aeons.
3. I show the place of extinction, I reveal to all beings a device to educate them, albeit I do not become extinct at the time, and in this very place continue preaching the law.
4. There I rule myself as well as all beings. But men of perverted minds, in their delusion, do not see me standing there.
5. In the opinion that my body is completely extinct, they pay worship, in many ways, to the relics, but me they see not. They feel however a certain aspiration by which their mind becomes right.
6. When such upright pious, mild, and gentle creatures leave off their bodies, then I assemble the crowd of disciples and show myself here on the Gridhrakuta.

7. And then I speak thus to them, in this very place: I was not completely extinct at that time; it was but a device of mine, monks; repeatedly am I born in the world of the living.
8. Honoured by other beings, I show them my superior enlightenment, but you would not obey my word, unless the Lord of the world enters Nirvana.
9. I see how the creatures are afflicted, but I do not show them my proper being. Let them first have an aspiration to see me; then I will reveal to them the true law.
10. Such has always been my firm resolve during an inconceivable number of thousands of kotis of Aeons, and I have not left this Gridhrakuta for other abodes.
11. And when creatures behold this world and imagine that it is burning, even then my Buddha-field is teeming with gods and men.
12. They dispose of manifold amusements, kotis of pleasure gardens, palaces, and aerial cars; this field is embellished by hills of gems and by trees abounding with blossoms and fruits.
13. And aloft gods are striking musical instruments and pouring a rain of Mandaras by which they are covering me, the disciples and other sages who are striving after enlightenment.
14. So is my field here, everlastingly; but others fancy that it is burning; in their view this world is most terrific, wretched, replete with a number of woes.
15. Ay, many kotis of years they may pass without ever having mentioned my name, the law, or my congregation. That is the fruit of sinful deeds.
16. But when mild and gentle beings are born in this world of men, they immediately see me revealing the law, owing to their good works.
17. I never speak to them of the infinitude of my action. Therefore, I am, properly, existing since long, and yet declare: The Jinas are rare or precious.
18. Such is the glorious power of my wisdom that knows no limit, and the duration of my life is as long as an endless

period; I have acquired it after previously following a due course.

19. Feel no doubt concerning it, O sages, and leave off all uncertainty: the word I here pronounce is really true; my word is never false.
20. For even as that physician skilled in devices for the sake of his sons whose notions were perverted, said that he had died although he was still alive, and even as no sensible man would charge that physician with falsehood;
21. So am I the father of the world, the Self-born, the Healer, the Protector of all creatures. Knowing them to be perverted, infatuated, and ignorant I teach final rest, myself not being at rest.
22. What reason should I have to continually manifest myself? When men become unbelieving, unwise, ignorant, careless, fond of sensual pleasures, and from thoughtlessness run into misfortune.
23. Then I, who know the .course of the world, declare: I am so and so, and consider: How can I incline them to enlighten-ment? how can they become partakers of the Buddha-laws?

◆ ◆ ◆ ◆ ◆

16

OF PIETY

Meritoriousness of the belief in the immense duration of the Tathagatas and all those who have once become the Buddhas.

While this exposition of the duration of the Tathagata's lifetime was being given, innumerable, countless creatures profited by it. Then the Lord addressed the Bodhisattva Mahasattva Maitreya: While this exposition of the duration of the Tathagata's lifetime was being given, Ajita, sixty-eight hundred thousand myriads of kotis of Bodhisattvas, comparable to the sands of the Ganges, have acquired the faculty to acquiesce in the law that has no origin. A thousand times more Bodhisattvas Mahasattvas have obtained Dharani; and other Bodhisattvas Mahasattvas, equal to the dust atoms of one third of a macrocosm, have by hearing this Dharmaparyaya obtained the faculty of unhampered view. Other Bodhisattvas Mahasattvas again, equal to the dust atoms of two-third parts of a macrocosm, have by hearing this Dharmaparyaya obtained the Dharani that makes hundred thousand kotis of revolutions.

Again, other Bodhisattvas Mahasattvas, equal to the dust atoms of a whole macrocosm, have by hearing this Dharmaparyaya moved forward the wheel that never rolls back. Some Bodhisattvas Mahasattvas, equal to the dust atoms of a mean universe, have by hearing this Dharmaparyaya moved forward the wheel of spotless radiance. Other Bodhisattvas Mahasattvas, equal to the dust atoms of a small universe, have by hearing this Dharmaparyaya come so far that they will reach supreme, perfect enlightenment after eight births. Other

Bodhisattvas Mahasattvas, equal to the dust atoms of four worlds of four continents, have by hearing this Dharmaparyaya become such as to require four births more before reaching supreme, perfect enlightenment. Other Bodhisattvas Mahasattvas, equal to the dust atoms of three four-continental worlds, have by hearing this Dharmaparyaya become such as to require three births more before reaching supreme, perfect enlightenment. Other Bodhisattvas Mahasattvas, equal to the dust atoms of two four-continental worlds, have by hearing this Dharmaparyaya become such as to require two births more before reaching supreme, perfect enlightenment. Other Bodhisattvas Mahasattvas, equal to the dust atoms of one four-continental world, have by hearing this Dharmaparyaya become such as to require but one birth before reaching supreme, perfect enlightenment. Other Bodhisattvas Mahasattvas, equal to the dust atoms of eight macrocosms consisting of three parts, have by hearing this Dharmaparyaya conceived the idea of supreme, perfect enlightenment.

No sooner had the Lord given this exposition determining the duration and periods of the law, than there fell from the upper sky a great rain of Mandarava and great Mandarava flowers that covered and overwhelmed all the hundred thousand myriads of kotis of Buddhas who were seated on their thrones at the foot of the jewel trees in hundred thousands of myriads of kotis of worlds. It also covered and overwhelmed the Lord Sakyamuni, the Tathagata, etc., and the Lord Prabhutaratna, the Tathagata, etc., the latter sitting fully extinct on his throne, as well as that entire host of Bodhisattvas and the four classes of the audience. A rain of celestial powder of sandal and agallochum trickled down from the sky, whilst higher up in the firmament the great drums resounded, without being struck, with a pleasant, sweet, and deep sound. Double pieces of fine heavenly cloth fell down by hundreds and thousands from the upper sky; necklaces, half-necklaces, pearl necklaces, gems, jewels, noble gems, and noble jewels were seen high in the firmament hanging down from every side in all directions of space, while all around thousands of jewel censers, containing priceless, exquisite incense, were moving of their own accord. Bodhisattvas Mahasattvas were seen holding above each

Tathagata, high aloft, a row of jewel umbrellas stretching as high as the Brahma-world. So acted the Bodhisattvas Mahasattvas in respect to all the innumerable hundred thousands of myriads of kotis of Buddhas. Severally they celebrated these Buddhas in appropriate stanzas, sacred hymns in praise of the Buddhas.

And on that occasion the Bodhisattva Mahasattva Maitreya uttered the following stanzas:

1. Wonderful is the law which the Sugata has expounded, the law we never heard before; how great the majesty of the Leaders is, and how infinit the duration of their life!
2. And on hearing such a law imparted by the Sugata from face to face, thousands of kotis of creatures, the genuine sons of the Leader of the world, have been pervaded with gladness.
3. Some have reached the point of supreme enlightenment from whence there is no return, others are standing on the lower stage; some have reached the standpoint of having an unhampered view, and others have obtained thousands of kotis of Dharanis.
4. There are others as atoms, who have reached supreme Buddha-knowledge. Some, again, will after eight births become Jinas seeing the infinite.
5. Among those who hear this law from the Master, some will obtain enlightenment and see the truth after four births, others after three, others after two.
6. Some among them will become all-knowing after one birth, in the next following existence. Such will be the perfect result of learning the duration of life of the Chief.
7. Innumerable, countless as the atoms of the eight fields, are the kotis of beings who by hearing this law have conceived the idea of superior enlightenment.
8. Such is the effect produced by the great Seer, when he reveals this Buddha-state that is endless and has no limit, which is as immense as the element of ether.
9. Many thousand kotis of angels, lndras, and Brahma-angels, like the sands of the Ganges, have flocked hither from

thousands of kotis of distant fields and have poured a rain of Mandaravas.

10. They move in the sky like birds, and strew fragrant powder of sandal and agallochum, to cover ceremoniously the Chief of Jinas withal.
11. High aloft tymbals without being struck emit sweet sounds; thousands of kotis of white cloth whirl down upon the Chiefs.
12. Thousands of kotis of jewel censers of costly incense move of their own accord on every side to honour the mighty Lord of the world.
13. Innumerable wise Bodhisattvas hold myriads of kotis of umbrellas, elevated and made of noble jewels, like chaplets, up to the Brahma-world.
14. The sons of Sugata, in their great joy, have attached beautiful triumphal streamers at the top of the banner staffs in honour of the Leaders whom they celebrate in thousands of stanzas.
15. Such a marvellous, extraordinary, prodigious, splendid phenomenon, O Leader, is being displayed by all those beings who are gladdened by the exposition of the duration of life of the Tathagata.
16. Grand is the matter now occurring in the ten points of space, and great the sound raised by the Leaders; thousands of kotis of living beings are refreshed and gifted with virtue for enlightenment.

Thereupon the Lord addressed the Bodhisattva Mahasattva Maitreya: Those beings, Ajita, who during the exposition of this Dharmaparyaya in which the duration of the Tathagata's life is revealed have entertained, were it but a single thought of trust, or have put belief in it, how great a merit are they to produce, be they young men and young ladies of good family? Listen then, and mind it well, how great the merit is they shall produce. Let us suppose the case, Ajita, that some young man or young lady of good family, desirous of supreme, perfect enlightenment, for eight hundred thousand myriads of kotis of Aeons practises the five perfections of virtue, Paramitas, perfect charity in alms, perfect morality, perfect forbearance, perfect energy, perfect meditation—perfect wisdom being excepted; let us, on the other hand, suppose the case, Ajita, that a young man or young lady of good family, on hearing this Dharmaparyaya containing the exposition of the duration of the Tathagata's life, conceives were it but a single thought of trust or puts belief in it; then that former accumulation of merit, that accumulation of good connected with the five perfections of virtue, that accumulation which has come to full accomplishment in eight hundred thousand myriads of kotis of Aeons, does not equal one hundredth part of the accumulation of merit in the second case; it does not equal one thousandth part; it admits of no calculation, no counting, no reckoning, no comparison, no approximation, no secret teaching. One who is possessed of such an accumulation of merit, Ajita, be he a young man or a young lady of good family, will not miss supreme, perfect enlightenment; no, that is not possible.

And on that occasion the Lord uttered the following stanzas:

17. Let a man who is seeking after this knowledge, superior Buddha-knowledge, undertake to practise in this world the five perfect virtues;
18. Let him, during eight thousand kotis of complete Aeons, continue giving repeated alms to Buddhas and disciples;
19. Regaling Pratyeka Buddhas and kotis of Bodhisattvas by giving meat, food and drink, clothing and lodging.
20. Let him build on earth refuges and monasteries of sandal-wood, and pleasant convent gardens provided with walks;
21. Let him after so bestowing gifts, various and diversified, during thousands of kotis of Aeons, direct his mind to enlightenment;
22. Let him then, for the sake of Buddha-knowledge, keep unbroken the pure moral precepts which have been recommended by the perfect Buddhas and acknowledged by the wise;
23. Let him further develop the virtue of forbearance, be steady in the stage of meekness, be constant, of good memory, and patiently endure many censures;

24. Let him, moreover, for the sake of Buddha-knowledge, bear the contemptuous words of unbelievers who are rooted in pride;
25. Let him, always zealous, strenuous, studious, of good memory, without any other preoccupation in his mind, practise meditation, during kotis of Aeons;
26. Let him, whether living in the forest or entering upon a vagrant life!, go about, avoiding sloth and torpor, for kotis of Aeons;
27. Let him as a philosopher, a great philosopher who finds his delight in meditation, in concentration of mind, pass eight thousand kotis of Aeons;
28. Let him energetically pursue enlightenment with the thought of his reaching all-knowingness, and so arrive at the highest degree of meditation;
29. Then the merit accruing to those who practise the virtues as described, during thousands of kotis of Aeans,
30. Is less than that of a man or a woman who, on hearing the duration of my life, for a single moment believes in it; this merit is endless.
31. He who renouncing doubt, vacillation, and misgiving shall believe even for a short moment, shall obtain such a reward.
32. The Bodhisattvas also, who have practised those virtues during kotis of Aeons, will not be startled at hearing of this inconceivably long life of mine.
33. They will bow their heads and think: 'May I also in future become such a one and release kotis of living beings!
34. 'As the Lord Sakyamuni, the Lion of the Sakya race, after he had occupied his seat on the terrace of enlightenment, raised his lion's roar;
35. 'So may I in future be sitting on the terrace of enlightenment, honoured by all mortals, to teach so long a life!'
36. Those who are possessed of firmness of intention and have learnt the principles, will understand the mystery and feel no uncertainty.

Again, Ajita, he who after hearing this Dharmaparyaya, which contains an exposition of the duration of the Tathagata's life, apprehends it, penetrates and understands it, will produce a yet more immeasurable accumulation of merit conducive to Buddha-knowledge; unnecessary to add that he who hears such a Dharmaparyaya as this or makes others hear it; who keeps it in memory, reads, comprehends or makes others comprehend it; who writes or has it written, collects or has it collected into a volume, honours, respects, worships it with flowers, incense, perfumed garlands, ointments, powder, cloth, umbrellas, flags, streamers, lighted oil lamps, ghee lamps or lamps filled with scented oil, will produce a far greater accumulation of merit conducive to Buddha-knowledge.

And, Ajita, as a test whether that young man or young lady of good family who hears this exposition of the duration of the Tathagata's life most decidedly believes in it may be deemed the following. They will behold me teaching the law here on the Gridhrakuta, surrounded by a host of Bodhisattvas, attended by a host of Bodhisattvas, in the centre of the congregation of disciples. They will behold here my Buddha-field in the Saha-world, consisting of lapis lazuli and forming a level plain; forming a chequered board of eight compartments with gold threads; set off with jewel trees. They will behold the towers that the Bodhisattvas use as their abodes. By this test, Ajita, one may know if a young man or young lady of good family has a most decided belief.

Moreover, Ajita, I declare that a young man of good family who, after the complete extinction of the Tathagata, shall not reject, but joyfully accept this Dharmaparyaya when hearing it, that such a young man of good family also is earnest in his belief; far more one who keeps it in memory or reads it. He who after collecting this Dharmaparyaya into a volume carries it on his shoulder carries the Tathagata on his shoulder. Such a young man or young lady of good family, Ajita, need make no Stupas for me, nor monasteries; need not give to the congregation of monks medicaments for the sick or other requisites. For, Ajita, such a young man or a young lady of good family has spiritually built for the worship of my relics Stupas of seven precious substances reaching up to the Brahma-world in height, and with a circumference in proportion, with the umbrellas thereto belonging, with triumphal streamers, with tinkling bells and baskets; has shown manifold marks of respect to those Stupas of relics with diverse celestial and earthly flowers, incense, perfumed garlands, ointments, powder, cloth, umbrellas, banners, flags, triumphal streamers, by various sweet, pleasant, clear-sounding tymbals and drums, by the tune, noise, sounds of musical instruments and castanets, by songs, nautch and dancing of different kinds, of many, innumerable kinds; has done those acts of worship during many, innumerable thousands of kotis of Aeons. One who keeps in memory this Dharmaparyaya after my complete extinction, who reads, writes, promulgates it, Ajita, shall also have built monasteries, large, spacious, extensive, made of red sandalwood, with thirty-two pinnacles, eight stories, fit for a thousand monks, adorned with gardens and flowers, having walks furnished with lodgings, completely provided with meat, food and drink and medicaments for the sick, well equipped with all comforts. And those numerous, innumerable beings, say a hundred or a thousand or ten thousand or a kotis or hundred kotis or thousand kotis or hundred thousand kotis or ten thousand times hundred thousand kotis, they must be considered to form the congregation of disciples seeing me from face to face, and must be considered as those whom I have fully blessed.

He who, after my complete extinction, shall keep this Dharmaparyaya, read, promulgate, or write it, he, I repeat, Ajita, need not build Stupas of relics, nor worship the congregation; not necessary to tell, Ajita, that the young man or young lady of good family who, keeping this Dharmaparyaya, shall crown it by charity in alms, morality, forbearance, energy, meditation, or wisdom, will produce a much greater accumulation of merit; it is, in fact, immense, incalculable, infinite. Just as the element of ether, Ajita, is boundless, to the east, south, west, north, beneath, above, and in the intermediate quarters, so immense and incalculable an accumulation of merit, conducive to Buddha-knowledge, will be produced by a young man or young lady of good family who shall keep, read, write, or cause to be written, this Dharmaparyaya. He will be zealous in worshipping the Tathagata shrines; he will laud the disciples of the Tathagata, praise the hundred thousands of myriads of kotis of virtues of the Bodhisattvas Mahasattvas, and expound them to others; he will be accomplished in forbearance, be moral, of good character, agreeable to live with, and tolerant, modest, not jealous of others, not wrathful, not vicious in mind, of good memory, strenuous and always busy, devoted to meditation in striving after the state of a Buddha, attaching great value to abstract meditation, frequently engaging in abstract meditation, able in solving questions and in avoiding hundred thousands of myriads of kotis of questions.

Any Bodhisattva Mahasattva, Ajita, who, after the Tathagata's complete extinction, shall keep this Dharmaparyaya, will have the good qualities I have described. Such a young man or young lady of good family, Ajita, must be considered to make for the terrace of enlightenment; that young man or young lady of good family steps towards the foot of the tree of enlightenment in order to reach enlightenment. And where that young man or young lady of good family, Ajita, stands, sits, or walks, there one should make a shrine, dedicated to the Tathagata, and the world, including the gods, should say: This is a Stupa of relics of the Tathagata.

And on that occasion the Lord uttered the following stanzas:

37. An immense mass of merit, as I have repeatedly mentioned, shall be his who, after the complete extinction of the Leader of men, shall keep this Sutra.
38. He will have paid worship to me, and built Stupas of relics, made of precious substances, variegated, beautiful, and splendid;
39. In height coming up to the Brahma-world, I with rows of umbrellas, great in circumference, gorgeous, and decorated with triumphal streamers;
40. Resounding with the clear ring of bells, and decorated with silk bands, while jingles moved by the wind form another ornament at the shrines of Jina relics,
41. He will have shown great honour to them by flowers, perfumes, and ointments; by music, clothes, and the repeated sound of tymbals.
42. He will have sweet musical instruments struck at those relics, and lamps with scented oil kept burning all around.

43. He who at the period of depravation shall keep and teach this Sutra, he will have paid me such an infinitely varied worship.
44. He has built many kotis of excellent monasteries of sandalwood, with thirty-two pinnacles, and eight terraces high;
45. Provided with couches, with food hard and soft; furnished with excellent curtains, and having cells by thousands.
46. He has given hermitages and walks embellished by flower-gardens; many elegant objects of various forms and variegated.
47. He has shown manifold worship to the host of disciples in my presence, he who, after my extinction, shall keep this Sutra.
48. Let one be ever so good in disposition, much greater merit will he obtain who shall keep or write this Sutra.
49. Let a man cause this to be written and have it well put together in a volume; let him always worship the volume with ointments.
50. Let him constantly place near it a lamp filled with scented oil, along with full-blown lotuses and suitable oblations of Michelia Champaka.
51. The man who pays such worship to the books will produce a mass of merit which is not to be measured.
52. Even as there is no measure of the element of ether, in none of the ten directions, so there is no measure of this mass of merit.
53. How much more will this be the case with one who is patient, meek, devoted, moral, studious, and addicted to meditation;
54. Who is not irascible, not treacherous, reverential towards the sanctuary, always humble towards monks, not conceited, nor neglectful;
55. Sensible and wise, not angry when he is asked a question; who, full of compassion for living beings, gives such instruction as suits them.

56. If there be such a man who at the same time keeps this Sutra, he will possess a mass of merit that cannot be measured.
57. If one meets such a man as here described, a keeper of this Sutra, one should do homage to him.
58. One should present him with divine flowers, cover him with divine clothes, and bow the head to salute his feet, in the conviction of his being a Tathagata.
59. And at the sight of such a man one may directly make the reflection that he is going towards the foot of the tree to arrive at superior, blessed enlightenment for the weal of all the world, including the gods.
60. And wherever such a sage is walking, standing, sitting, or lying down; wherever the hero pronounces were it but a single stanza from this Sutra;
61. There one should build a Stupa for the most high of men, a splendid, beautiful Stupa, dedicated to the Lord Buddha, the Chief, and then worship it in manifold ways.
62. That spot of the earth has been enjoyed by myself; there have I walked myself, and there have I been sitting; where that son of Buddha has stayed, there I am.

◆ ◆ ◆ ◆ ◆

17

OF JOYFUL ACCEPTANCE

The Lord details the great merit attending a ready acceptance of the preaching of the law.

Thereupon the Bodhisattva Mahasattva Maitreya said to the Lord: O Lord, one who, after hearing this Dharmaparyaya being preached, joyfully accepts it, be that person a young man of good family or a young lady, how much merit, O Lord, will be produced by such a young man or young lady of good family?

And on that occasion the Bodhisattva Mahasattva Maitreya uttered this stanza:

1. How great will be the merit of him who, after the extinction of the great Hero, shall hear this exalted Sutra and joyfully accept it?

And the Lord said to the Bodhisattva Mahasattva Maitreya: If anyone, Ajita, either a young man of good family or a young lady, after the complete extinction of the Tathagata, hears the preaching of this Dharmaparyaya, let it be a monk or nun, a male or female lay devotee, a man of ripe understanding or a boy or girl; if the hearer joyfully accepts it, and then after the sermon rises up to go elsewhere, to a monastery, house, forest, street, village, town, or province, with the motive and express aim to expound the law such as he has understood, such as he has heard it, and according to the measure of his power, to another person, his mother, father, kinsman, friend, acquaintance, or any other person; if the latter, after hearing, joyfully accepts, and, in consequence, communicates it to another; if the latter, after hearing, joyfully accepts, and communicates it to another; if this other, again, after hearing, joyfully accepts it, and so on in succession until a number of fifty is reached; then, Ajita, the fiftieth person to hear and joyfully accept the law so heard, let it be a young man of good family or a young lady, will have acquired an accumulation of merit connected with the joyful acceptance, Ajita, which I am going to indicate to thee. Listen, and take it well to heart; I will tell thee.

It is, Ajita, as if the creatures existing in the four hundred thousand Asankhyeyas of worlds in any of the six states of existence, born from an egg, from a womb, from warm humidity, or from metamorphosis, whether they have a shape or have not, be they conscious or unconscious, neither conscious nor unconscious, footless, two-footed, four-footed, or many-footed, as many beings as are contained in the world of creatures,—as if all those had flocked together to one place. Further, suppose some man appears, a lover of virtue, a lover of good, who gives to that whole body the pleasures, sports, amusements, and enjoyments they desire, like, and relish. He gives to each of them all Jambudvipa for his pleasures, sports, amusements, and enjoyments; gives bullion, gold, silver, gems, pearls, lapis lazuli, conches, stones coral, carriages yoked with horses, with bullocks, with elephants; gives palaces and towers. In this way, Ajita, that master of munificence, that great master of munificence continues spending his gifts for fully eighty years.

Then, Ajita, that master of munificence, that great master of munificence reflects thus: All these beings have I allowed to sport and enjoy themselves, but now they are covered with wrinkles and grey-haired, old, decrepit, eighty years of age, and near the term of their life. Let me therefore initiate them in the discipline of the law revealed by the Tathagata, and instruct them. Thereupon, Ajita, the man exhorts all those beings, thereafter initiates them in the discipline of the law revealed by the Tathagata, and makes them adopt it. Those beings learn the law from him, and in one moment, one instant, one bit of time, all become Srotapannas, obtain the fruit of the rank of Sakridagamin and of Anagamin, until they become Arhats, free from all imperfections, adepts in meditation, adepts in great meditation and in the meditation with eight emancipations. Now, what is thine opinion, Ajita, will that master of munificence, that great master of munificence, on account of his doings, produce great merit, immense, incalculable merit? Whereupon the Bodhisattva Mahasattva Maitreya said in reply to the Lord: Certainly, Lord; certainly, Sugata; that person, Lord, will already produce much merit on that account, because he gives to the beings all that is necessary for happiness; how much more then if he establishes them in Arhatship!

This said, the Lord spoke to the Bodhisattva Mahasattva Maitreya as follows: I announce to thee, Ajita, I declare to thee; take on one side the master of munificence, the great master of munificence, who produces merit by supplying all beings in the four hundred thousand Asankhyeyas of worlds with all the necessaries for happiness and by establishing them in Arhatship; take on the other side the person who, ranking the fiftieth in the series of the oral tradition of the law, hears, were it but a single stanza, a single word, from this Dharmaparyaya and joyfully accepts it; if we compare the mass of merit connected with the joyful acceptance and the mass of merit connected with the charity of the master of munificence, the great master of munificence, then the greater merit will be his who, ranking the fiftieth in the series of the oral tradition of the law, after hearing were it but a single stanza, a single word, from this Dharmaparyaya, joyfully accepts it. Against this accumulation of merit, Ajita, this accumulation of roots of goodness connected with that joyful acceptance, the former accumulation of merit connected with the charity of that master of munificence, that great master of munificence, and connected with the confirmation in Arhatship, does not fetch the 1/100 part, not the 1/100,000 1/10,000,000 not the 1/1000,000,000 not the 1/1000 × 10,000,000 not the 1/100,000 × 10,000,000 not the 1/100,000 × 10,000 × 10,000,000 part; it admits of no calculation, no counting, no reckoning, no comparison, no approximation, no secret teaching. So immense, incalculable, Ajita, is the merit which a person, ranking the fiftieth in the series of the tradition of the law, produces by joyfully accepting, were it but a single stanza, a single word, from this Dharmaparyaya; how much more then will he produce Ajita, who hears this Dharmaparyaya in my presence and then joyfully accepts it? I declare, Ajita, that his accumulation of merit shall be even more immense, more incalculable.

And further, Ajita, if a young man of good family or a young lady, with the design to hear this discourse on the law, goes from home to a monastery, and there hears this Dharmaparyaya for a single moment, either standing or sitting, then that person, merely by the mass of merit resulting from that action, will after the termination of his present life, and at the time of his second existence when he receives another body, become a possessor of carriages yoked with bullocks, horses, or elephants, of litters, vehicles yoked with bulls, and of celestial aerial cars. If further that same person at that preaching sits down, were it but a single moment, to hear this Dharmaparyaya, or persuades another to sit down or shares with him his seat, he will by the store of merit resulting from that action gain seats of Indra, seats of Brahma, thrones of a Chakravartin.

And, Ajita, if someone, a young man of good family or a young lady, says to another person: Come, friend, and hear the Dharmaparyaya of the Lotus of the True Law, and if that other person owing to that exhortation is persuaded to listen, were it but a single moment, then the former will by virtue of that root of goodness, consisting in that exhortation, obtain the advantage of a connection with Bodhisattvas who have acquired Dharani. He will become the reverse of dull, will get keen faculties, and have wisdom; in the course of a hundred thousand existences he will never have a fetid mouth, nor an offensive one; he will have no diseases of the tongue, nor of the mouth; he will have no black teeth, no unequal, no yellow, no ill-ranged, no broken teeth, no teeth fallen out; his lips will not be pendulous, not turned inward, not gaping, not mutilated, not loathsome; his nose will not be flat, nor wry; his face will not be long, nor wry, nor unpleasant. On the contrary, Ajita, his tongue, teeth, and lips will be delicate and well-shaped; his nose long; his face perfectly round; the eyebrows well-shaped; the forehead well-formed. He will receive a very complete organ of manhood. He will have the advantage that the Tathagata renders sermons intelligible to him and soon come in connection with Lords, Buddhas. Mark, Ajita, how much good is produced by one's inciting were it but a single creature; how much more then by him who reverentially hears, reverentially reads, reverentially preaches, reverentially promulgates the law!

And on that occasion the Lord uttered the following stanzas:

2. Listen how great the merit is of one who, the fiftieth in the series of tradition hears a single stanza from this Sutra and with placid mind joyfully adopts it.
3. Suppose there is a man in the habit of giving alms to myriads of kotis of beings, whom I have here before indicated by way of comparison; all of them he satisfies during eighty years.
4. Then seeing that old age has approached for them, that their brow is wrinkled and their head grey, he thinks: Alas, how all beings come to decay! Let me therefore admonish them by speaking of the law.
5. He teaches them the law here on earth and points to the state of Nirvana hereafter. All existences, he says, are like a mirage; hasten to become disgusted with all existence.'
6. All creatures, by hearing the law from that charitable person, become at once Arhats, free from imperfections, and living their last life.
7. Much more merit than by that person will be acquired by him who through unbroken tradition shall hear were it but a single stanza and joyfully receive it. The mass of merit of the former is not even so much as a small particle of the latter's.
8. So great will be one's merit, endless, immeasurable, owing to one's hearing merely a single stanza, in regular tradition; how much more then if one hears from face to face!
9. And if somebody exhorts were it but a single creature and says: Go, hear the law, for this Sutra is rare in many myriads of kotis of Aeons;
10. And if the creature so exhorted should hear the Sutra even for a moment, hark what fruit is to result from that action. He shall never have a mouth disease;
11. His tongue is never sore; his teeth shall never fall out, never be black, yellow, unequal; his lips never become loathsome;

12. His face is not wry, nor lean, nor long; his nose not flat; it is well-shaped, as well as his forehead, teeth, lips, and round face.
13. His aspect is ever pleasant to men; his mouth is never fetid, it constantly emits a smell sweet as the lotus.
14. If some wise man, to hear this Sutra, goes from his home to a monastery and there listen, were it but for a single moment, with a placid mind, hear what results from it.
15. His body is very fair; he drives with horse-carriages, that wise man, and is mounted on elevated carriages drawn by elephants and variegated with gems.
16. He possesses litters covered with ornaments and carried by numerous men. Such is the blessed fruit of his going to hear preaching.
17. Owing to the performance of that pious work he shall, when sitting in the assembly there, obtain seats of Indra, seats of Brahma, seats of kings.

◆ ◆ ◆ ◆ ◆

18

RELIGIOUS PREACHER

Exposition of the advantages, worldly and spiritual, enjoyed by the ministers of religion.

The Lord then addressed the Bodhisattva Mahasattva Satatasamitabhiyukta (*i.e.*, ever and constantly strenuous). Anyone, young man of good family, who shall keep, read, teach, write this Dharmaparyaya or have it written, let that person be a young man of good family or a young lady, shall obtain eight hundred good qualities of the eye, twelve hundred of the ear, eight hundred of the nose, twelve hundred of the tongue, eight hundred of the body, twelve hundred of the mind. By these many hundred good qualities the whole of the six organs shall be perfect, thoroughly perfect. By means of the natural, carnal eye derived from his parents being perfect, he shall see the whole triple universe, outwardly and inwardly, with its mountains and woody thickets, down to the great hell Avichi and up to the extremity of existence. All that he shall see with his natural eye, as well as the creatures to be found in it, and he shall know the fruit of their works.

And on that occasion the Lord uttered the following stanzas:

1. Hear from me what good qualities shall belong to him who unhesitatingly and undismayed shall preach this Sutra to the congregated assembly.
2. First, then, his eye or, organ of vision shall possess eight hundred good qualities by which it shall be correct, clear, and untroubled.
3. With the carnal eye derived from his parents he shall see the whole world from within and without.

4. He shall see the Meru and Sumeru, all the horizon and other mountains, as well as the seas.
5. He, the hero, sees all, downward to the Avichi and upward to the extremity of existence. Such is his carnal eye.
6. But he has not yet got the divine eye, it having not yet been produced in him; such as here described is the range of his carnal eye.

Further, Satatasamitabhiyukta, the young man of good family or the young lady who proclaims this Dharmaparyaya and preaches it to others, is possessed of the twelve hundred good qualities of the ear. The various sounds that are uttered in the triple universe, downward to the great hell Avichi and upward to the extremity of existence, within and without, such as the sounds of horses, elephants, cows, goats, cars; the sounds of weeping and wailing; of horror, of conch-trumpets, bells, tymbals; of playing and singing; of camels, of tigers; of women, men, boys, girls; of righteousness piety and unrighteousness, impiety; of pleasure and pain; of ignorant men and aryas; pleasant and unpleasant sounds; sounds of gods, Nagas, goblins, Gandharvas, demons, Garudas, Kinnaras, great serpents, men, and beings not human; of monks, disciples, Pratyeka Buddhas, Bodhisattvas, and Tathagatas; as many sounds as are uttered in the triple world, within and without, all those he hears with his natural organ of hearing when perfect. Still he does not enjoy the divine ear, although he apprehends the sounds of those different creatures, understands, discerns the sounds of those different creatures, and when with his natural organ of hearing he hears the sounds of those creatures, his ear is not overpowered by any of those sounds. Such, Satatasamitabhiyukta, is the organ of hearing that the Bodhisattva Mahasattva acquires; yet he does not possess the divine ear.

Thus spoke the Lord; thereafter he, the Sugata, the Master, added:

7. The organ of hearing of such a person becomes or, is cleared and perfect, though as yet it be natural; by it he perceives the various sounds, without any exception, in this world.

8. He perceives the sounds of elephants, horses, cars, cows, goats, and sheep; of noisy kettle-drums, tabours, lutes, flutes, Vallaki-lutes.
9. He can hear singing, lovely and sweet, and, at the same time, is constant enough not to allow himself to be beguiled by it; he perceives the sounds of kotis of men, whatever and wherever they are speaking.
10. He, moreover, always hears the voice of gods and Nagas; he hears the tunes, sweet and affecting, of song, as well as the voices of men and women, boys and girls.
11. He hears the cries of the denizens of mountains and glens; the tender notes of Kalavinkas, cuckoos, peafowls, pheasants, and other birds.
12. He also hears the heart-rending cries of those who are suffering pains in the hells, and the yells uttered by the Spirits, vexed as they are by the difficulty to get food;
13. Likewise the different cries produced by the demons and the inhabitants of the ocean. All these sounds the preacher is able to hear from his place on earth, without being overpowered by them.
14. From where he is stationed here on the earth he also hears the different and multifarious sounds through which the inhabitants of the realm of brutes are conversing with each other.
15. He apprehends all the sounds, without any exception, whereby the numerous angels living in the Brahma-world, the Akanishthas and Abhasvaras, call one another.
16. He likewise always hears the sound which the monks on earth are raising when engaged in reading, and when preaching the law to congregations, after having taken orders under the command of the Sugatas.
17. And when the Bodhisattvas here on earth have a reading together and raise their voices in the general synods, he hears them severally.
18. The Bodhisattva who preaches this Sutra shall, at one time, also hear the perfect law that the Lord Buddha, the tamer of men, announces to the assemblies.

19. The numerous sounds produced by all beings in the triple world, in this field, within and without, downward to the Avichi and upward to the extremity of existence, are heard by him.
20. In short, he perceives the voices of all beings, his ear being open. Being in the possession of his six senses, he will discern the different sources of sound, and that while his organ of hearing is the natural one;
21. The divine ear is not yet operating in him; his ear continues in its natural state. Such as here told are the good qualities belonging to the wise man who shall be a keeper of this Sutra.

Further, Satatasamitabhiyukta, the Bodhisattva Mahasattva who keeps, proclaims, studies, writes this Dharmaparyaya becomes possessed of a perfect organ of smell with eight hundred good qualities. By means of that organ he smells the different smells that are found in the triple world, within and without, such as fetid smells, pleasant and unpleasant smells, the fragrance of diverse flowers, as the great-flowered jasmine, Arabian jasmine, Michelia Champaka, trumpet-flower; likewise the different scents of aquatic flowers, as the blue lotus, red lotus, white esculent water-lily and white lotus. He smells the odour of fruits and blossoms of various trees bearing fruits and blossoms, such as sandal, Xanthochymus, Tabernaemontana, agallochum. The manifold hundred-thousand mixtures of perfumes he smells and discerns, without moving from his standing-place.

He smells the diverse smells of creatures, as elephants, horses, cows, goats, beasts, as well as the smell issuing from the body of various living beings in the condition of brutes. He perceives the smells exhaled by the body of women and men, of boys and girls. He smells, even from a distance, the odour of grass, bushes, herbs, trees. He perceives those smells such as they really are, and is not surprised nor stunned by them. Staying on this very earth he smells the odour of gods and the fragrance of celestial flowers, such as Erythrina, Bauhinia, Mandarave: and great Mandarava, Mansha and great Malyosha. He smells the perfume of the divine powders of sandal and agallochum, as well as that of the hundred-thousands of mixtures of different divine flowers. He smells the odour exhaled by the body of the gods, such as Indra, the chief of the gods, and thereby knows whether the god is sporting, playing, and enjoying himself in his palace Vaijayanta or is speaking the law to the gods of paradise in the assembly-hall of the gods, Sudharma, or is resorting to the pleasure-park for sport. He smells the odour proceeding from the body of the sundry other gods, as well as that proceeding from the girls and wives of the gods, from the youths and maidens amongst the gods, without being surprised or stunned by those smells.

He likewise smells the odour exhaled by the bodies of all Devanikayas, Brahmakayikas, and Mahabrahmas. In the same manner he perceives the smells coming from disciples, Pratyeka-Buddhas, Bodhisattvas, and Tathagatas. He smells the odour arising from the seats of the Tathagatas and so discovers where those Tathagatas, Arhats, etc., abide. And by none of all those different smells is his organ of smell hindered, impaired, or vexed; and, if required, he may give an account of those smells to others without his memory being impaired by it.

And on that occasion the Lord uttered the following stanzas:

22. His organ of smell is quite correct, and he perceives the manifold and various smells, good or bad, which exist in this world;
23. The fragrance of the great-flowered jasmine, Arabian jasmine, Xanthochymus, sandal, agallochum, of several blossoms and fruits.
24. He likewise perceives the smells exhaled by men, women, boys, and girls, at a considerable distance, and by the smell he knows where they are.
25. He recognises emperors, rulers of armies, governors of provinces, as well as royal princes and ministers, and all the ladies of the harem by their peculiar scent.
26. It is by the odour that the Bodhisattva discovers sundry jewels of things, such as are found on the earth and such as serve as jewels for women.
27. That Bodhisattva likewise knows by the odour the various kinds of ornament that women use for their body, robes, wreaths, and ointments.

28. The wise man who keeps this exalted Sutra recognises, by the power of a good-smelling organ, a woman standing, sitting, or lying; he discovers wanton sport and magic power.
29. He perceives at once where he stands, the fragrance of scented oils, and the different odours of flowers and fruits, and thereby knows from what source the odour proceeds.
30. The discriminating man recognises by the odour the numerous sandal-trees in full blossom in the glens of the mountains, as well as all creatures dwelling there.
31. All the beings living within the compass of the horizon or dwelling in the depth of the sea or in the bosom of the earth the discriminating man knows how to distinguish from the peculiar smell.
32. He discerns the gods and demons, and the daughters of demons; he discovers the sports of demons and their luxury. Such, indeed is the power of his organ of smell.
33. By the smell he tracks the abodes of the quadrupeds in the woods, lions, tigers, elephants, snakes, buffaloes, cows, gayals.
34. He infers from the odour, whether the child that women, languid from pregnancy, bear in the womb be a boy or a girl.
35. He can discern if a woman is big with a dead child; he discerns if she is subject to throes, and, further, if a woman, the pains being removed, shall be delivered of a healthy boy.
36. He guesses the various designs of men, he smells so to say an air of design; he finds out the odour of passionate, wicked, hypocritical, or quiet persons.
37. That Bodhisattva by the scent smells treasures hidden in the ground, money, gold, bullion, silver, chests, and metal pots.
38. Necklaces of two sorts, gems, pearls, nice priceless jewels he knows by the scent, as well as things priceless and brilliant in general.

39. That great man from his very place on earth smells the flowers here above in the sky with the gods, such as Mandaravas, Manjushakas, and those growing on the coral tree.
40. By the power of his organ of smell he, without leaving his stand on earth, perceives how and whose are the aerial cars, of lofty, low, and middling size, and other brilliant forms shooting through the firmament.
41. He likewise finds out the paradise, the gods in the hall of Sudharma and in the most glorious palace of Vaijayanta, and the angels who there are diverting themselves.
42. He perceives, here on earth, an air of them; by the scent he knows the angels, and where each of them is acting, standing, listening, or walking.
43. That Bodhisattva tracks by the scent the houris who are decorated with many flowers, decked with wreaths and ornaments and in full attire; he knows wherever they are dallying or staying at the time.
44. By smell he apprehends the gods, Brahmas, and Brahmakayas moving on aerial cars aloft, upwards to the extremity of existence; he knows whether they are absorbed in meditation or have risen from it.
45. He perceives the Abhasvara angels falling and shooting and appearing, even those that he never saw before. Such is the organ of smell of the Bodhisattva who keeps this Sutra.
46. The Bodhisattva also recognises all monks under the rule of the Sugata, who are strenuously engaged in their walks and find their delight in their lessons and reading.
47. Intelligent as he is, he discerns those among the sons of Jina who are disciples and those who used to live at the foot of trees, and he knows that the monk so and so is staying in such and such a place.
48. The Bodhisattva knows by the odour whether other Bodhisattvas are of good memory, meditative, delighting in their lessons and reading, and assiduous in preaching to congregations.

49. In whatever point of space the Sugata, the great Seer, so benign and bounteous, reveals the law in the midst of the crowd of attending disciples, the Bodhisattva by the odour recognises him as the Lord of the universe.
50. Staying on earth, the Bodhisattva also perceives those beings who hear the law and rejoice at it, and the whole assembly of the Jina.
51. Such is the power of his organ of smell. Yet it is not the divine organ he possesses, but the natural one prior to the perfect, divine faculty of smell.

Further, Satatasamitabhiyukta, the young man of good family or the young lady who keeps, teaches, proclaims, writes this Dharmaparyaya shall have an organ of taste possessed of twelve hundred good faculties of the tongue. All flavours he takes on his tongue will yield a divine, exquisite relish. And he tastes in such a way that he is not to relish anything unpleasant; and even the unpleasant flavours that are taken on his tongue will yield a divine relish. And whatever he shall preach in the assembly, the creatures will be satisfied by it; they will be content, thoroughly content, filled with delight. A sweet, tender, agreeable, deep voice goes out from him, an amiable voice which goes to the heart, at which those creatures will be ravished and charmed; and those to whom he preaches, after having heard his sweet voice, so tender and melodious, will, even if they are gods, be of opinion that they ought to go and see, venerate, and serve him. And the angels and houris will be of opinion, etc. The Indras, Brahmas, and Brahmakayikas will be of opinion, etc. The Nagas and Naga girls will be of opinion, etc. The demons and their girls will be of opinion, etc. The Garudas and their girls will be of opinion; etc.

The Kinnaras and their girls, the great serpents and their girls, the goblins and their girls, the imps and their girls will be of opinion that they ought to go and see, venerate, serve him, and hear his sermon, and all will show him honour, respect, esteem; worship, reverence, and veneration. Monks and nuns, male and female lay devotees will likewise be desirous of seeing him. Kings, royal princes, and grandees or ministers will also be desirous of seeing him. Kings, ruling armies and emperors possessed of the seven treasures, along with the princes royal, ministers, ladies of the harem, and their retinue will be desirous of seeing him and paying him their homage. So sweet will be the speech delivered by that preacher, so truthful and according to the teaching of the Tathagata will be his words. Others also, Brahmins and laymen, citizens and peasants, will always and ever follow that preacher till the end of life. Even the disciples of the Tathagata will be desirous of seeing him; likewise the PratyekaBuddhas and the Lords Buddhas. And wherever that young man of good family or young lady shall stay, there he or she will preach, the face turned to the Tathagata, and he or she will be a worthy vessel of the Buddha-qualities. Such, so pleasant, so deep will be the voice of the going out from him.

And on that occasion the Lord uttered the following stanzas:

52. His organ of taste is most excellent, and he will never relish anything of inferior flavour; the flavours are no sooner put on his tongue than they become divine and possessed of a divine taste.
53. He has a tender voice and delivers sweet words, pleasant to hear, agreeable, charming; in the midst of the assembly he is used to speak with a melodious and deep voice.
54. And whosoever hears him when he is delivering a sermon with myriads of kotis of examples, feels a great joy and shows him an immense veneration.
55. The gods, Nagas, demons, and goblins always long to see him, and respectfully listen to his preaching. All those good qualities are his.
56. If he would, he might make his voice heard by the whole of this world; his voice is so fine, sweet, deep, tender, and winning.
57. The emperors on earth, along with their children and wives, go to him with the purpose of honouring him, and listen all the time to his sermon with joined hands.
58. He is constantly followed by goblins, crowds of Nagas, Gandharvas, imps, male and female, who honour, respect, and worship him.
59. Brahma himself becomes his obedient servant; the gods Isvara and Mahesvara, as well as Indra and the numerous heavenly nymphs, approach him.

60. And the Buddhas, benign and merciful for the world, along with their disciples, hearing his voice, protect him by showing their face, and feel satisfaction in hearing him preaching.

Further, Satatasamitabhiyukta, the Bodhisattva Mahasattva who keeps, reads, promulgates, teaches, writes this Dharmaparyaya shall have the eight hundred good qualities of the body. It will be pure, and show a hue clear as the lapis lazuli; it will be pleasant to see for the creatures. On that perfect body he will see the whole triple universe; the beings who in the triple world disappear and appear, who are low or lofty, of good or of bad colour, in fortunate or in unfortunate condition, as well as the beings dwelling within the circular plane of the horizon and of the great horizon, on the chief mountains Meru and Sumeru, and the beings dwelling below in the Avichi and upwards to the extremity of existence; all of them he will see on his own body. The disciples, Pratyeka Buddhas, Bodhisattvas, and Tathagatas dwelling in the triple universe, and the law taught by those Tathagatas and the beings serving the Tathagatas, he will see all of them on his own body, because he receives the proper body of all those beings, and that on account of the perfectness of his body.

And on that occasion the Lord uttered the following stanzas:

61. His body becomes thoroughly pure, clear as if consisting of lapis lazuli; he who keeps this sublime Sutra is always a pleasant sight for all creatures.

62. As on the surface of a mirror an image is seen, so on his body this world. Being self-born, he sees no other beings. Such is the perfectness of his body.

63. Indeed, all beings who are in this world, men, gods, demons, goblins, the inhabitants of hell, the spirits, and the brute creation are seen reflected on that body.

64. The aerial cars of the gods up to the extremity of existence, the rocks, the ridge of the horizon, the Himalaya, Sumeru, and great Meru, all are seen on that body.

65. He also sees the Buddhas on his body, along with the disciples and other sons of Buddha; likewise the

Bodhisattvas who lead a solitary life, and those who preach the law to congregations.

66. Such is the perfectness of his body, though he has not yet obtained a divine body; the natural property of his body is such.

Further, Satatasamitabhiyukta, the Bodhisattva Mahasattva who after the complete extinction of the Tathagata keeps, teaches, writes, reads this Dharmaparyaya shall have a mental organ possessed of twelve hundred good qualities of intellect. By this perfect mental organ he will, even if he hears a single stanza, recognise its various meanings. By fully comprehending the stanza he will find in it the text to preach upon for a month, for four months, nay, for a whole year. And the sermon he preaches will not fade from his memory. The popular maxims of common life, whether sayings or counsels, he will know how to reconcile with the rules of the law. Whatever creatures of this triple universe are subject to the mundane whirl, in any of the six conditions of existence, he will know their thoughts, doings, and movements. He will know and discern their motions, purposes, and aims. Though he has not yet attained the state of an Arya, his intellectual organ will be thoroughly perfect. And all he shall preach after having pondered on the interpretation of the law will be really true; he speaks what all Tathagatas have spoken, all that has been declared in the Sutras of former Jinas.

And on that occasion the Lord uttered the following stanzas:

67. His mental organ is perfect, lucid, right, and untroubled. By it he finds out the various laws, low, high, and mean.

68. On hearing the contents of a single stanza, the wise man catches the manifold significations hidden in it, and he is able for a month, four months, or even a year to go on expounding both its conventional and its true sense.

69. And the beings living in this world, within or without, gods, men, demons, goblins, Nagas, brutes.

70. The beings stationed in any of the six conditions of existence, all their thoughts the sage knows instantaneously. These are the advantages of keeping this Sutra.

71. He also hears the holy sound of the law which the Buddha, marked with a hundred blessed signs, preaches all over the world, and he catches what the Buddha speaks.
72. He reflects much on the supreme law, and is in the wont of constantly dilating upon it; he is never hesitating. These are the advantages of keeping this Sutra.
73. He knows the connections and knots; he discerns in all laws contrarieties; he knows the meaning and the interpretations, and expounds them according to his knowledge.
74. The Sutra which since so long a time has been expounded by the ancient Masters of the world is the law which he, never flinching, is always preaching in the assembly.
75. Such is the mental organ of him who keeps or reads this Sutra; he has not yet the knowledge of emancipation, but one that precedes it.
76. He who keeps this Sutra of the Sugata stands on the stage of a master; he may preach to all creatures and is skilful in kotis of interpretations.

◆ ◆ ◆ ◆ ◆

19

THE STORY OF SADAPARIBHUTA

A story exemplifying the superiority of simple-mindedness and pure-heartedness to wordly wisdom.

The Lord then adressed the Bodhisattva Mahasattva Mahasthamaprapta. In a similar way, Mahasthamaprapta, one may infer from what has been said that he who rejects such a Dharmaparyaya as this, who abuses monks, nuns, lay devotees male or female, keeping this Sutra, insults them, treats them with false and harsh words, shall experience dire results, to such an extent as is impossible to express in words. But those that keep, read, comprehend, teach, amply expound it to others, shall experience happy results, such as I have already mentioned: they shall attain such a perfection of the eye, ear, nose, tongue, body, and mind as just described.

In the days of yore, Mahasthamaprapta, at a past period, before incalculable Aeons, nay, more than incalculable, immense, inconceivable, and even long before, there appeared in the world a Tathagata, named Bhishmagarjitasvaraja, endowed with science and conduct, a Sugata, etc. etc. in the Aeon Vinirbhoga, in the world Mahasambhava. Now, Mahasthamaprapta, that Lord Bhishmagarjitasvararaja, the Tathagata, etc., in that world Vinirbhoga, showed the law in the presence of the world, including gods, men, and demons; the law containing the four noble truths and starting from the chain of causes and effects, tending to overcome birth, decrepitude, sickness, death, sorrow, lamentation, woe, grief, despondency, and finally leading to Nirvana, he showed to the disciples; the law connected with the six Perfections of virtue and terminating in the knowledge of the Omniscient, after the attainment of supreme, perfect enlightenment, he showed to the Bodhisattvas. The lifetime of that Lord Bhishmagarjitasvararja, the Tathagata, etc., lasted forty hundred thousand myriads of kotis of Aeons equal to the sands of the river Ganges.

After his complete extinction his true law remained hundred thousands of myriads of kotis of Aeons equal to the atoms contained in Jambudvipa, and the counterfeit of the true law continued hundred thousands of myriads of kotis of Aeons equal to the dust-atoms in the four continents. When the counterfeit of the true law of the Lord Bhishmagarjitasvaraja, the Tathagata, etc., after his complete extinction, had disappeared in the world Mahasambhava, Mahasthamaprapta, another Tathagata Bhishmajarjaita-svaraja, Arhat, etc., appeared, endowed with science and conduct. So in succession, Mahasthamaprapta, there arose in that world Mahasambhava twenty hundred thousand myriads of kotis of Tathagatas, etc., called Bhishmagarjitasvararja. At the time, Mahasthamaprapta, after the complete extinction of the first Tathagata amongst all those of the name of Bhishmagarjitasvaraja, Tathagata, etc., endowed with science and conduct, etc., when his true law had disappeared and the counterfeit of the true law was fading; when the reign of the law was being oppressed by proud monks, there was a monk, a Bodhisattva Mahasattva, called Sadaparibhuta. For what reason, Mahasthamaprapta, was that Bodhisattva: Mahasattva called Sadaparibhuta? It was Mahasthamaprapta, because that Bodhisattva Mahasattva was in the habit of exclaiming to every monk or nun, male or female lay devotee, while approaching them: I do not contemn you, worthies. You deserve no contempt, for you all observe the course of duty of Bodhisattvas and are to become Tathagatas, etc.

In this way, Mahasthamaprapta, that Bodhisattva Mahasattva, when a monk, did not teach nor study; the only thing he did was, whenever he decried from afar a monk or nun, a male or female lay devotee, to approach them and exclaim: I do not contemn you, sisters. You deserve no contempt, for you all observe the course of duty of Bodhisattvas and are to become Tathagatas, etc. So, Mahasthamaprapta, the Bodhisattva Mahasattva at that time used to address every monk or nun, male or female devotee. But all were extremely irritated and angry at it, showed him their displeasure, abused and insulted him: Why does he, unasked, declare that he feels no contempt for us? Just by so doing he shows a contempt for us. He renders himself contemptible by predicting our future destiny to supreme, perfect enlightenment; we do not care for what is not true. Many years, Mahasthamaprapta, went on during which that Bodhisattva Mahasattva was being abused, but he was not angry at anybody, nor felt malignity, and to those who, when he addressed them in the said manner, cast a clod or stick at him, he loudly exclaimed from afar: I do not contemn you. Those monks and nuns, male and female lay devotees, being always and ever addressed by him in that phrase gave him the nick name of Sadaparibhuta.

Under those circumstances, Mahasthamaprapta, the Bodhisattva Mahasattva Sadaparibhuta happened to hear this Dharmaparyaya of the Lotus of the True Law when the end of his life was impending, and the moment of dying drawing near. It was the Lord Bhishmagarjitasvaraja, the Tathagata, etc., who expounded this Dharmaparyaya in twenty times twenty hundred thousand myriads of kotis of stanzas, which the Bodhisattva Mahasattva Sadaparibhuta heard from a voice in the sky, when the time of' his death was near at hand. On hearing that voice from the sky, without there appearing a person speaking, he grasped this Dharmaparyaya and obtained the perfections already mentioned: the perfection of sight, hearing, smell, taste, body, and mind. With the attainment of these perfections he at the same time made a vow to prolong his life for twenty hundred thousand myriads of kotis of years, and promulgated this Dharmaparyaya of the Lotus of the True Law. And all those proud beings, monks, nuns, male and female lay devotees to whom he had said: I do not contemn you, and who had given him the name of Sadaparibhuta, became all his followers to hear the law, after they had seen the power and strength of his sublime magic faculties, of his vow, of his readiness of wit, of his wisdom. All those and many hundred thousand myriads of kotis of other beings were by him roused to supreme, perfect enlightenment.

Afterwards, Mahasthamaprapta, that Bodhisattva Mahasattva disappeared from that place and propitiated twenty hundred kotis of Tathagatas, etc., all bearing the same name of Chandraprabhasraja, under all of whom he promulgated this Dharmaparyaya. By virtue of his previous root of goodness he, in course of time, propitiated twenty hundred thousand myriads of kotis of Tathagatas, etc., all bearing the name of Dundubhisvararaja, and under all he obtained this very Dharmaparyaya of the Lotus of the True Law and promulgated it to the four classes. By virtue of his previous root of goodness he again, in course of time, propitiated twenty hundred thousand myriads of kotis of Tathagatas, etc., all bearing the name of Meghasvararaja, and under all he obtained this very Dharmaparyaya of the Lotus of the True Law and promulgated it to the four classes. And under all of them he was possessed of the aforementioned perfectness of sight, hearing, smell, taste, body, and mind.

Now, Mahasthamaprapta, that Bodhisattva Mahasattva Sadaparibhuta, after having honoured, respected, esteemed, worshipped, venerated, revered so many hundred thousand myriads of kotis of Tathagatas, and after having acted in the same way towards many hundred thousand myriads of kotis of other Buddhas, obtained under all of them this very Dharmaparyaya of the Lotus of the True Law, and owing to his former root of goodness having come to full development, gained supreme, perfect enlightenment. Perhaps, Mahasthamaprapta, thou wilt have some doubt, uncertainty, or misgiving, and think that he who at that time, at that juncture was the Bodhisattva Mahasattva called Sadaparibhuta was one, and he who under the rule of that Lord Bhishmagarjitasvararaja the Tathagata, etc., was generally catted Sadaparibhuta by the four classes, by whom so many Tathagatas were propitiated, was another. But thou shouldst not think so. For it is myself who at that time, at that juncture was the Bodhisattva Mahasattva Sadaparibhuta. Had I not formerly grasped and kept this Dharmaparyaya, Mahasthamaprapta, should not so soon have arrived at supreme, perfect enlightenment. It is because I have kept, read, preached this Dharmaparyaya derived from the teaching of the ancient Tathagatas, etc., Mahasthamaprapta, that I have so soon arrived at supreme, perfect enlightenment. As to the hundreds of monks, nuns, male and female lay devotees, Mahasthamaprapta, to whom under that Lord the Bodhisattva Mahasattva Sadaparibhuta promulgated this Dharmaparyaya by saying: I do not contemn you; you all observe the course of duty of Bodhisattvas; you are to become Tathagatas, etc., and in whom awoke a feeling of malignity towards that Bodhisattva, they in twenty hundred thousand myriads of kotis of Aeons never saw a Tathagata, nor heard the call of the law, nor the call of the assembly, and for ten thousand Aeons they suffered terrible pain in the great hell Avichi. Thereafter released from the ban, they by the instrumentality of that Bodhisattva Mahasattva were all brought to full ripeness for supreme, perfect enlightenment. Perhaps, Mahasthamaprapta, thou wilt have some doubt, uncertainty, or misgiving as to who at that time, at that juncture were the persons hooting and laughing at the Bodhisattva Mahasattva. They are, in this very assembly, the five hundred Bodhisattvas headed by Bhadrapala, the five hundred nuns following Simhachandra, the five hundred lay devotees following Sugataketana, who all of them have been rendered inflexible in supreme, perfect enlightenment. So greatly useful it is to keep and preach this Dharmaparyaya, as it tends to result for Bodhisattvas Mahasattvas in supreme, perfect enlightenment. Hence, Mahasthamaprapta, the Bodhisattvas Mahasattvas should, after the complete extinction of the Tathagata, constantly keep, read, and promulgate this Dharmaparyaya.

And on that occasion the Lord uttered the following stanzas:

1. I remember a past period, when king Bhishmasvara, the Jina, lived, very mighty, and revered by gods and men, the leader of men, gods, goblins, and giants.
2. At the time succeeding the complete extinction of that Jina, when the decay of the true law was far advanced, there was a monk, a Bodhisattva, called by the name of Sadaparibhuta.
3. Other monks and nuns who did not believe but in what they saw, he would approach and say: I never am to contemn you, for you observe the course leading to supreme enlightenment.
4. It was his wont always to utter those words, which brought him but abuse and taunts from their part. At the time when his death was impending he heard this Sutra.

5. The sage, then, did not expire; he resolved upon a very long life, and promulgated this Sutra under the rule of that leader.
6. And those many persons who only acknowledged the evidence of sensual perception were by him brought to full ripeness for enlightenment. Then, disappearing from that place, he propitiated thousands of kotis of Buddhas.
7. Owing to the successive good actions performed by him, and to his constantly promulgating this Sutra, that son of Jina reached enlightenment. That Bodhisattva then is myself, Sakyamuni.
8. And those persons who only believed in perception by the senses, those monks, nuns, male and female lay devotees who by the sage were admonished of enlightenment,
9. And who have seen many kotis of Buddhas, are the monks here before me,—no less than five hundred,—nuns, and female lay devotees.
10. All of them have been by me brought to complete ripeness, and after my extinction they will all, full of wisdom, keep this Sutra.
11. Not once in many, inconceivably many kotis of Aeons has such a Sutra as this been heard. There are, indeed, hundreds of kotis of Buddhas, but they do not elucidate this Sutra.
12. Therefore let one who has heard this law exposed by the Self-born himself, and who has repeatedly propitiated him, promulgate this Sutra after my extinction in this world.

◆ ◆ ◆ ◆ ◆

20

THE TRANSCENDENT POWER OF THE TATHAGATAS

Grand show exhibited by two Tathagatas, Sakyamuni and Prabhutaratna, which creates a great stir in the cosmos, and the Tathagata extols the Lotus Sutra.

Thereupon those hundred thousands of myriads of kotis of Bodhisattvas equal to the dust atoms of a macrocosm, who had issued from the gaps of the earth, all stretched their joined hands towards the Lord, and said unto him: We, O Lord, will, after the complete extinction of the Tathagata, promulgate this Dharmaparyaya everywhere for every occasion in all Buddha-fields of the Lord, wherever or whenever the Lord shall be completely extinct. We are anxious to obtain this sublime Dharmaparyaya, O Lord, in order to keep, read, publish, and write it.

Thereupon the hundred thousands of myriads of kotis of Bodhisattvas, headed by Manjusri; the monks, nuns, male and female lay devotees living in this world; the gods, Nagas, goblins, Gandharvas, demons, Garudas, Kinnaras, great serpents, men, and beings not human, and the many Bodhisattvas Mahasattvas equal to the sands of the river Ganges, said unto the Lord: We also, O Lord, will promulgate this Dharmaparyaya after the complete extinction of the Tathagata. While standing with an invisible body in the sky, O Lord, we will send forth a voice, and plant the roots of goodness of such creatures as have not yet planted roots of goodness.

Then the Lord addressed the Bodhisattva Mahasattva Visishtacharitra, followed by a troop, a great troop, the master of a troop, who was the very first of those aforementioned Bodhisattvas Mahasattvas followed by a troop, a great troop, masters of a troop: Very well, Visishtacharitra, very well; so you should do; it is for the sake of this Dharmaparyaya that the Tathagata has brought you to ripeness.

Thereupon the Lord Sakyamuni, the Tathagata, etc., and the wholly extinct Lord Prabhutaratna, the Tathagata, etc., both seated on the throne in the centre of the Stupa, commenced smiling to one another, and from their opened mouths stretched out their tongues, so that with their tongues they reached the Brahma-world, and from those two tongues issued many hundred thousand myriads of kotis of rays. From each of those rays issued many hundred thousand myriads of kotis of Bodhisattvas, with gold-coloured bodies and possessed of the thirty-two characteristic signs of a great man, and seated on thrones consisting of the interior of lotuses. Those Bodhisattvas spread in all directions in hundred; thousands of worlds, and while on every side stationed in the sky preached the law. Just as the Lord Sakyamuni, the Tathagata, etc., produced a miracle of magic by his tongue, so, too, Prabhutaratna, the Tathagata, etc., and the other Tathagatas, etc., who, having flocked from hundred thousands of myriads of kotis of other worlds, were seated on thrones at the foot of jewel trees, by their tongues produced a miracle of magic.

The Lord Sakyamuni, the Tathagata, etc., and all those Tathagatas, etc., produced that magical effect during fully a thousand years. After the lapse of that millennium those Tathagatas, etc., pulled back their tongue, and all simultaneously, at the same moment, the same instant, made a great noise as of expectoration and of snapping the fingers, by which sounds all the hundred thousands of myriads of kotis of Buddha-fields in every direction of space were moved, removed, stirred, wholly stirred, tossed, tossed forward, tossed along, and all beings in all those Buddha-fields, gods, Nagas, goblins, Gandharvas, demons, Garudas, Kinnaras, great serpents, men, and beings not human beheld, by the power of the Buddha, from the place where they stood, this Saha-world. They beheld the hundred thousands of myriads of kotis of Tathagatas seated severally on their throne at the foot of a jewel tree, and the Lord Sakyamuni, the Tathagata, etc., and the Lord Prabhutaratna, the Tathagata, etc., wholly extinct, sitting on the throne in the centre of the

Stupa of magnificent precious substances, along with the Lord Sakyamuni, the Tathagata, etc.; they beheld, finally, those four classes of the audience. At this sight they felt struck with wonder, amazement, and rapture. And they heard a voice from the sky calling: Worthies, beyond a distance of an immense, incalculable number of hundred thousands of myriads of kotis of worlds there is the world named Saha; there the Tathagata called Sakyamuni, the Arhat, etc., is just now revealing to the Bodhisattvas Maha-sattvas the Dharmaparyaya of the Lotus of the True Law, a Sutranta of great extent, serving to instruct Bodhisattvas, and belonging in proper to all Buddhas. Ye accept it joyfully with all your heart, and do homage to the Lord Sakyamuni, the Tathagata, etc., and the Lord Prabhutaratna, the Tathagata, etc.

On hearing such a voice from the sky all those beings exclaimed from the place where they stood, with joined hands: Homage to the Lord Sakyamuni, the Tathagata. Then they threw towards the Saha-world various flowers, incense, fragrant wreaths, ointment, gold, cloth, umbrellas, flags, banners, and triumphal streamers, as well as ornaments, parures, necklaces, gems and jewels of all sorts, in order to worship the Lord Sakyamuni, the Tathagata, and this Dharmaparyaya of the Lotus of the True Law. Those flowers, incense, etc., and those necklaces, etc., came down upon this Saha-world, where they formed a great canopy of flowers hanging in the sky above the Tathagatas there sitting, as well as those in the hundred thousands of myriads of kotis of other worlds.

Thereupon the Lord addressed the Bodhisattvas Mahasattvas headed by Visishtacharitra: Inconceivable, young men of good family, is the power of the Tathagatas. In order to transmit this Dharmaparyaya, young men of good family, I might go on for hundred thousands of myriads of kotis of Aeons explaining the manifold virtues of this Dharmaparyaya through the different principles of the law, without reaching the end of those virtues. In this Dharmaparyaya I have succinctly taught all Buddha-laws or Buddha-qualities, all the superiority, all the mystery, all the profound conditions of the Buddhas. Therefore, young men of good family, you should, after the complete extinction of the Tathagata, with reverence keep, read, promulgate, cherish, worship it. And wherever on earth, young men of good family, this Dharmaparyaya shall be made known, read, written, meditated, expounded, studied or collected into a volume, be it in a monastery or at home, in the wilderness or in a town, at the foot of a tree or in a palace, in a building or is a cavern, on that spot one should erect a shrine in dedication to the Tathagata. For such a spot must be regarded as a terrace of enlightenment; such a spot must be regarded as one where all Tathagatas etc. have arrived at supreme, perfect enlightenment; on that spot have all Tathagatas moved forward the wheel of the law; on that spot one may hold that all Tathagatas have reached complete extinction.

And on that occasion the Lord uttered the following stanzas:

1. Inconceivable is the power to promote the weal of the world possessed by those who, firmly established in transcendent knowledge, by means of their unlimited sight display their magic faculty in order to gladden all living beings on earth.
2. They extend their tongue over the whole world, darting thousands of beams to the astonishment .of those to whom this effect of magic is displayed and who are making for supreme enlightenment.
3. The Buddhas made a noise of expectoration and of snapping the fingers, and by it called the attention of the whole world, of all parts of the world in the ten directions of space.
4. Those .and other miraculous qualities they display in their benevolence and compassion with the view that the creatures, gladly excited at the time, may also keep the Sutra after the complete extinction of the Sugata.
5. Even if I continued for thousands of kotis of Aeons speaking the praise of those sons of Sugata who shall keep this eminent Sutra after the extinction of the Leader of the world.
6. I should not have terminated the enumeration of their qualities; inconceivable as the qualities of infinite space are the merits of those who constantly keep this holy Sutra.
7. They behold me as well as these chiefs, and the Leader of the world now extinct; they behold all these numerous Bodhisattvas and the four classes.

8. Such a one now here propitiates me and all these leaders, as well as the extinct chief Jinas and the others in every quarter.
9. The future and past Buddhas stationed in the ten points of space will all be seen and worshipped by him who keeps this Sutra.
10. He who keeps this Sutra, the veritable law, will fathom the mystery of the highest man; will soon comprehend what truth it was that was arrived at on the terrace of enlightenment.
11. The quickness of his apprehension will be unlimited; like the wind he will nowhere meet impediments; he knows the purport and interpretation of the law, he who keeps this exalted Sutra.
12. He will, after some reflection, always find out the connection of the Sutras spoken by the leaders; even after the complete extinction of the leader he will grasp the real meaning of the Sutras.
13. He resembles the moon and the sun; he illuminates all around him, and while roaming the earth in different directions he rouses many Bodhisattvas.
14. The wise Bodhisattvas who, after hearing the enumeration of such advantages, shall keep this Sutra after my complete extinction will doubtless reach enlightenment.

◆ ◆ ◆ ◆ ◆

21

SPELLS

Efficacy of talismanic spells, or Dharanis.

Thereupon the Bodhisattva Mahasattva Bhaishajyaraja rose from his seat, and having put his upper robe upon one shoulder and fixed the right knee upon the ground lifted his joined hands up to the Lord and said: How great, O Lord, is the pious merit which will be produced by a young man of good family or a young lady who keeps this Dharmaparyaya of the Lotus of the True Law, either in memory or in a book? Whereupon the Lord said to the Bodhisattva Mahasattva Bhaishajyaraja: Suppose, Bhaishajyaraja, that some man of good family or a young lady honours, respects, reveres, worships hundred thousands of myriads of kotis of Tathagatas equal to the sands of eighty Ganges rivers; dost thou think, Bhaishajyarja, that such a young man or young lady of good family will on that account produce much pious merit? The Bodhisattva Bhaishajyarja replied: Yes, Lord; yes, Sugata. The Lord said: I announce to thee, Bhaishajyarja, I declare to thee: a young man or young lady of good family, Bhaishjyaraja, who shall keep, read, comprehend, and in practice follow, were it but a single stanza from this Dharmaparyaya of the Lotus of the True Law, that young man or young lady of good family, Bhaishjyaraja, will on that account produce far more pious merit.

Then the Bodhisattva Mahasattva Bhaishajyaraja immediately said to the Lord: To those young men or young ladies of good family, O Lord, who keep this Dharmaparyaya of the Lotus of the True Law in their memory or in a book, we will give talismanic words for guard, defence, and protection; such as, *anye manye mane mamane litte larite same, simitavi, sante, mukte, muktatame, same avishame, samasame, Jaye, kshaye, akshine, sante sani, dharalni alokabhashe, partyavekshani, nidhini, abhyantavisishte, utkule mutkule, asade, parade, sukanikshi, asamasame, buddhavilokite, dharmaparikshite, sanghanirghoshani, nirghoshani bhayabhayasodhani, mantre mantrakshayate, rutakausalye, akshaye, akshavanataya, vakule valoda, amanyataya.* These words of charms and spells, O Lord, have been pronounced by reverend Buddhas in number equal to the sands of sixty-two Ganges rivers. All these Buddhas would be offended by anyone who would attack such preachers, such keepers of the Sutranta.

The Lord expressed his approval to the Bodhisattva Mahasattva Bhaishjyarja by saying: Very well, Bhaishajyaraja, by those talismanic words being pronounced out of compassion for creatures, the common weal of creatures is promoted; their guard, defence, and protection is secured.

Thereupon the Bodhisattva Mahasattva Pradanasura said unto the Lord: I also, O Lord, will, for the benefit of such preachers, give them talismanic words, that no one seeking for an occasion to surprise such preachers may find the occasion, be it a demon, giant, goblin, sorcerer, imp or ghost; that none of these when seeking and spying for an occasion to surprise may find the occasion. And then the Bodhisattva Mahasattva Pradanasura instantly pronounced the following words of a spell: *jvale mahajvale, ukke mukke, ade, adavati, tritye, trityavati, itini vitini chitini, tritti trityavati svaha.* These talismanic words, O Lord, have been pronounced and approved by Tathagatas, etc., in number equal to the sands of the river Ganges. All those Tathagatas would be offended by anyone who would attack such preachers.

Thereupon Vaisravana, one of the four rulers of the cardinal points, said unto the Lord: I also, O Lord, will pronounce talismanic words for the benefit and weal of those preachers, out of compassion to them, for their guard, defence, and protection: *natte vanatte anade, nadi kunadi svaha.* With these spells, O Lord, I shall guard those preachers over an extent of a hundred yojanas. Thus will those young men or young ladies of good family who keep this Sutranta, be guarded, be safe.

At that meeting was present Virudhaka, another of the four rulers of the cardinal points sitting surrounded and attended by hundred thousands of myriads of kotis of Kumbhandas. He rose from his seat, put his upper robe upon one shoulder, lifted his joined hands up to the Lord, and spoke to him as follows: I also, O Lord, will pronounce talismanic words for the benefit of people at large, and to guard, defend, protect such preachers as are qualified, who keep the Sutranta as mentioned: *agane gane gauri gandhari chandali matangi pukkasi sankule vrusali svaha*. These talismanic words, Lord, have been pronounced by forty-two hundred thousand myriads of kotis of Buddhas. All those Buddhas would be offended by anyone who would attack such preachers as are qualified.

Thereupon the giantesses called Lamba, Vilamba, Kutadanta, Pushpadantt, Makutadanti, Kesint, Achala, Maladhart, Kuntt, Sarvasattvojahari, and Hariti, all with their children and suite went up to the place where the Lord was, and with one voice said unto him : We also, O Lord, will afford guard, defence, and protection to such preachers as keep this Sutranta; we will afford them safety, that no one seeking for an occasion to surprise those preachers may find the occasion. And the giantesses all simultaneously and in a chorus gave to the Lord the following words of spells: *iti me, iti me, iti me, iti me, iti me; nime nime nime nime nime; ruhe ruhe ruhe ruhe ruhe; stuhe stuhe stuhe stuhe stuhe, svaha.* No one shall overpower and hurt such preachers; no goblin, giant, ghost, devil, imp, sorcerer, spectre, gnome; no spirit causing epilepsy, no sorcerer of goblin race, no sorcerer of not-human race, no sorcerer of human race; no sorcerer producing tertian ague, quartian ague, quotidian ague. Even if in his dreams he has visions of women, men, boys or girls, it shall be impossible that they hurt him.

And the giantesses simultaneously and in a chorus addressed the Lord with the following stanzas:

1. His head shall be split into seven pieces, like a sprout of Symplocos Racemosa, who after hearing this spell would attack a preacher.
2. He shall go the way of patricides and matricides, who would attack a preacher.

3. He shall go the way of oil-millers and sesamum-pounders, who would attack a preacher.
4. He shall go the way of those who use false weights and measures, who would attack a preacher.

Thereafter the giantesses headed by Kuntt said unto the Lord : We also, O Lord, will afford protection to such preachers; we will procure them safety; we will protect them against assault and poison. Whereupon the Lord said to those giantesses: Very well, sisters, very well; you do well in affording guard, defence, and protection to those preachers, even to such who shall keep no more than the name of this Dharmaparyaya; how much more then to those who shall keep this Dharmaparyaya wholly and entirely, or who, possessing the text of it in a volume, honour it with flowers, incense, fragrant garlands, ointment, powder, cloth, flags, banners, lamps with sesamum oil, lamps with scented oil, lamps with champaka-scented oil, with Varshika-scented oil, with lotus-scented oil, with jasmine-scented oil; who by such-like manifold hundred thousand manners of worshipping shall honour, respect, revere, venerate, this Sutra, deserve to be guarded by thee and thy suite, Kunti!

And while this chapter on spells was being expounded sixty-eight thousand living beings received the faculty of acquiescence in the law that has no origin.

◆ ◆ ◆ ◆ ◆

22

BODHISATTVA BHAISHAJYARAJA

Self-sacrifice of the Bodhisattva and glorification of the Lotus Sutra as the most eminent.

Thereupon the Bodhisattva Mahasattva Nakshatraja-sankusumitabhijna spoke to the Lord as follows: Wherefore, O Lord, does the Bodhisattva Bhaishjyaraja pursue his course in this Saha-world, while he is fully aware of the many hundred thousands of myriads of kotis of difficulties he has to meet? Let the Lord, the Tathagata, etc., deign to tell us any part of the course of duty of the Bodhisattva Mahasattva Bhaishajyaraja, that by hearing it the gods, Nagas, goblins, Gandharvas, demons, Garudas, Kinnaras, great serpents, men, and beings not human, as well as the Bodhisattvas Mahasattvas from other worlds here present, and these great disciples here may be content, delighted, overjoyed.

And the Lord, out of regard to that request of the Bodhisattva Mahasattva Nakshatrarajasankusumitabhijna, told him the following: Of yore, young man of good family, at a past epoch, at a time as many Aeons ago as there are grains of sand in the river Ganges, there appeared in the world a Tathagata, etc., by the name of Chandravimalasuryaprabhasasri, endowed with science and conduct, a Sugata, etc. etc. Now that Tathagata, etc., Chandravimalasuryaprabhasasri had a great assembly of eighty kotis of Bodhisattvas Mahasattvas and an assembly of disciples equal to the sands of seventy-two Ganges rivers. His spiritual rule was exempt from the female sex, and his Buddha-field had no hell, no brute creation, no ghosts, no demons; it was level, neat, smooth as the palm of the hand. Its floor consisted of heavenly lapis lazuli, and it was adorned with trees of jewel and sandalwood; inlaid with a multitude of jewels, and hung with long bands of silk, and scented by censors made of jewels. Under each jewel tree, at a distance not farther than a bow-shot, was made a small jewel-house, and on the top of those small jewel-houses stood a hundred kotis of angels performing a concert of musical instruments and castanets, in order to honour the Lord Chandravimalasuryaprabhasasri, the Tathagata, etc., while that Lord was extensively expounding this Dharma-paryaya of the Lotus of the True Law to the great disciples and Bodhisattvas, directing himself to the Bodhisattva Mahasattva Sarvasattvapriyadarsana. Now, Nakshatrarajasankusumita-bhijna, the lifetime of that Lord Chandravimalasuryapra-bhasasri, the Tathagata, etc., lasted forty-two thousand Aeons, and likewise that of the Bodhisattvas Mahasattvas and great disciples. It was under the spiritual rule of that Lord that the Bodhisattva Mahasattva Sarvasattvapriyadarsana applied himself to his difficult course.

He wandered twelve thousand years strenuously engaged in contemplation. After the expiration of those twelve thousand years he acquired the Samadhi termed Sarvarupasandarsana, the sight or display of forms. No sooner had he acquired that Samadhi than satisfied, glad, joyful, rejoicing, and delighted he made the following reflection: It is owing to this Dharmaparyaya of the Lotus of the True Law that I have acquired the Samadhi of Sarvarupasandarsana. Then he made another reflection: Let me do homage to the Lord Chandravimalasuryaprabhasasri and this Dharmaparyaya of the Lotus of the True Law. No sooner had he entered upon such a meditation than a great rain of Mandarava and great Mandarava flowers fell from the upper sky. A cloud of Kalanusarin sandal was formed, and a rain of Uragasara sandal poured down. And the nature of those essences was so noble that one karsha of it was worth the whole Saha-world.

After a while, Nakshatrarajasankusumitabhijna, the Bodhisattva Mahasattva Sarvasattvapriyadarsana rose from that meditation with memory and full consciousness, and reflected thus: This display of magic power is not likely to honour the Lord and Tathagata so much as the sacrifice of my own body will do. Then the Bodhisattva Mahasattva Sarvasattvapriyadarsana instantly began to eat Agallochum, Olibanum, and the resin of Boswellia Thurifera, and to drink oil of Champaka. So, Nakshatrarajasankusumitabhijna, the Bodhisattva Mahasattva Sarvasattvapriyadarsana passed twelve years in always and constantly eating those fragrant substances and drinking oil of Champaka. After the expiration of those twelve years the Bodhisattva Mahasattva Sarvasattvapriyadarsana wrapped his body in divine garments, bathed it in oil, made his last vow, and thereafter burnt his own body with the object to pay worship to the Tathagata and this Dharmaparyaya of the Lotus of the True Law.

Then, Nakshatrarajasankusumitabhijna, eighty worlds equal to the sands of the river Ganges were brightened by the glare of the flames from the blazing body of the Bodhisattva Mahasattva Sarvasattvapriyadarsana, and the eighty Lords Buddhas equal to the sands of the Ganges in those worlds all shouted their applause, and exclaimed; Well done, well done, young man of good family, that is the real heroism which the Boddhisattvas Mahasattvas should develop; that is the real worship of the Tathagata, the real worship of the law. No worshipping with flowers, incense, fragrant wreaths, ointment, powder, cloth, umbrellas, flags, banners; no worshipping with material gifts or with Uragasara sandal equals it. This, young man of good family, is the sublimest gift, higher than the abandoning of royalty, the abandoning of beloved children and wife. Sacrificing one's own body, young man of good family, is the most distinguished, the chiefest, the best, the very best, the most sublime worship of the law. After pronouncing this speech, Nakshatrarjasankusumitabhijna, those Lords Buddhas were silent.

The body of Sarvasattvapriyadarsana continued blazing for twelve thousand years without ceasing to burn. After the expiration of those twelve thousand years the fire was extinguished. Then, Nakshatrarjasankusumitabhijna, the Bodhisattva Mahasattva Sarvasattvapriyadarsana, having paid such worship to the Tathagata, disappeared from that place, and reappeared under the spiritual reign of that very Lord Chandravimalasuryaprabhasasrt, the Tathagata, etc., in the house of king Vimaladatta, by apparitional birth, and sitting cross-legged. Immediately after his appearance the Bodhisattva Mahasattva Sarvasattvapriyadarsana addressed his father and mother in the following stanza:

1. This, O exalted king, is the walk in which I have acquired meditation; I have achieved a heroical feat, fulfilled a great vote by sacrificing my own dear body.

After uttering this stanza, Nakshatrarajasankusumitabhijna, the Bodhisattva Mahasattva Sarvasattvapriyadarsana said to his father and mother: Even now, father and mother, the Lord Chandravimalasuryaprabhasasri, the Tathagata, etc., is still living, existing, staying in the world, the Lord by worshipping whom I have obtained the spell of knowing all sounds and this Dharmaparyaya of the Lotus of the True Law, consisting of eighty hundred thousand myriads of kotis of stanzas, of a hundred Niyutas, of Vivaras, of a hundred Vivaras, which I have heard from that Lord. Therefore, father and mother, I should like to go to that Lord and worship him again. Instantaneously, Nakshatrarajasankusumitabhijna, the Bodhisattva Mahasattva Sarvasattvapriyadarsana rose seven talas high into the sky and sat cross-legged on the top of a tower of seven precious substances. So he went up to the presence of that Lord, and having approached him humbly saluted him, circumambulated him seven times from left to right, stretched the joined hands towards the Lord, and after thus paying his homage addressed him with the following stanza:

2. O thou whose face is so spotless and bright; thou, king and sage! How thy lustre sparkles in all quarters! After having anciently paid thee homage, O Sugata, I now come again to behold thee, O Lord.

Having pronounced this stanza, the Bodhisattva Mahasattva Sarvasattvapriyadarsana said to the Lord Chandravimalasuryaprabhasasri, the Tathagata, etc.: Thou art then still alive, Lord? Whereon the Lord Chandravimalasuryaprabhasasri, the Tathagata, etc., replied: The time of my final extinction, young man of good family, has arrived; the time of my death has arrived. Therefore, young man of good family, prepare my couch; I am going to enter complete extinction. Then, Nakshatrarajasankusumitabhijna the Lord Chandravimalasuryaprabhasasri said to the Bodhisattva Mahasattva Sarvasattvapriyadarsana: I entrust to thee, young man of good family, my commandment or mastership, rule; I entrust to thee these Bodhisattvas Mahasattvas, these great disciples, this Buddha-enlightenment, this world, these jewel cars, these jewel trees, and these angels, my servitors. I entrust to thee also, young man of good family, my relics after my complete extinction. Thou shouldst pay a great worship to my relics, young man of good family, and also distribute them and build many thousands of Stupas. And, Nakshatrarajasankusumitabhijna, after the Lord Chandravimalasuryaprabhasasri, the Tathagata, etc., had given these instructions to the Bodhisattva Mahasattva Sarvasattvapriyadarsana he in the last watch of the night entered absolute final extinction.

Thereupon, Nakshatrarajasankusumitabhijna, the Bodhisattva Mahasattva Sarvasattvapriyadarsana, perceiving that the Lord Chandravimalasuryaprabhasasri, the Tathagata, etc., had expired, made a pyre of Uragasara sandalwood and burnt the body of the Tathagata. When he saw that the body was burnt to ashes and the fire extinct, he took the bones and wept, cried and lamented. After having wept, cried and lamented, Nakshatrarajasankusumitabhijna, the Bodhisattva Mahasattva Sarvasattvapriyadarsana caused to be made eighty-four thousand urns of seven precious substances, deposed in them the bones of the Tathagata, founded eighty-four thousand Stupas, reaching in height to the Brahma-world, adorned with a row of umbrellas, and equipped with silk bands and bells. After founding those Stupas he made the following reflection: I have paid honour to the Tathagata-relics of the Lord Chandravimalasuryaprabhasasri, but I will pay to those relics a yet loftier and most distinguished honour. Then, Nakshatrarajasankusumitabhijna, the Bodhisattva Mahasattva Sarvasattvapriyadarsana addressed that entire assembly of Bodhisattvas, those great disciples, those gods, Nagas, goblins, Gandharvas, demons, Garudas, Kinnaras, great serpents, men, and beings not human: Ye all, young men of good family, unanimously vow to pay worship to the relics of the Lord. Immediately after, Nakshatrarajasankusumitabhijna, the Bodhisattva Mahasattva Sarvasattvapriyadarsana, in presence of those eighty-four thousand Stupas, burnt his own arm which was marked by the one hundred auspicious signs, and so paid worship to those Stupas containing the relics of the Tathagata, during seventy-two thousand years. And while paying worship, he educated countless hundred thousands of myriads of kotis of disciples from that assembly, in consequence whereof all those Bodhisattvas acquired the Samadhi termed Sarvarupasan-darsana.

Then, Nakshatrarajasankusumitabhijna, the entire assembly of Bodhisattvas and all great disciples, seeing the Bodhisattva Mahasattva Sarvasattvapriyadarsana deprived of a limb, said, with tears in their eyes, weeping, crying, lamenting: The Bodhisattva Mahasattva Sarvasattvapriyadarsana, our master and instructor, is now deprived of a limb, deprived of one arm. But the Bodhisattva Mahasattva Sarvasattvapri-yadarsana addressed those Bodhisattvas, great disciples, and angels in the following terms: Do not, young men of good family, weep, cry, lament at the sight of my being deprived of one arm. All the Lords Buddhas who be, exist, live in the endless, limitless worlds in every direction of space, have I taken to witness. Before their face have I pronounced a vow of truth, and by that truth, by that word of truth shall I, after the sacrifice of my own arm in honour of the Tathagata, have a body of gold colour. By this truth, by this word of truth let this arm of mine become such as it was before, and let the great earth shake in six different ways, and let the angels in the sky pour down a rain of flowers.

No sooner, Nakshatrarajasankusumitabhijna, had the Bodhisattva Mahasattva Sarvasattvapriyadarsana made that vow of truth, than the whole triple macrocosm was shaken in six different ways, and from the sky aloft fell a great rain of flowers. The arm of the Bodhisattva Mahasattva Sarvasattvapriyadarsana became again as it was before, and that by the power of knowledge and by the power of pious merit belonging to that Bodhisattva Mahasattva. Perhaps, Nakshatrarajasankusumitabhijna, thou wilt have some doubt, uncertainty or misgiving, and think that the Bodhisattva Mahasattva Sarvasattvapriya-darsana at that time, and that epoch, was another. But do not think so; for the Bodhisattva Mahasattva Bhaishajyaraja here was at that time, and that epoch, the Bodhisattva Mahasattva Sarvasattvapriyadarsana. So many hundred thousand myriads of kotis of difficult things, Nakshatrarajasankusumitabhijna, and sacrifices of his body does this Bodhisattva Mahasattva Sarvasattvapriyadarsana accomplish. Now, Nakshatrarajasank-usumitabhijna, the young man or young lady of good family striving in the Bodhisattva vehicle towards the goal and longing for supreme, perfect enlightenment, who at the Tathagata shrines shall burn a great toe, a finger, a toe, or a whole limb, such a young man or young lady of good family, I assure thee, shall produce far more pious merit, far more than results from giving up a kingdom, sons, daughters, and wives, the whole triple world with its woods, oceans, mountains, springs: streams, tanks, wells, and gardens.

And, Nakshatrarajasankusumitabijna, the young man or young lady of good family, striving in the Bodhisattva-vehicle for the goal, who after filling with the seven precious substances this whole triple world should give it in alms to all Buddhas, Bodhisattvas, disciples, Pratyeka Buddhas, that young man or young lady of good family, Nakshatrarajasankusumitabhijna, does not produce so much pious merit as a young man or young lady of good family who shall keep, were it but a single verse from this Dharmaparyaya of the Lotus of the True Law. I positively declare that the accumulation of merit of the latter is greater than if a person, after filling the whole triple world with the seven precious substances, bestows it in alms on all Buddhas, Bodhisattvas, disciples, or Pratyeka Buddhas.

Just as the great ocean, Nakshatrarajasankusumitibijna, surpasses all springs, streams, and tanks, so, Nakshatrarajasankusumitabhjina, this Dharmaparyaya of the Lotus of the True Law surpasses all Sutras spoken by the Tathagata, Just as the Sumeru, the king of mountains, Nakshatrarajasankusumitabhijna, all elevations at the cardinal points, horizon circles and great horizons, so, Nakshatrarajasankusumitabhijna, this Dharmaparyaya of the Lotus of the True Law surpasses as a king all the Sutrantas spoken by the Tathagata. As the moon, Nakshatrarajasankusumitabhijna, as a luminary, takes the first rank amongst the whole of the asterisms, so, Nakshatrarajasankusumitabhijna, this Dharmaparyaya of the Lotus of the

True Law ranks first amongst all Sutrantas spoken by the Tathagata, though it surpasses hundred thousands of myriads of kotis of moons. As the orb of the sun, Nakshatrarajasankusumitabhijna, dispels gloomy darkness, so, Nakshatrarajasankusumitabhijna, this Dharmapayaya of the Lotus of the True Law dispels all the gloomy darkness of unholy works. As Indra, Nakshatrarajasankusumitabhijna, is the chief of the gods of paradise, so, Nakshatrarajasankusumitabhijna, this Dharmaparyaya of the Lotus of the True Law is the chief of Sutrantas spoken by the Tathagata. As Brahma Sahampati, Nakshatrarajasankusumitabhijna, is the king of all Brahmakayika gods and exercises the function of a father in the Brahma-world, so, Nakshatrarajasankusumitabhijna, this Dharmaparyaya of the Lotus of the True Law exercises the function of a father to all beings, whether under training or past it, to all disciples, Pratyeka Buddhas, and those who in the Bodhisattva-vehicle are striving for the goal. As the Srotapanna, Nakshatrarajasankusumitabhijna, as well as the Sakridagamin, Anagamin, Arhat and Pratyeka Buddha, excels the ignorant people and the *profanum vulgus*, so, Nakshatrarajasankusumitabhijna, the Dharmaparyaya of the Lotus of the True Law must be held to excel and surpass all Sutrantas spoken by the Tathagata; and such as shall keep this king of Sutras, Nakshatrarajasankusumitabhijna, must be held to surpass others who do not.

As a Bodhisattva is accounted superior to all disciples and Pratyekabuddhas, so, Nakshatrajasankusumitabhijna, this Dharmaparyaya of the Lotus of the True Law is accounted superior to all Sutrantas spoken by the Tathagata. Even as the Tathagata is the crowned king of the law of all disciples, Pratyeka Buddhas, and Bodhisattvas, so, Nakshatrarajasankusumitabhijna, this Dharmaparyaya is a Tathagata in respect to those who in the vehicle of Bodhisattvas are striving to reach the goal. This Dharmaparyaya of the Lotus of the True Law, Nakshatrarajasankusumitabhijna, saves all beings from all fear, delivers them from all pains. It is like a tank for the thirsty, like a fire for those who suffer from cold, like a garment for the naked, like the caravan leader for the merchants, like a mother for her children, like a boat for those who ferry over, like a leech for the sick, like a lamp for those who are wrapt in darkness, like a jewel for those who want wealth, like the ocean for the rivers, like a torch for the dispelling of darkness. So, Nakshatrarajasankusumitabhijna, this Dharmaparyaya of the Lotus of the True Law delivers from all evils, extirpates all diseases, releases from the narrow bonds of the mundane whirl.

And he who shall hear this Dharmaparyaya of the Lotus of the True Law, who shall write it and cause it to be written, will produce an accumulation of pious merit the term of which is not to be arrived at even by Buddha-knowledge; so great is the accumulation of pious merit that will be produced by a young man of good family or a young lady who after teaching or learning it, writing it or having it collected into a volume, shall honour, respect, venerate, worship it with flowers, incense, fragrant garlands, ointment, powder, umbrellas, flags, banners, triumphal streamers, with music, with joining of hands, with lamps burning with ghee, scented oil, Champaka oil, jasmine oil, trumpet-flower oil, Varshika oil or double jasmine oil.

Great will be the pious merit, Nakshatrarajasankusumitabhijna, to be produced by a young man of good family or a young lady striving to reach the goal in the Bodhisattva-vehicle, who shall keep this chapter of the Ancient Devotion of Bhaishajyaraja, who shall read and learn it. And, Nakshatraraja, should a female, after hearing this Dharmaparyaya, grasp and keep it, then this existence will be her last existence as a woman. Any female, Nakshatrarajasatikusumitabhijna, who in the last five hundred years of the millennium shall hear and penetrate this chapter of the Ancient Devotion of Bhaishajyaraja, will after disappearing from earth be reborn in the world Sukhavati, where the Lord Amitayus, the Tathagata, etc., dwells, exists, lives surrounded by a host of Bodhisattvas. There will he who formerly was a female appear seated on a throne consisting of the interior of a lotus; no affection, no hatred, no infatuation, no pride, no envy, no wrath, no malignity will vex him. With his birth he will also receive the five transcendent faculties, as well as the acquiescence in the eternal law, and, once in possession thereof, Nakshatrarajasankusumitabhijna, he as a Bodhisattva Mahasattva will see Tathagatas equal to the sands of seventy-two rivers Ganges. So perfect will be his organ of sight that by means thereof he shall see those Lords Buddhas, which Lords

Buddhas will applaud him and say: Well done, well done, young man of good family, that after hearing this Dharmaparyaya of the Lotus of the True Law which has been promulgated by the spiritual proclamation of the Lord Sakyamuni, the Tathagata, etc., thou hast studied, meditated, examined, minded it, and expounded it to other beings, other persons. This accumulation of thy pious merit, young man of good family, cannot be burnt by fire, nor swept away by water. Even a thousand Buddhas would not be able to determine this accumulation of thy pious merit, young man of good family. Thou hast subdued the opposition of the Evil One, young man of good family. Thou, young man of good family, hast victoriously emerged from the battle of mundane existence, hast crushed the enemies annoying thee. Thou young man of good family, hast been superintended by thousands of Buddhas; thine equal, young man of good family, is not to be found in the world, including the gods, with the only exception of the Tathagata; there is no other, be he disciple, Pratyeka Buddha, or Bodhisattva, able to surpass thee in pious merit, knowledge, wisdom or meditation. Such a power of knowledge, Nakshatrarajasankusumitabhijna, will be acquired by that Bodhisattva.

Anyone, Nakshatrarajasankusumitabhijna, who on hearing this chapter of the ancient devotion of Bhaishajyarja approves it, will emit from his mouth a breath sweet as of the lotus, and from his limbs a fragrance as of sandalwood. Such temporal advantages as I have just now indicated will belong to him who approves this Dharmaparyaya. On that account then, Nakshatrarajasankusumitabhijna, I transmit to thee this chapter of the Ancient Devotion of the Bodhisattva Mahasattva Sarvasattvapriyadarsana, that at the end of time, the last period, in the latter half of the millennium it may have course here in Jambudvipa and not be lost; that neither Mara the Fiend, nor the celestial beings called Marakayikas, Nagas, goblins, imps may find the opportunity of hurting it. Therefore, Nakshatrarajasankusumitabhijna, I bequeath this Dharmaparyaya; it is to be like a medicament for sick and suffering creatures in Jambudvipa. No sickness shall overpower him who has heard this Dharmaparyaya, no decrepitude, no untimely death. Whenever a person striving to reach the goal in the vehicle of

Bodhisattvas happens to see such a monk as keeps this Sutranta, then he should strew him with sandal-powder and blue lotuses, and reflect thus: This young man of good family is going to reach the terrace of enlightenment; he will spread the bundle of grass on the terrace of enlightenment; he will put to flight the party of Mara, blow the conch trumpet of the law, beat the drum of the law, cross the ocean of existence. Thus, Nakshatrarajasankusumitabhijna, should a young man of good family, striving to reach the goal in the vehicle of Bodhisattva, reflect when seeing a monk who keeps this Sutra, and he will acquire such advantages as have been indicated by the Tathagata.

While this chapter of the Ancient Devotion of Bhaishajyaraja was being expounded, eighty-four thousand Bodhisattvas attained the spell connected with skill in all sounds. And the Lord Prabhutaratna, the Tathagata, etc., intimated his approval by saying: Well done, well done, Nakshatrarajasankusumitabhijna; thou hast done well in thus questioning the Tathagata, who is endowed with such inconceivable qualities and properties.

◆ ◆ ◆ ◆ ◆

23

BODHISATTVA GADGADASVARA

Visit of the Bodhisattva to the Saha-world and narration of his extraordinary qualities by the Tathagata.

At that moment the Lord Sakyamuni, the Tathagata, etc., darted a flash of light from the circle of hair between his eyebrows, one of the characteristic signs of a great man, by which flash of light hundred thousands of myriads of kotis of Buddha-fields, equal to the sands of eighteen rivers Ganges, became illuminated. Beyond those Buddha-fields, equal, etc., is the world called Vairochanarasmipratimandita (*i.e.*, embellished by the rays of the sun). There dwells, lives, exists the Tathagata named Kamaladalavimalanakshatrarajasankusumitabhijna, who, surrounded and attended by a large and immense assembly of Bodhisattvas, preached the law. Immediately the ray of light flashing from the circle of hair between the eyebrows of the Lord Sakyamuni, the Tathagata, etc., filled the world Vairochanarasmipratimandita with a great lustre. In that world Vairochanarasmipratimandita there was a Bodhisattva Mahasattva called Gadgadasvara, who had planted roots of goodness, who had before seen similar luminous flashes emitted by many Tathagatas, etc., and who had acquired many Samadhis, such as the Samadhi Dhvajagrakeyura (*i.e.*, bracelet at the upper end of the banner staff), Saddharma Pundarika (*i.e.*, the Lotus of the True Law). Vimaladatta (*i.e.*, given by Vimala), Nakshatrarajavikridita (*i.e.*, sport of the king of asterisms, the moon god), Anilambha, Jnanamudra (*i.e.*, the seal of science), Chandrapradipa (*i.e.*, moon-light), Sarvarutakausalya (*i.e.*, skill in all sounds), Sarvapunyasamuchchaya (*i.e.*, compendium or collection of all piety), Prasadavati (*i.e.* the favourably-disposed lady), Riddhivikridita (*i.e.*, sport of magic), Jnanolka (*i.e.* torch of knowledge), Vyuharaja (*i.e.*, king of expansions or speculations), Vimalaprabha (*i.e.*, spotless lustre), Vimalagarbha (*i.e.*, of spotless, interior part), Apkritsna, Suryavarta (*i.e.*, sun-turn); in short, he had acquired many hundred thousand myriads of kotis of Samadhis equal to the sands of the river Ganges. Now, the flash of light came down upon that Bodhisattva Mahasattva Gadgadasvara. Then the Bodhisattva Mahasattva Gadgadasvara rose from his seat, put his upper robe upon one shoulder, fixed his right knee on the ground, stretched his joined hands towards the Lord Buddha, and said to the Tathagata Kamaladalavimalanakshatrarajasankusumitabhijna: O Lord, I would resort to the Saha-world to see, salute, wait upon the Lord Sakyamuni, the Tathagata, etc.; to see and salute Manjusri, the prince royal; to see the Bodhisattvas Bhaishajyaraja, Pradanasura, Nakshtrarajasankusumitabhijna, Visishtajaritra, Vyuharaja, Bhaishajyarajasamudgata.

Then the Lord Kamaladalavimalanakshatrarajasankusumitabhijna, the Tathagata, etc, said to the Bodhisattva Mahasattva Gadgadasvara: On coming to the Saha-world, young man of good family, thou must not conceive a low opinion of it. That world, young man of good family, has ups and downs, consists of earth, is replete with mountains of Kala, filled with gutters. The Lord Sakyamuni, the Tathagata, etc., is short of stature, and so are the Bodhisattvas Mahasattvas, whereas thou, young man of good family, hast got a body forty-two hundred thousand yojanas high, and myself have got a body sixty-eight hundred thousand yojanas high. And, young man of good family, thou art lovely, handsome, of pleasant appearance, endowed with a full bloom of extremely fine colour, and abundantly blest with hundred thousands of holy signs. Therefore then, young man of good family, when you have come to the Saha-world, do not conceive a low opinion of the Tathagata, nor of the Bodhisattvas, nor of that Buddha-field.

Thus addressed, the Bodhisattva Mahasattva Gadgadasvara said to the Lord Kamaladalavimalanakshatrarajasankusumitabhijna, the Tathagata, etc: I shall do, Lord, as the Lord commands; I shall go to that Saha-world by virtue of the Lord's resolution, of the Lord's power, of the Lord's might, of the Lord's disposal, of the Lord's foresight. Where on the Bodhisattva Mahasattva Gadgadasvara, without leaving that Buddha-field and without leaving his seat, plunged into so deep a meditation that immediately after, on a sudden, there appeared before the Tathagata on the Gridharakuta mountains in the Saha-world eighty-four hundred thousand myriads of kotis of lotuses on gold stalks with silver leaves and with cups of the hue of rosy lotuses and Butea Frondosa.

On seeing the appearance of this mass of lotuses the Bodhisattva Mahasattva Manjusri, the prince royal, asked the Lord Sakyamuni, the Tathagata, etc: By what cause and by whom, O Lord, have been produced these eighty-four hundred thousand myriads of kotis of lotuses on gold stalks with silver leaves and with cups of the hue of rosy lotuses and Butea Frondosa? Whereon the Lord replied to Manjusri, the prince royal: It is, Manjusri, the Bodhisattva Mahasattva Gadgadasvara, who accompanied and attended by eighty-four hundred thousand myriads of kotis of Bodhisattvas arrives from the east, from the world Vairochanarasmipratimandita, the Buddha-field of the Lord Kamaladalavimalanakshatrarajasankusumitabhijna, the Tathagata, etc., at this Saha-world to see, salute, wait upon me, and to hear this Dharmaparyaya of the Lotus of the True Law. Then Manjusri, the prince royal, said to the Lord: What mass of roots of goodness, O Lord, has that young man of good family collected, that he has deserved to obtain such a distinction? And what meditation is it, O Lord, that the Bodhisattva practises? Let us also learn that meditation, O Lord, and practise that meditation. And let us see that Bodhisattva, Lord; see how the colour, outward shape, character, figure, and behaviour of that Bodhisattva is. May the Lord deign to produce such a token that the Bodhisattva Mahasattva be admonished by it to come to this Saha-world.

Then the Lord Sakyamuni, the Tathagata, etc., said to the Lord Prabhutaratna, the Tathagata, etc., who was completely extinct: Produce such a token, Lord, that the Bodhisattva Mahasattva Gadgadasvara be admonished by it to come to this Saha-world. And the Lord Prabhutaratna, the Tathagata, etc., who was completely extinct, instantly produced a token in order to admonish the Bodhisattva Mahasattva Gadgadasvara and said: Come, young man of good family, to this Saha-world; Manjusri, the prince royal, will hail thy coming. And the Bodhisattva Mahasattva Gadgadasvara, after humbly saluting the feet of the Lord Kamaladalavimalanakshatrarajasankusumitabhijna, the Tathagata, etc., and after three times circumambulating him from left to right, vanished from the world Vairochanarasmipratimandita, along with eighty-four hundred thousand myriads of kotis of Bodhisattvas who surrounded and followed him, and arrived at this Saha-world, among a stir of Buddha-fields, a rain of lotuses, a noise of hundred thousands of myriads of kotis of musical instruments. His face showed eyes resembling blue lotuses, his body was gold-coloured, his person marked by a hundred thousand of holy signs; he sparkled with lustre, glowed with radiance, had limbs marked by the characteristic signs, and a body compact as Narayana's.

Mounted on a tower made of seven precious substances, he moved through the sky to a height of seven Talas, surrounded by a host of Bodhisattvas, in the direction of this Saha-world, and approached the Gridhrakuta, the king of mountains. At his arrival, he alighted from the tower, and went, with a necklace of pearls worth a hundred thousands, to the place where the Lord was sitting. After humbly saluting the feet of the Lord, and circumambulating him seven times from left to right, he offered him the necklace of pearls in token of homage, whereafter he said to the Lord: The Lord Kamaladalavimalanakshatraragasankusumitabhijna, the Tathagata, etc., inquires after the Lord's health, welfare, and sprightliness; whether he feels free from affliction and at ease. That Lord has also charged me to ask: Is there something thou hast to suffer or allow? the humours of the body are not in an unfavourable state? thy creatures are decent in manners, tractable, and easy to be healed? their bodies are clean? They are not too passionate, I hope, not too irascible, not too unwise in their doings? They are not jealous, Lord, not envious, not ungrateful to their father and mother, not impious, not heterodox, not unsubdued in mind, not unrestrained in sexual desires? Are the creatures able to resist the Evil One? Has the Lord Prabhutaratna, the Tathagata, etc., who is completely extinct, come to the Saha-world in order to hear the law, sitting in the centre of a Stupa made of seven precious substances? And as to that, Lord Prabhutaratna, the Tathagata, etc., the Lord Kamaladalavimalanakshatrarasakusumi tabhijna, inquires: Is there something that the Lord Prabhutaratna, etc., has to suffer or allow? Is the Lord Prabhutaratna, etc., to stay long? We also, O Lord, are desirous of seeing the rudimentary frame of that Lord Prabhutaratna, the Tathagata, etc. May the Lord therefore please to show us the rudimentary frame of the Lord Prabhutaratna, the Tathagata, etc.

Then the Lord Sakyamuni, the Tathagata, etc., said to the Lord Prabhutaratna, the Tathagata, etc., who was completely extinct: Lord, the Bodhisattva Mahasattva Gadgadasvara here wishes to see the Lord Prabhutaratna, the Tathagata, etc., who is completely extinct. Whereon the Lord Prabhutaratna, the Tathagata, etc., spoke to the Bodhisattva Mahasattva Gadgadasvara in this strain: Well done, well done, young gentleman, that thou hast come hither in the desire to see the Lord Sakyamuni, the Tathagata, etc.; to hear this Dharmaparyaya of the Lotus of the True Law, and see Manjusri, the prince royal.

Subsequently, the Bodhisattva Mahasattva Padmasri said to the Lord: What root of goodness has the Bodhisattva Mahasattva Gadgadasvara formerly planted? And in presence of which Tathagata? And the Lord Sakyamuni, the Tathagata, etc., said to the Bodhisattva Mahasattva Padmasri: In the days of yore, young man of good family, at a past period there appeared in the world a Tathagata called Meghadundubhisvararaja (*i.e.*, the king of the drum-sound of the clouds), perfectly enlightened, endowed with science and conduct, a Sugata, etc., in the world Sarvabuddhasandarsana (*i.e.*, sight or display of all Buddhas), in the Aeon Priyadarsana. To that Lord Meghadundubhisvararaja the Bodhisattva Mahasattva Gadgadasvara paid homage by making resound hundred thousands of musical instruments during twelve thousand years. He presented to him also eighty-four thousand vessels of seven precious substances. Under the reaching of the Tathagata Meghadundubhisvararaja, young man of good family, has the Bodhisattva Mahasattva Gadgadasvara obtained such a beauty as he now displays. Perhaps, young man of good family, thou hast some doubt, uncertainty or misgiving, and thinkest that at that time, that epoch, there was another Bodhisattva Mahasattva called Gadgadasvara, who paid that homage to the Lord Meghadundubhisvararaja, the Tathagata, and presented him the eighty-four thousand vessels.

But, young man of good family, do not think so. For, it was the very same Bodhisattva Mahasattva Gadgadasvara, young man of good family, who paid that homage to the Lord Meghadundubhisvararaja, the Tathagata, and presented to him the eighty-four thousand vessels. So, young man of good family, the Bodhisattva Mahasattva Gadgadasvara has waited upon many Buddhas, has planted good roots under many Buddhas, and prepared the soil under each of them. And this. Bodhisattva Mahasattva Gadgadasvara had previously seen Lords Buddhas similar to the sands of the river Ganges. Dost thou see, Padmasri, how the Bodhisattva Mahasattva Gadgadasvara now looks? Padmasri replied: I do, Lord; I do, Sugata. The Lord said: Now, Padmasri, this Bodhisattva Mahasattva Gadgadasvara preaches this Dharmaparyaya of the Lotus of the True Law under many shapes he assumes; sometimes under the shape of Brahma, sometimes under that of Indra, sometimes under that of Siva, sometimes under that of Kubera, sometimes under that of a sovereign, sometimes under that of a duke, sometimes under that of a chief merchant, sometimes under that of a citizen, sometimes under that of a villager, sometimes under that of a Brahman. Sometimes again the Bodhisattva Mahasattva Gadgadasvara preaches this Dharmaparyaya of the Lotus of the True Law under a monk's shape, sometimes under a nun's, sometimes under a male lay devotee's, sometimes under a female lay devotee's, sometimes under that of a chief merchant's wife, sometimes under that of a citizen's wife, sometimes under a boy's, sometimes under a girl's shape.

With so many variations in the manner to show himself, the Bodhisattva Mahasattva Gadgadasvara preaches this Dharmaparyaya of the Lotus of the True Law to creatures. He has even assumed the shape of a goblin to preach this Dharmaparyaya to such as were to be converted by a goblin. To some he has preached this Dharmaparyaya of the Lotus of the True Law under the shape of a demon, to some under a Garuda's, to some under a Kinnara's, to some under a great serpent's shape. Even to the beings in any of the wretched states, in the hells, the brute creation, Yama's realm, the Bodhisattva

Mahasattva Gadgadasvara is a supporter. Even to the creatures in the gynaeceums of this Saha-world has the Bodhisattva Mahasattva Gadgadasvara, after metamorphosing himself into a woman, preached this Dharmaparyaya of the Lotus of the True Law. Verily, Padmasri, the Bodhisattva Mahasattva Gadgadasvara is the supporter of the creatures living in this Saha-world. Under so many shapes, assumed at will, has the Bodhisattva Mahasattva Gadgadasvara preached this Dharmaparyaya of the Lotus of the True Law to creatures. Yet, there is no diminution of wisdom, nor diminution of magic power in that good man. So many, young man of good family, are the manifestations of knowledge by which this Bodhisattva Mahasattva Gadgadasvara has made himself known in this Saha-world. In other worlds also, similar to the sands of the river Ganges, he preaches the law, under the shape of Bodhisattva to such as must be converted by a Bodhisattva; under the shape of a disciple to such as must be converted by a disciple; under the shape of a Pratyeka Buddha to such as must be converted by a Pratyeka Buddha; under the shape of a Tathagata to such as must be converted by a Tathagata. Nay, he will show to those who must be converted by a relic of the Tathagata himself such a relic, and to those who must be converted by complete extinction he will show himself completely extinct. Such is the powerful knowledge, Padmasri, the Bodhisattva Mahisattva is possessed of.

Thereafter the Bodhisattva Mahisattva Padmasri said to the Lord: The Bodhisattva Mahasattva Gadgadasvara then has planted good roots, Lord. What meditation is it, Lord, whereby the Bodhisattva Mahasattva Gadgadasvara, with unshaken firmness, has converted for educated so many creatures? Whereupon the Lord Sakyamuni, the Tathagata, etc., replied to the Bodhisattva Mahasattva Padmasri; It is, young man of good family, the meditation termed Sarvarupasandarsana. By steadiness in it has the Bodhisattva Mahasattva Gadgadasvara so immensely promoted the weal of creatures.

While this chapter of Gadgadasvara was being expounded, all the eighty-four hundred thousand myriads of kotis of Bodhisattvas Mahasattvas who, along with the Bodhisattva Mahasattva Gadgadasvara, had come to the Saha-world, obtained the meditation Sarvarupasandarsana, and as to the number of Bodhisattvas Mahasattvas of this Saha-world obtaining the meditation Sarvarupasandarsana, it was beyond calculation.

Then the Bodhisattva Mahasattva Gadgadasvara, after having paid great and ample worship to the Lord Sakyamuni, the Tathagata, etc., and at the Stupa of relics of the Lord Prabhutaratna, the Tathagata, etc., again mounted the tower made of seven precious substances, among the stir of the fields, the rain of lotuses, the noise of hundred thousands of myriads of kotis of musical instruments, and with the eighty-four hundred thousand myriads of kotis of Bodhisattvas surrounding and following him, returned to his own Buddha-field. At his arrival there he said to the Lord Kamaladalavimalanakshatrarajasankusumitabhijna, the Tathagata, etc.: O Lord, I have in the Saha-world promoted the weal of creatures; I have seen and saluted the Stupa of relics of the Lord Prabhutaratna, the Tathagata, etc.; I have seen and saluted the Lord Sakyamuni, the Tathagata, etc.; I have seen Manjusri, the prince royal, as well as the Bodhisattva Bhaishajyaraja, who is possessed of mighty knowledge and impetuosity, and the Bodhisattva Mahasattva Pradanasura; and these eighty-four hundred thousand myriads of kotis of Bodhisattvas Mahasattvas have all obtained the meditation termed Sarvarupasandarsana.

And while this relation of the going and coming of the Bodhisattva Mahisattva Gadgadasvara was being delivered, forty-two thousand Bodhisattvas acquired the faculty of acquiescence in future things, and the Bodhisattva Mahasattva Padmasri acquired the meditation called the Lotus of the True Law.

◆ ◆ ◆ ◆ ◆

24

TRANSFORMATIONS OF AVALOKITESVARA

The grandeur of the Bodhisattva Arvalokitesvara.

Thereafter the Bodhisattva Mahasattva Akshayamati rose from his seat, put his upper robe upon one shoulder, stretched his joined hands towards the Lord, and said: For what reason, O Lord, is the Bodhisattva Mahasattva Avalokitesvara called Avalokitesvara? So he asked, and the Lord answered to the Bodhisattva Mahasattva Akshayamati: All the hundred thousands of myriads of kotis of creatures, young man of good family, who in this world are suffering troubles will, if they hear the name of the Bodhisattva Mahasattva Avalokitesvara, be released from that mass of troubles. Those who shall keep the name of this Bodhisattva Mahasattva Avalokitesvara, young man of good family, will, if they fall into a great mass of fire, be delivered therefrom by virtue of the lustre of the Bodhisattva Mahasattva. In case, young man of good family, creatures, carried off by the current of rivers, should implore the Bodhisattva Mahasattva Avalokitesvara, all rivers will afford them a ford. In case, young man of good family, many hundred thousand myriads of kotis of creatures, sailing in a ship on the ocean, should see their bullion, gold, gems, pearls, lapis lazuli, conch shells, stones, corals, emeralds, Musaragalvas, red pearls, and other goods lost, and the ship by a vehement, untimely gale cast on the island of Giantesses, and if in that ship a single being implores Avalokitesvara, all will be saved from that island of Giantesses. For that reason, young man of good family, the Bodhisattva Mahasattva Avalokitesvara is named Avalokitesvara.

If a man given up to capital punishment implores Avalokitesvara, young man of good family, the swords of the executioners shall snap asunder, Further, young man of good family, if the whole triple chiliocosm were teeming with goblins and giants, they would by virtue of the name of the Bodhisattva Mahasattva Avalokitesvara being pronounced lose the faculty of sight in their wicked designs. If some creature, young man of good family, shall be bound in wooden or iron manacles, chains or fetters, be he guilty or innocent, then those manacles, chains or fetters shall give way as soon as the name of the Bodhisattva Mahasattva Avalokitesvara is pronounced. Such, young man of good family, is the power of the Bodhisattva Mahasattva Avalokitesvara. If this whole triple chiliocosm, young man of good family, were teeming with knaves, enemies, and robbers armed with swords, and if a merchant leader of a caravan marched with a caravan rich in jewels; if then they perceived those robbers, knaves, and enemies armed with swords, and in their anxiety and fright thought themselves helpless; if, further, that leading merchant spoke to the caravan in this strain: Be not afraid, young gentlemen, be not frightened; invoke, all of you, with one voice the Bodhisattva Mahasattva Avalokitesvara, the giver of safety; then you shall be delivered from this danger by which you are threatened at the hands of robbers and enemies; if then the whole caravan with one voice invoked Avalokitesvara with the words: Adoration, adoration be to the giver of safety, to Avalokitesvara Bodhisattva Mahasattva then, by the mere act of pronouncing that name, the caravan would be released from all danger. Such, young man of good family, is the power of the Bodhisattva Mahasattva Avalokitesvara.

In case creatures act under the impulse of impure passion, young man of good family, they will, after adoring the Bodhisattva Mahasattva Avalokitesvara, be freed from passion. Those who act under the impulse of hatred will, after adoring the Bodhisattva Mahasattva Avalokitesvara, be freed from hatred. Those who act under the impulse of infatuation will, after adoring the Bodhisattva Mahasattva Avalokitesvara, be freed from infatuation. So mighty, young man of good family, is the Bodhisattva Mahasattva Avalokitesvara. If a woman, desirous of male offspring, young man of good family, adores the Bodhisattva Avalokitesvara, she shall get a son, nice, handsome, and beautiful; one possessed of the characteristics of a male child, generally beloved and winning, who has planted good roots. If a woman is desirous of getting a daughter, a nice, handsome, beautiful girl shall be born to her; one possessed of the good characteristics of a girl, generally beloved and winning, who has planted good roots. Such, young man of good family, is the power of the Bodhisattva Mahasattva Avalokitesvara.

Those who adore the Bodhisattva Mahasattva Avalokitesvara will derive from it an unfailing profit. Suppose, young man of good family, on one hand some one adoring the Bodhisattva Mahasattva Avalokitesvara and cherishing his name; on the other hand another adoring a number of Lords Buddhas equal to sixty-two times the sands of the river Ganges, cherishing their names and worshipping so many Lords Buddhas during their stay, existence, and life, by giving robes, alms-bowls, couches, medicaments for the sick; how great is then in thine opinion, young man of good family, the accumulation of pious merit which that young gentleman or young lady will produce in consequence of it? So asked, the Bodhisattva Mahasattva Akshayamati said to the Lord: Great, O Lord, great, O Sugata, is the pious merit which that young gentleman or young lady will produce in consequence of it. The Lord proceeded: Now, young man of good family, the accumulation of pious merit produced by that young gentleman paying homage to so many Lords Buddhas, and the accumulation of pious merit produced by him who performs were it but a single act of adoration to the Bodhisattva Mahasattva Avalokitesvara and cherishes his name, are equal. He who adores a number of Lords Buddhas equal to sixty-two times the sands of the river Ganges and cherishes their names, and he who adores the Bodhisattva Mahasattva Avalokitesvara and cherishes his name, have an equal accumulation of pious merit; both masses of pious merit are not easy to be destroyed even in hundred thousands of myriads of kotis of Aeons. So immense, young man of good family, is the pious merit resulting from cherishing the name of the Bodhisattva Mahasattva Avalokitesvara.

Again the Bodhisattva Mahasattva Akshayamati said to the Lord: How, O Lord, is it that the Bodhisattva Mahasattva

Avalokitesvara frequents this Saha-world? And how does he preach the law? And which is the range of the skilfulness of the Bodhisattva Mahasattva Avalokitesvara? So asked, the Lord replied to the Bodhisattva Mahasattva Akshayamati: In some worlds, young man of good family, the Bodhisattva Mahasattva Avalokitesvara preaches the law to creatures in the shape of a Buddha; in others he does so in the shape of a Bodhisattva. To some beings he shows the law in the shape of a Pratyeka Buddha; to others he does so in the shape of a disciple; to others again under that of Brahma, Indra, or a Gandharva. To those who are to be converted by a goblin, he preaches the law assuming the shape of a goblin; to those who are to be converted by Isvara, he preaches the law in the shape of Isvara; to those who are to be converted by Mahesvara, he preaches assuming the shape of Mahesvara. To those who are to be converted by a Chakravartin, he shows the law after assuming the shape of a Chakravartin; to those who are to be converted by an imp, he shows the law under the shape of an imp; to those who are to be converted by Kubera, he shows the law by appearing in the shape of Kubera; to those who are to be converted by Senapati, he preaches in the shape of Senapati; to those who are to be converted by assuming a Brahmin, he preaches in the shape of a Brahmin; to those who are to be converted by Vajrapani, he preaches in the shape of Vajrapani. With such inconceivable qualities, young man of good family, is the Bodhisattva Mahasattva Avalokitesvara endowed. Therefore then, young man of good family, honour the Bodhisattva Mahasattva Avalokitesvara. The Bodhisattva Mahasattva Avalokitesvara, young man of good family, affords safety to those who are in anxiety. On that account one calls him in this Saha-world Abhayandada (*i.e.*, Giver of Safety).

Further, the Bodhisattva Mahasattva Akshayamati said to the Lord: Shall we give a gift of piety, a decoration of piety, O Lord, to the Bodhisattva Mahasattva Avalokitesvara? The Lord replied: Do so, if thou thinkest it opportune. Then the Bodhisattva Mahasattva Akshayamati took from his neck a pearl necklace, worth a hundred thousand gold pieces, and presented it to the Bodhisattva Mahasattva Avalokitesvara as a decoration of piety, with the words: Receive from me this decoration of piety, good man. But he would not accept it. Then the Bodhisattva

Mahasattva Akshayamati said to the Bodhisattva Mahasattva Avalokitesvara: Out of compassion to us, young man of good family, accept this pearl necklace. Then the Bodhisattva Mahasattva Avalokitesvara accepted the pearl necklace from the Bodhisattva Mahasattva Akshayamati, out of compassion to the Bodhisattva Mahasattva Akshayamati and the four classes, and out of compassion to the gods, Nagas, goblins, Gandharvas, demons, Garudas, Kinnaras, great serpents, men, and beings not human. Thereafter he divided the necklace into two parts, and offered one part to the Lord Sakyamuni, and the other to the jewel Stupa of the Lord Prabhutaratna, the Tathagata, etc., who had become completely extinct.

With such a faculty of transformation, young man of good family, the Bodhisattva Mahasattva Avalokitesvara is moving in this Saha-world.

And on that occasion the Lord uttered the following stanzas:

1. Chitradhvaja asked Akshayamati the following question: For what reason, son of Jina, is Avalokitesvara so called?
2. And Akshayamati, that ocean of profound insight, after considering how the matter stood, spoke to Chitradhvaja: Listen to the conduct of Avalokitesvara.
3. Hear from my indication how for numerous, inconceivable Aeons he has accomplished his vote under many thousand kotis of Buddhas.
4. Hearing, seeing, regularly and constantly thinking will infallibly destroy all suffering mundane existence, and grief of living beings here on earth.
5. If one be thrown into a pit of fire, by a wicked enemy with the object of killing him, he has but to think of Avalokitesvara, and the fire shall be quenched as if sprinkled with water.
6. If one happens to fall into the dreadful ocean, the abode of Nagas, marine monsters, and demons he has but to think of Avalokitesvara, and he shall never sink down in the king of waters.
7. If a man happens to be hurled down from the brink of the Meru, by some wicked person with the object of killing him,

he has but to think of Avalokitesvara, and he shall, sunlike, stand firm in the sky.

8. If rocks of thunderstone and thunderbolts are thrown at a man's head to kill him, he has but to think of Avalokitesvara, and they shall not be able to hurt one hair of the body.
9. If a man be surrounded by a host of enemies armed with swords, who have the intention of killing him, he has but to think of Avalokitesvara, and they shall instantaneously become kindhearted.
10. If a man, delivered to the power of the executioners, is already standing at the place of execution, he has but to think of Avalokitesvara, and their swords shall go to pieces.
11. If a person happens to be fettered in shackles of wood or iron, he has but to think of Avalokitesvara, and the bonds shall be speedily loosened.
12. Mighty spells, witchcraft, herbs, ghosts, and spectres, pernicious to life, revert thither whence they come, when one thinks of Avalokitesvara.
13. If a man is surrounded by goblins, Nagas, demons, ghosts, or giants, who are in the habit of taking away bodily vigour, he has but to think of Avalokitesvara, and they shall not be able to hurt one hair of his body.
14. If a man is surrounded by fearful beasts with sharp teeth and claws, he has but to think of Avalokitesvara, and they shall quickly fly in all directions.
15. If a man is surrounded by snakes malicious and frightful on account of the flames and fires they emit he has but to think of Avalokitesvara, and they shall quickly lose their poison.
16. If a heavy thunderbolt shoots from a cloud pregnant with lightning and thunder, one has but to think of Avalokitesvara, and the fire of heaven shall quickly, instantaneously be quenched.
17. He, Avalokitesvara, with his powerful knowledge beholds all creatures who are beset with many hundreds of troubles and afflicted by many sorrows, and thereby is a saviour in the world, including the gods.

18. As he is thoroughly practised in the power of magic, and possessed of vast knowledge and skilfulness, he shows himself in all directions and in all regions of the world.
19. Birth, decrepitude, and disease will come to an end for those who are in the wretched states of existence, in hell, in brute creation, in the kingdom of Yama, for all beings in general.

Then Akshayamati In the joy of his heart uttered the following stanzas.

20. O thou whose eyes are dear, whose eyes are kind, distinguished by wisdom and knowledge, whose eyes are full of pity and benevolence; thou so lovely by thy beautiful face and beautiful eyes!
21. Pure one, whose shine is spotless bright, whose knowledge is free from darkness, thou shining as the sun, not to be beaten away, radiant as the blaze of fire, thou spreadest in thy flying course thy lustre in the world.
22. O thou who rejoicest in kindness having its source in compassion, thou great cloud of good qualities and of benevolent mind, thou quenchest the fire that vexes living beings, thou pourest out nectar, the rain of the law.
23. In quarrel, dispute, war, battle, in any great danger one has to think of Avalokitesvara, who shall quell the wicked troop of foes.
24. One should think of Avalokitesvara, whose sound is as the cloud's and the drum's, who thunders like a rain-cloud, possesses a good voice like Brahma, a voice going through the whole gamut of tones.
25. Think, O think with tranquil mood of Avalokitesvara, that pure being; he is a protector, a refuge, a recourse in death, disaster, and calamity.
26. He who possesses the perfection of all virtues, and beholds all beings with compassion and benevolence, he, an ocean of virtues, Virtue itself, he, Avalokitesvara, is worthy of adoration.
27. He, so compassionate for the world, shall once become a Buddha, destroying all dangers and sorrows; I humbly bow to Avalokitesvara.

28. This universal Lord, chief of kings, who is a rich mine of monastic virtues, he, universally worshipped, has reached pure, supreme enlightenment, after plying his course of duty during many hundreds of Aeons.
29. At one time standing to the right, at another to the left of the Chief Amitabha, whom he is fanning, he, by dint of meditation, like a phantom, in all regions honours the Jina.
30. In the west, where the pure world Sukhakara is situated, there the Chief Amitabha, the tamer of men, has his fixed abode.
31. There no women are to be found; there sexual intercourse is absolutely unknown; there the sons of Jina, on springing into existence by apparitional birth, are sitting in the undefiled cups of lotuses.
32. And the Chief Amitabha himself is seated on a throne in the pure and nice cup of a lotus, and shines as the Sala-king.
33. The Leader of the world, whose store of merit has been praised, has no equal in the triple world. O supreme of men, let us soon become like thee!

Thereupon the Bodhisattva Mahasattva Dharanindhara rose from his seat, put his upper robe upon one shoulder, fixed his right knee against the earth, stretched his joined hands towards the. Lord and said: They must be possessed of not a few good roots, O Lord, who are to hear this chapter from the Dharmaparyaya about the Bodhisattva Mahasattva Avalokitesvara and this miraculous power of transformation of the Bodhisattva Mahasattva Avalokitesvara.

And while this chapter of the All-sided One was being expounded by the Lord, eighty-four thousand living beings from that assembly felt their minds drawn to that supreme and perfect enlightenment, with which nothing else can be compared.

◆ ◆ ◆ ◆ ◆

25

CONVERSION OF A KING

Wonderful and edifying story of the conversion of King Subhavyuha through his two sons.

Thereupon the Lord addressed the entire assemblage of Bodhisattvas: Of yore, young men of good family, at a past epoch, incalculable, more than incalculable Aeons ago, at that time there appeared in the world a Tathagata named Galadharagarjitaghoshasusvaranakshatrarajasankusumitabhijna, an Arhat, etc., endowed with science and conduct, etc. etc., in the Aeon Priyadarsana, in the world Vairochanarasmipratimandita. Now, there was, young men of good family, under the spiritual rule of the Tathagata Jaladharagarjitaghoshasusvaranakshatrarajapsankusumitabhijna a king called Subhavyuha. That king Subhavyuha, young men of good family, had a wife called Vimaladatta, and two sons, one called Vimalagarbha, the other Vimalanetra. These two boys, who possessed magical power and wisdom, applied themselves to the course of duty of Bodhisattvas, to the perfect virtues (Paramitas) of almsgiving, morality, forbearance, energy, meditation, wisdom, and skilfulness; they were accomplished in benevolence, compassion, joyful sympathy and indifference, and in all the thirty seven consituents of true knowledge.

They had perfectly mastered the meditation Vimala (*i.e.*, spotless), the meditation Nakshatrarajaditya, the meditation Alankarasura, the meditation Mahatejogarbha. Now at that time, that period the said Lord preached the Dharmaparyaya of the Lotus of the True Law out of compassion for the beings then living and the king Subhavyuha.

Then, young men of good family, the two young princes went to their mother, to whom they said, after stretching their joined hands: We should like to go, mother, to the Lord

Jaladharagarjitaghoshasusvaranakshatrarajasan-kusumitabhijna, the Tathagata, etc., and that, mother, because the Lord Jaladharagarjitaghoshasusvaranakshatrarajasankusumitabhijna, the Tathagata, etc., expounds, in great extension, before the world, including the gods, the Dharmaparyaya of the Lotus of the True Law. We should like to hear it. Whereupon the queen Vimaladatta said to the two young princes, Vimalagarbha and Vimalanetra: Your father, young gentlement, the king Subhavyuha, favours the Brahmins. Therefore you will not obtain the permission to go and see the Tathagata. Then the two young princes Vimalagarbha and Vimalanetra, stretching their joined hands, said to their mother: Though born in a family that adheres to a false doctrine, we feel, as sons to the king of the law. Then, young men of good family, the queen Vimaladatta said to the young princes: Well, young gentlemen, out of compassion for your father, the king Subhavyuha, display some miracle, that he may become favourably inclined to you, and on that account grant you the permission of going to the Lord Jaladharagargitaghoshasusvaranakshatrarajasankusumitabhijna, the Tathagata, etc.

Immediately the young princes Vimalagarbha and Vimalanetra rose into the atmosphere to a height of seven Tal trees and performed miracles such as are allowed by the Buddha, out of compassion for their father, the king Subhavyuha. They prepared in the sky a couch and raised dust; there they also emitted from the lower part of their body a shower of rain, and from the upper part a mass of fire; then again they emitted from the upper part of their body a shower of rain, and from the lower part a mass of fire. While in the firmament they became now big, then small; and now small, then big. Then they vanished from the sky to come up again from the earth and reappear in the air. Such, young men of good family, were the miracles produced by the magical power of the two young princes, whereby their father, the king Subhavyuha, was converted. At the sight of the miracle produced by the magical power of the two young princes, the king Subhavyuha was content, in high spirits, ravished, rejoiced, joyful, and happy, and, the joined hands raised, he said to the boys: Who is your master, young gentlemen? whose pupils are you? And the two young princes answered the king Subhavyuha: There is, noble king, there exists and lives a Lord Jaladharagarjitaghoshasusvaranakshatrarajasankusumitabhijna, a Tathagata, etc.; seated on the stool of law at the foot of the tree of enlightenment; he extensively reveals the Dharmaparyaya of the Lotus of the True Law to the world, including the gods. That Lord is our Master, O noble king; we are his pupils. Then, young gentlemen of good family, the king Subhavyuha said to the young princes: I will see your Master, young gentlemen; I am to go myself to the presence of that Lord.

After the two young princes had descended from the sky, young gentlemen, they went to their mother and with joined hands stretched forward said to her: Mother, we have converted our father to supreme and perfect knowledge; we have performed the office of masters towards him; therefore let us go now; we wish to enter on the ecclesiastical life in the face of the Lord. And on that occasion, young men of good family, the young princes Vimalagarbha and Vimalanetra addressed their mother in the following two stanzas:

1. Allow us, O mother, to go forth from home and to embrace the houseless life; ay, we will become ascetics, for rare to be met with, is a Tathagata.
2. As the blossom of the glomerated fig-tree, nay, more rare is the Jina. Let us depart; we will renounce the world; the favourable moment is precious or not often to be met with.

Vimaladatta said:

3. Now I grant you leave; go, my children, give my consent. I myself will likewise renounce the world, for rare to be met with 'or precious' is a Tathagata.

Having uttered these stanzas, young men of good family, the two young princes said to their parents: Pray, father and mother, you also go together with us to the Lord Jaladhargarjitaghoshasusvaranakshatrarajasankusumitabhijna, the Tathagata, etc., in order to see, humbly salute and wait upon him, and to hear the law. For, father and mother, the appearance of a Buddha is rare to be met with as the blossom of the glomerated fig-tree, as tne entering of the tortoise's neck into the hole of the yoke formed by the great ocean. The appearance of Lords Buddhas, father and mother, is rare. Hence, father and mother, it is a happy lot we have been blessed with, to have been born at the time of such a prophet. Therefore, father and mother, give us leave; we would go and become ascetics in presence of the Lord Jaladharagarjitaghoshasusvaranakshatrarajasankusumitabhijna, the Tathagata, etc., for the seeing of a Tathagata is something rare. Such a king of the law is rarely met with; such a favourable occasion is rarely met with.

Now at that juncture, young men of good family, the eighty-four thousand women of the harem of the king Subhavyuha became worthy of being receptacles of this Dharmaparyaya of the Lotus of the True Law. The young prince Vimalanetra exercised himself in this Dharmaparyaya, whereas the young prince Vimalagarbha for many hundred thousand myriads of kotis of Aeons practised the meditation Sarvasattvapapajahana, with the object that all beings should abandon all evils. And the mother of the two young princes, the queen Vimaladatta, acknowledged the harmony between all Buddhas and all topics treated by them. Then, young men of good family, the king Subhavyuha, having been converted to the law of the Tathagata by the instrumentality of the two young princes, having been initiated and brought to full maturity in it, along with all his relations and retinue; the queen Vimaladatta with the whole crowd of women in her suite, and the two young princes, the sons of the king Subhavyuha, accompanied by forty-two thousand living beings, along with the women of the harem and the ministers, went all together and unanimously to the Lord Jaladharagarjitaghoshasusvaranakshatrarajasankusumitabhijna the Tathagatha, etc. On arriving at the place where the Lord was, they humbly saluted his feet, circumambulated him three times from left to right and took their stand at some distance.

Then, young men of good family, the Lord Jaladharagarjitaghoshasusvaranakshatrarajasatikusumitabhijna, the Tathagata, etc., perceiving the king Subhavyuha, who had arrived with his retinue, instructed, roused, excited and comforted him with a sermon. And the king Subhavyuha, young men of good family, after he had been well and duly instructed, roused, excited, and comforted by the sermon of the Lord, was so content, glad, ravished, joyful, rejoiced, and delighted, that he put his diadem on the head of his younger brother and established him in the government, whereafter he himself with his sons, kinsmen, and retinue, as well as the queen Vimaladatta and her numerous train of women, the two young princes accompanied by forty-two thousand living beings went all together and unanimously forth from home to embrace the houseless life, prompted as they were by their faith in the preaching of the Lord Jaladharagajitaghoshasusvaranakshatrarajasailkusumitabhijna, the Tathagata, etc. Having become an ascetic, the king Subhavyuha, with his retinue, remained for eighty-four thousand years applying himself to studying, meditating, and thoroughly penetrating this Dharmaparyaya of the Lotus of the True Law. At the end of those eighty-four thousand years, young men of good family, the king Subhavyuha acquired the meditation termed Sarvagunalankaravyuha. No sooner had he acquired that meditation, than he rose seven Tals up to the sky, and while staying in the air, young men of good family, the king Subhavyuha said to the Lord Jaladharagajita-ghoshasusvaranakshatrarajasankusumitabhijna, the Tathagata, etc.: My two sons, O Lord, are my masters, since it is owing to the miracle produced by their magical power that I have been diverted from that great heap of false doctrines, been established in the command of the Lord, brought to full ripeness in it, introduced to it, and exhorted to see the Lord. They have acted as true friends to me, O Lord, those two young princes who as sons were born in my house, certainly to remind me of my former roots of goodness.

At these words the Lord Jaladharagajitaghoshasusvaranak-shatrarajasankusumitabhijna, the Tathagata, etc., spoke to the king Subhavyuha: It is as thou sayest, noble king. Indeed, noble king, such young men or young ladies of good family as possess roots of goodness, will in any existence, state, descent, rebirth or place easily find true friends, who with them shall perform the task of a master, who shall admonish, introduce, fully prepare them to obtain supreme and perfect enlightenment. It is an exalted position, noble king, the office of a true friend who rouses another to see the Tathagata. Dost thou see these two young princes, noble king? I do, Lord; I do, Sugata, said the king. The Lord proceeded: Now, these two young gentlemen, noble king, will pay worship to sixty-five times the number of Tathagatas, etc., equal to the sands of the Ganges; they will pay this Dharmaparyaya of the Lotus of the True Law, out of compassion for beings who hold false doctrines, and with the aim to produce in those beings an earnest striving after the right doctrine.

Thereupon, young men of good family, the king Subhavyuha came down from the sky, and, having raised his joined hands, said to the Lord Jaladharagarjitaghoshasusvara-nakshatrarajasankusumitabhijna, the Tathagata, etc.: Please, Lord, deign to tell me, what knowledge the Tathagata is possessed of, so that the protuberance on his head is shining;

that the Lord's eyes are so clear; that between his brows the Urna (circle of hair) is shining, resembling in whiteness the moon; that in his mouth a row of equal and close-standing teeth is glittering; that the Lord has lips red as the Bimba and such beautiful eyes.

As the king Subhavyuha, young men of good family, had celebrated thy Lord Jaladharagajitaghoshasusvaranakshatrarajasankusumitabhijna, the Tathagata, etc., by enumerating so many good qualities and hundred thousands of myriads of kotis of other good qualities besides, he said to the Lord Jaladharagajitaghoshasusvaranakshatrarajasankusumitabhijna, the Tathagata, etc.: It is wonderful, O Lord, how valuable the Tathagata's teaching is, and with how many inconceivable virtues the religious discipline proclaimed by the Tathagata is attended; how beneficial the moral precepts proclaimed by the Tathagata are. From henceforward, O Lord, we will no more be slaves to our own mind; no more be slaves to false doctrine; no more slaves to rashness; no more slaves to the sinful thoughts arising in us. Being possessed of so many good qualities, O Lord, I do not wish to go away from the presence of the Lord.

After humbly saluting the feet of the Lord Jaladharagajitaghoshasusvaranakshatrarajasankusumitabhijna, the Tathagata, etc, the king rose up to the sky and there stood. Thereupon the king Subhavyuha and the queen Vimaladatta from the sky threw a pearl necklace worth a hundred thousand gold pieces upon the Lord; and that pearl necklace no soon came down upon the head of the Lord than it assumed the shape of a tower with four columns, regular, well-constructed, and beautiful. On the summit of the tower appeared a couch covered with many hundred thousand pieces of fine cloth, and on the couch was seen the image of a Tathagata sitting cross-legged. Then the following thought presented itself to the king Subhavyuha: The Buddha-knowledge must be very powerful, and the Tathagata endowed with inconceivable good qualities that this Tathagata-image shows itself on the summit of the tower, an image so nice, beautiful, possessed of an extreme abundance of good colours. Then the Lord Jaladharagarjitaghoshasusvaranakshatrarajasankusumitabhijna, the Tathagata, etc., addressed the four classes and asked: Do you see, monks, the king Subhavyuha who, standing in the sky, is emitting a lion's roar? They answered: We do, Lord.

The Lord proceeded: This king Subhavyuha, monks, after having become a monk under my rule shall become a Tathagata in the world, by the name of Salendraraja, endowed with science and conduct, etc. etc., in the world Vistirnavati; his epoch shall be called Abhyudgataraja. That Tathagata Salendrararaja, monks, the Arhat, etc., shall have an immense congregation of Bodhisattvas, an immense congregation of disciples. The said world Vistirnavati shall be level as the palm of the hand, and consist of lapis lazuli. So he shall be an inconceivably great Tathagata, etc. Perhaps, young men of good family, you will have some doubt, uncertainty or misgiving and think that the king Subhavyuha at that time, that juncture was another. But you must not think so; for it is the very same Bodhisattva Mahasattva Padmasri here present, who at that time, that juncture was the king Subhavyuha. Perhaps, young men of good family, you will have some doubt, uncertainty or misgiving and think that the queen Vimaladatta at that time, that juncture was another.

But you must not think so; for it is the very same Bodhisattva Mahasattva called Vairochanarasmipratimanditaraja, who at that time, that juncture was the queen Vimaladatta, and who out of compassion for the king Subhavyuha and the creatures had assumed the state of being the wife of king Subhavyuha. Perhaps, young men of good family, you will have some doubt, uncertainty or misgiving and think that the two young princes were others. But you must not think so; for it was Bhaishajyaraja and Bhaishajyarajasamudgata, who at that time, that juncture were sons to the king Subhavyuha. With such inconceivable qualities, young men of good family, were the Bodhisattvas Mahasattvas Bhaishajyaraja and Bhaishajyarajasamudgata endowed, they, the two good men, having planted good roots under many hundred thousand myriads of kotis of Buddhas. Those that shall cherish the name of these two good men shall all become worthy of receiving homage from the world, including the gods.

While this chapter was being expounded, the spiritual insight of eighty-four thousand living beings in respect to the law was purified so as to become unclouded and spotless.

◆ ◆ ◆ ◆ ◆

26

BODHISATTVA SAMANTABHADRA

The Bodhisattva changes himself with the task of being a protector of religion after the Lord's nirvana.

Thereupon Bodhisattva Mahasattva Samantabhadra, in the east, surrounded and followed by Bodhisattvas Mahasattvas surpassing all calculation, amid the stirring of fields, a rain of lotuses, the playing of hundred thousands of myriads of kotis of musical instruments, proceeded with the great pomp of a Bodhisattva, the great display of transformations proper to a Bodhisattva, the great magnificence of a Bodhisattva, the great power of a Bodhisattva, the great lustre of a glorious Bodhisattva, the great stately march of a Bodhisattva, the great miraculous display of a Bodhisattva, a great phantasmagorical sight of gods, Nagas, goblins, Gandharvas, demons, Garudas, Kinnaras, great serpents, men, and beings not human, who, produced by his magic, surrounded and followed him; Samantabhadra, then, the Bodhisattva, amid such inconceivable miracles worked by magic, arrived at this Saha-world. He went up to the face of the Lord on the Gridhrakuta, the king of mountains, and on approaching he humbly saluted the Lord's feet, made seven circumambulations from left to right, and said to the Lord: I have come hither, O Lord, from the field of the Lord Ratnatejobhyudgata, the Tathagata, etc., as I am aware, Lord, that here in the Saha-world is taught the Dharmaparyaya of the Lotus of the True Law, to hear which from the mouth of the Lord Sakyamuni have come accompanied by these hundred thousands of Bodhisattvas Mahasattvas. May the Lord deign to expound, in extension, this Dharmaparyaya of the Lotus of the True Law to these Bodhisattvas Mahasattvas.

So addressed, the Lord said to the Bodhisattva Mahasattva Samantabhadra: These Bodhisattvas, young man of good family, are, indeed, quick of understanding, but this is the

Dharmaparyaya of the Lotus of the True Law, that is to say, an unmixed truth. The Bodhisattvas exclaimed: Indeed Lord; indeed, Sugata. Then in order to confirm, in the Dharmaparyaya of the Lotus of the True Law, the females among the monks, nuns, and lay devotees assembled at the gathering, the Lord again spoke to the Bodhisattva Mahasattva Samantabhadra: This Dharmaparyaya of the Lotus of the True Law, young man of good family, shall be entrusted to a female if she be possessed of four requisites, she shall stand under the superintendence of the Lords Buddhas; she shall have planted good roots she shall keep steadily to the mass of disciplinary regulations; she shall, in order to save creatures, have the thoughts fixed on supreme and perfect enlightenment. These are the four requisites, young man of good family, a female must be possessed of, to whom this Dharmaparyaya of the Lotus of the True Law is to be entrusted.

Then the Bodhisattva Mahasattva Samantabhadra said to the Lord: At the end of time, at the end of the period, in the second half of the millennium, I will protect the monks who keep this Sutranta; I will take care of their safety, avert blows, and destroy poison, so that no one laying snares for those preachers may surprise them, neither Mara the Evil One, nor the sons of Mara, the angels called Marakayikas, the daughters of Mara, the followers of Mara, and all other servitors to Mara; that no gods, goblins, ghosts, imps, wizards, spectres laying snares for those preachers may surprise them. Incessantly and constantly, O Lord, will I protect such a preacher. And when a preacher who applies himself to this Dharmaparyaya shall take a walk, then, O Lord, will I mount a white elephant with six tusks, and with a train of Bodhisattvas betake myself to the place where that preacher is walking, in order to protect this Dharmaparyaya. And when that preacher, applying himself to this Dharmaparyaya, forgets, be it but a single word or syllable, then will I mount the white elephant with six tusks, show my face to that preacher, and repeat this entire Dharmaparyaya. And when the preacher has seen my proper body and heard from me this entire Dharmaparyaya, he, content, in high spirits, ravished, rejoiced, joyful, and delighted, will the more do his utmost to study this Dharmaparyaya, and immediately after beholding me he will acquire meditation and obtain spells, termed the talisman of preservation, the talisman of hundred thousand kotis, and the talisman of skill in all sounds.

Again, Lord, the monks, nuns, male or female lay devotees, who at the end of time, at the end of the period, in the second half of the millennium, shall study this Dharmaparyaya, when walking for three weeks for twenty-one days, to them will I show my body, at the sight of which all beings rejoice. Mounted on that same white elephant with six tusks, and surrounded by a troop of Bodhisattvas, I shall on the twenty-first day betake myself to the place where the preachers are walking; there I shall rouse, excite, and stimulate them, and give them spells where by those preachers shall become inviolable, so that no being, either human or not human, shall be able to surprise them, and no women able to beguile them. I will protect them, take care of their safety, avert blows, and destroy poison. I will, besides, O Lord, give those preachers words of talismanic spells, such as, *Adanda dandapati, dandavartani dandakusale dandasudhari dhari sudharapati, buddhapasyani dharani, avartani samvartani sanghaparikshite sanghanirghatani dharmaparikshite sarvesattvarutakausalyanugate simhavikri-dite.* The Bodhisattva Mahasattva, whose organ of hearing is struck by these talismanic words, Lord, shall be aware that the Bodhisattva Mahasattva Samantabhadra is their ruling power.

Further, Lord, the Bodhisattvas Mahasattvas to whom this Dharmaparyaya of the Lotus of the True Law shall be entrusted, as long as it continues having course in Jambudvipa, those preachers, Lord, should take this view: It is owing to the power and grandeur of the Bodhisattva Mahasattva Samantabhadra that this Dharmaparyaya has been entrusted to us. Those creatures who shall write and keep this Sutra, O Lord, are to partake of the course of duty of the Bodhisattva Mahasattva Samantabhadra; they will belong to those who have planted good roots under many Buddhas, O Lord, and whose heads are caressed by the hands of the Tathagata. Those who shall write and keep this Sutra, O Lord, will afford me pleasure. Those who shall write this Sutra, O Lord, and comprehend it, shall, when they disappear from this world, after having written it, be reborn in the company of the gods of paradise, and at that birth shall eighty-four thousand heavenly nymphs immediately come near them.

Adorned with a high crown, they shall as angels dwell amongst those nymphs. Such is the mass of merit resulting from writing this Dharmaparyaya; how much greater will be the mass of merit reaped by those who recite, study, meditate, remember it! Therefore, young men of good family, one ought to honour this Dharmaparyaya of the Lotus of the True Law, and write it with the utmost attention. He who writes it with undistracted attention shall be supported by the hands of a thousand Buddhas, and at the moment of his death he shall see another thousand of Buddhas from face to face. He shall not sink down into a state of wretchedness, and after disappearing from this world he shall enter the company of the Tushita-gods, where the Bodhisattva Mahasattva Maitreya is residing, and where, marked by the thirty-two sublime characteristics, surrounded by a host of Bodhisattvas, and waited upon by hundred thousands of myriads of kotis of heavenly nymphs he is preaching the law. Therefore, then, young men of good family, a wise young man or young lady of good family should respectfully write this Dharmaparyaya of the Lotus of the True Law, respectfully recite it, respectfully study it, respectfully treasure it up in his or her mind. By writing, reciting, studying this Dharmaparyaya, and by treasuring it up in one's mind, young men of good family, one is to acquire innumerable good qualities-Hence a wise young man or young lady of good family ought to keep this Dharmaparyaya of the Lotus of the True Law. I myself, O Lord, will superintend this Dharmaparyaya, that through my superintendence it may here spread in Jambudvipa.

Then the Lord Sakyamuni, the Tathagata, etc., expressed his approval to the Bodhisattva Mahasattva Samantabhadra: Very well, very well, Samantabhadra. It is happy that thou art so well disposed to promote the weal and happiness of the people at large, out of compassion for the people, for the benefit, weal, and happiness of the great body of men; that thou art endowed with such inconceivable qualities, with a mind so full of compassion, with intentions so inconceivably kind, so that of thine own accord thou wilt take those preachers under thy protection. The young men of good family who shall cherish the name of the Bodhisattva Mahasattva Samantabhadra may be convinced that they have seen Sakyamuni, the Tathagata, etc. that they have heard this Dharmaparyaya of the Lotus of the True Law from the Lord Sakyamuni: that they have paid homage to the Tathagata Sakyamuni; that they have applauded the preaching of the Tathagata Sakyamuni.

They will have joyfully accepted this Dharmaparyaya; the Tathagata Sakyamuni will have laid his hand upon their head, and they will have decked the Lord Sakyamuni with their robes. Those young men or young ladies of good family, Samantabhadra, must be held to have accepted the command of the Tathagata. They will have no pleasure in worldly philosophy; no persons fondly addicted to poetry will please them; no dancers, athletes, vendors of meat, mutton-butchers, poulterers, pork-butchers, or profligates will please them. After having heard, written, kept, or read such Sutrantas; this, they will find no delight in those persons. They must be held to be possessed of natural righteousness; they will be rightminded from themselves, possess a power to do good of their own accord, and make an agreeable impression on others. Such will be the monks who keep this Sutranta. No passionate attachment will hinder them, no hatred, no infatuation, no jealousy, no envy, no hypocrisy, no pride, no conceitedness, no mendaciousness. Those preachers, Samantabhadra, will be content with what they receive. He, Samantabhadra, who at the end of time, at the end of the period, in the second half of the millennium, sees a monk keeping this Dharmaparyaya of the Lotus of the True Law, must think thus: This young man of good family will reach the terrace of enlightenment; this young man will conquer the troop of the wicked Mara, move forward the wheel of the law, strike the drum of the law, blow the conch trumpet of the law, spread the rain of the law, and ascend the royal throne of the law.

The monks who at the end of time, at the end of the period, in the second half of the millennium, keep this Dharmaparyaya, will not be covetous, nor greedy of robes or vehicles. Those preachers will be honest, and possessed of three emancipations; they will refrain from worldly business. Such persons as lead into error monks who know this Sutranta, shall be born blind; and such as openly defame them, shall have a spotted body in this very world. Those who scoff and hoot at the monks who copy this Sutranta, shall have the teeth broken and separated far from each other; disgusting lips, a flat nose, contorted hands and feet, squinting eyes; a putrid body, a body covered with stinking boils, eruptions, scabs, and itch. If one speaks an unkind word, true or not true, to such writers, readers, and keepers of this Sutranta, it must be considered a very heinous sin. Therefore then, Samanta-bhadra, people should, even from afar, rise from their seats before the monks who keep this Dharmaparyaya and show them the same reverence as to the Tathagata.

While this chapter of the encouragement of Samantabhadra was being expounded, hundred thousands of kotis of Bodhisattvas Mahasattvas, equal to the sands of the river Ganges, acquired the talismanic spell Avarta.

◆ ◆ ◆ ◆ ◆

27

THE PERIOD OF THE LAW

Thereupon the Lord Sakyamuni, the Tathagata, etc., rose from his pulpit, collected the Bodhisattvas, took their right hands with his own right hand, which had become strong by the exercise of magic, and spoke on that occasion as follows: Into your hands, young men of good family, I transfer and transmit, entrust and deposit this supreme and perfect enlightenment arrived at by me after hundred thousands of myriads of kotis of incalculable Aeons. Ye, young men of good family, do your best that it may grow and spread.

A second time, a third time the Lord spoke to the host of Bodhisattvas after taking them by the right hands: Into your hands, young men of good family, I transfer and transmit, entrust and deposit this supreme and perfect enlightenment arrived at by me after hundred thousands of myriads of kotis of incalculable Aeons. Receive it, young men of good family, keep, read, fathom, teach, promulgate, and preach it to all beings. I am not avaricious, young men of good family, nor narrow-minded; I am confident and willing to impart Buddha-knowledge, to impart the knowledge of the Tathagata, the knowledge of the Self-born. I am a bountiful giver, young men of good family, and ye, young men of good family, follow my example; imitate me in liberally showing this knowledge of the Tathagata, and in skilfulness, and preach this Dharmaparyaya to the young men and young ladies of good family who successively shall gather round you. And as to unbelieving persons, rouse them to accept this law. By so doing, young men of good family, you will acquit your debt to the Tathagatas.

So addressed by the Lord Sakyamuni, the Tathagata, etc., the Bodhisattvas filled with delight and joy, and with a feeling of great respect they lowered, bent, and bowed their body towards the Lord, and, the head inclined and the joined hands stretched out, they spoke in one voice to the Lord Sakyamuni, the Tathagata, etc., the following words: We shall do, O Lord, what the Tathagata commands; we shall fulfil the command of all Tathagatas. Let the Lord be at ease as to this, and perfectly quiet. A second time, a third time the entire host of Bodhisattvas spoke in one voice the same words: Let the Lord be at ease as to this, and perfectly quiet. We shall do, O Lord, what the Tathagata commands us; we shall fulfil the command of all Tathagatas.

Thereupon the Lord Sakyamuni, the Tathagata, etc., dismissed all those Tathagatas, etc., who had come to the gathering from other worlds, and wished them a happy existence, with the words: May the Tathagatas, etc., live happy. Then he restored the Stupa of precious substances of the Lord Prabhutaratna, the Tathagata, etc., to its place, and wished him also a happy existente.

Thus spoke the Lord. The incalculable, innumerable Tathagatas, etc., who had come from other worlds and were sitting on their thrones at the foot of jewel trees, as well as Prabhutaratna, the Tathagata, etc., and the whole host of Bodhisattvas headed by Visishtacharitra, the innumerable, incalculable Bodhisattvas Mahasattvas who had issued from the gaps of the earth, the great disciples, the four classes, the world, including gods, men, demons, and Gandharvas, in ecstasy applauded the words of the Lord.

◆ ◆ ◆ ◆ ◆